THEORY IN EDUCATIONAL ADMINISTRATION

FENWICK W. ENGLISH

University of Kentucky

HarperCollins*CollegePublishers*

Acquisitions Editor: Christopher Jennison
Project Coordination and Text Design: Proof Positive/Farrowlyne Associates, Inc.
Cover Design: Kay Petronio
Production Manager: Kewal Sharma
Compositor: Proof Positive/Farrowlyne Associates, Inc.
Printer and Binder: R. R. Donnelley & Sons Company
Cover Printer: The Lehigh Press, Inc.

Theory in Educational Administration, First Edition

Copyright © 1994 by HarperCollins College Publishers

Library of Congress Cataloging-in-Publication Data

English, Fenwick W.
    Theory in educational administration / Fenwick W. English.
        p.   cm.
    Includes bibliographical references (p.) and index.
    ISBN 0-06-500934-7
    1. School management and organization—United States—Philosophy.
    2. Educational leadership—United States—Philosophy.   I. Title.
    LB2805.E66 1993
    371.2'00973—dc20   93-29246
                                                                        CIP

93 94 95 96 9 8 7 6 5 4 3 2 1

CONTENTS

INTRODUCTION

This book is about the past, present, and possible future uses of theory in educational administration. It is ground breaking in seven ways:

1. It recognizes that there are no privileged positions or privileged theories in educational administration. Previous books about administrative theory were really about one particular theory or point of view, or they critiqued previous theories without necessarily exposing the assumptions of the theory being used in shaping the critique. This text is an attempt to fully break with this pattern.

2. It begins with the concept that theories are simply stories or narratives. If they become privileged stories, or metanarratives, they represent vested interests, hidden agendas, and power–knowledge relationships that should be exposed. These discourses (enunciating metanarratives) irrevocably shape perception and transform experience prior to any observation. There is little that is remotely objective about such discursive practices. Theories spun from them are not likely to challenge or change practice unless they become self-critical or reflective in nature. This is extremely difficult to do, for as Charles Sanders Peirce (1934) notes, reality is "swimming" in indeterminancy, and is so complex and overwhelming that it defies our attempts to ever fully capture it. Reality is always multitheoretical as a result.

3. It views theories as language and culturally dependent. As such, they are contextually bound, finite, and limited responses to a very closed reality. The idea of *reality* is simply not possible as the old positivistic science conceptualized it—i.e., as a kind of objective and idealistic world of universal laws and numbers that produced *truth*. Reality is far more immediate, temporal, subjective, and corruptible than those who were interested in "scientizing" educational administration ever perceived. This book suggests the need for a counter ontology by which to expand the field and enhance its grasp of leadership in the future.

4. It acknowledges that many of the theories we believe to be true or deserving of our support in educational administration today are quite likely to be false or wrong paths, taken in good faith at the time because theories, embedded in paradigms, have no easy way to be criticized or tested. Theories in the social sciences are especially apt to go without a hard cri-

tique because they deal with concepts that have no immediate realm in human experience, and because most are self-enclosed systems that are relational and circular. As such, they turn out to be ideologies or pseudoscience, long before they are discovered to be so.

5. It posits that theories are omnipresent in human affairs. The most potent are those that remain hidden in our perceptions and culturalization patterns. These theories often catch us blind, and never permit us to see what is in front of us. We must be taught to see. In this respect, there is never a "theory–practice" gap. All practices are embedded in some theory or another. We may not know what they are, but their presence is the shaping force in the development of all knowledge.

6. It proffers that the purpose of theory is neither to predict nor control, but to search for meaning and to understand in order to become more fully human. Theory in educational administration has become entangled with management ideologies that are centered on prediction and control. Such theories lead to constrained and passive people occupying positions of authority. These managers or bureaucrats become chiefly interested in preserving their own roles and the place of the organization in society, and the perpetuation of systems of schooling that are clearly deficient, dysfunctional, and counterproductive to the political ideals of a democracy.

7. The book takes the position that educational administration is part of a much larger perspective in preparing school executives. This perspective belongs to the tradition of biography and the humanities. While most professional books in educational administration posit the beginnings of the field around 1900, this book links the tradition to Homer—several thousand years prior to the industrial age. If educational leadership is some kind of captaincy, the Western mindscape is first etched on the plains of Priam's City in Asia Minor.

It was Michel Foucault's (1972) observation that all discourses, of which this book represents but one, are part of a webbed set of interrelationships. I was particularly fortunate to present the basic typology of the metanarratives at the 1992 Danforth Preconference of the University Council of Educational Administration in Minneapolis, and later at the 1993 American Educational Research Association in Atlanta, in a Division A symposium. I learned from both of these experiences. I am also indebted to the serious consideration of my concepts and ideas by colleagues at many universities—particularly those who comprised the Danforth Group (Indiana University at Bloomington, University of Nebraska, Hofstra University, Fordham University, and Miami University of Ohio), and specifically to Nelda Cambron-McCabe and the late Thomas Mulkeen who were the Danforth Project Directors. I want to personally thank those who read prior drafts and offered helpful and encouraging comments: Colleen Capper at the University of Wisconsin at Madison, Patricia First at the University of Oklahoma, William Foster at Indiana University at Bloomington, and Spencer Maxcy at Lousiana State University. I would also like to thank Thomas Sergiovanni—Lillian Radford Professor of Educational Administration at Trinity University in San Antonio—for his comments on the concept of typologies, as well as Bonnie Sigafus, a doctoral student in the Department of Educational Administration and Supervision at the University of Kentucky, who assisted me in proofreading most of the chapters in the book. My colleagues at the University of Kentucky also deserve mention for their patience in listening to me ramble at times as we restructured our doctoral program around some of the themes in this book: Eddy Van Meter, Jane Lindle, Betty Steffy, Richard Donelan, Patricia Dardaine Ragguet, Susan Scollay, Charles Russo, and Jim Rinehart.

Because the book is different, I would suggest that the reader scan the key chapter concepts and terms prior to tackling each chapter. This will serve as a preview and will establish a strategy for encountering unfamiliar terrain.

Finally, let me take this occasion to dedicate the book to the memory of my friend and colleague, Robert Emil Lundgren (1936–1992), Deputy Director of the Department of Defense's Dependents Schools in Wiesbaden, Germany. I met Bob shortly after he received his doctorate from Stanford University, and continued his administrative career in Temple City, California. Bob had a profound respect and understanding of humanity that guided me in crafting the book, its perspective, and most importantly, its tone. We can never fully capture so complex an educator, but it is my hope that in some small way this book will be worthy of the man we miss very much.

Fenwick W. English, College of Education
Lexington, Kentucky

References

Foucault, M. (1972). *The Archaeology of Knowledge*. New York: Pantheon Books.
Peirce, C. S. (1934–1948). *Collected Papers* (4 volumes). Cambridge, Massachusetts: Harvard University Press.

LANGUAGE AND DISCOURSE

Imagine that in your town, city, or region there is a group of people who periodically meet to determine the future of the place. They decide what is to happen, who is to carry it out, under what circumstances people will be allowed to talk, and what problems will be addressed. This group of people, by virtue of their positions, could enforce their will on all the others. It would be a powerful group!

Suppose you found out where this group met, and you could become a fly on the wall and listen to their conversation. If you wanted to know where to invest, what streets were going to be laid, and what projects were going to be undertaken, all you would have to do is gain access to the meeting.

Now imagine that you meet someone who is a member of the group. She invites you to attend as a guest. What a chance! At the next meeting, you calmly sit to one side and listen to the group engage in a discussion.

As the group begins their discussion, right away you determine that there is something strange about the way they talk. You understand most of the words they use. Some of the phrases and ideas seem similar, but there is a general level of language usage that sounds strange. The conversation just isn't right. At the end of the meeting, you are hard pressed to know exactly what was discussed and what was decided.

THE MANY LEVELS OF HUMAN DISCUSSION

There are several levels to human discussion. First, there is the level of common talk, where words stand for concrete objects and firsthand experience in speech called *parole* (after Saussure, see Gadet, 1986). Second, there is an order to words. Sentences are formed and meaning shifts with the sentences and the order or sequence of words within them. This second level is the grammatical structure, called *langue,* and words must fall under its rules in order to be understood in all human communications (see Palmer, 1990, p. 8).

The third level of discussion is concerned about reflections on the second level, and about debating which assumptions, perceptions, values and predilections will shape, support, extend, and limit what can be discussed within a discourse. A discourse is simply thought in a particular linguistic form (Shumway, 1992, p. 16). At this level, one comes to understand the limitations of language rules (its structure) on any discussion. Language rules are embedded in a culture, which is a peculiar time-bound, value-laden context of events, interactions, perceptions, and motivations shared by a specific people. *Language* is a special kind of artifact in human life. It is both an *objective* body of rules and conventions as well as a *subjective* and personal medium of expression. Language is a product and a process. As a process, it is restless, always changing and shifting meanings. This phenomenon lies at the core of much theoretical discussion today in all of the social sciences.

If language shifts, then those things it represents—particularly abstractions—must shift as well. Thus, categorical distinctions used in the social sciences are not all that hard and fast. Someone seeking refuge in permanence and irrefutable "facts" will find the prospect of perpetual impermanence unsettling, for it means that there may be nothing at all except *change.*

Diagram 1   THE THREE LEVELS OF MEANING IN HUMAN LANGUAGE (LANGUE)

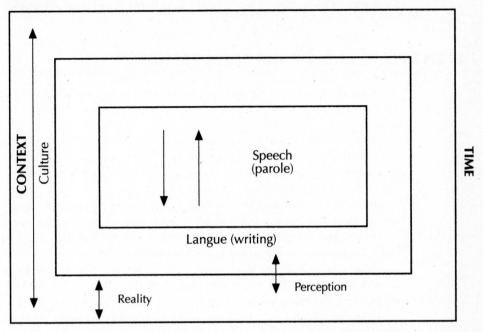

Diagram 1 indicates the three parts of human language levels. At the vortex of these human interactions lie the great branches of **philosophy: axiology,** a study of values to answer the question, "What is good?" **ontology,** a study of reality to answer the question, "What is real?" and **epistemology,** a study of knowledge to answer the question, "What is true?" Modern philosophers such as Martin Heidegger (1889–1976) have brought into question whether the traditional philosophical responses beginning with Aristotle are adequate as questions or traditions in thinking about the questions themselves. Heidegger's work represents a fundamental "turning" of questions regarding truth, values, and knowledge to concerns long abandoned in Western thinking.

Although these questions have been posed in nearly every culture and on nearly every continent throughout time, the answers have not always been the same. In fact, the questions have differed within the framework that they have been asked. This framework is a *discourse.* Heidegger's work represented an attempt to redefine the parameters of the discourse itself to include what was unsaid as significant (Bernasconi, 1991, pp. 49–63).

Language, especially written language, both erases and silences alternative positions or voices by flattening expression to a single, linear line and forcing words to follow given contextual sequences. Language reveals and conceals. Language is not only how humans communicate, it is also how humans perceive the world in which they live.

Think of a discourse as a discussion somewhere in a specific time, space, and culture. It includes not only what is spoken, but what is also written as well. It includes a speaker and a listener (Cherryholmes, 1988, p. 3). Let's examine some examples of the different levels of discussion for illustrative purposes.

HELEN KELLER AND ANNE SULLIVAN MACY

One of the most poignant and well-remembered anecdotes in the early life of Helen Keller occurred when she connected her sense perceptions to words or names.

Helen Keller was almost a year and a half old when she was struck with a disease that eventually left her blind and deaf. She grew up, in her own words, "a wild, destructive little animal" (Lash, 1980, p. 46). Little Helen would come to the dining table, mess up everyone's food, and break plates and lamps. She often cried out in emotional tirades and kicked things. She invented about 60 signs to show what she wanted. For ice cream, she imitated a freezer turning followed by a shiver. When she put on glasses, it symbolized her father. She did not, however, understand language or words as symbols of something else.

When Anne Sullivan Macy arrived to be Helen's teacher, she began by spelling into Helen's hand. The event that unlocked this relationship for Helen Keller was an incident involving a water spigot. As the cool liquid was pumped from the spout over one of Helen's hands, Anne Sullivan spelled the word *water* into the other, first slowly and then over and over again more rapidly.

At last, Helen made the connection. "Everything had a name, and each name gave birth to a new thought," she wrote (Lash, 1980, p. 55). The next morning, Helen rushed to objects and wanted to know each one's name. Her vocabulary then expanded to include hundreds of words.

It was at this point that Anne Sullivan Macy made an important adjustment in Helen Keller's language lesson. Anne notes:

> It occurred to me the other day that it is absurd to require a child to come to a certain place at a certain time and recite certain lessons when he has not yet acquired a working vocabulary. I sent Helen away and sat down to think. I asked myself, 'How does a normal child learn language?' The answer was simple. 'By imitation.' The child comes into the world with the ability to learn, and he learns himself, provided he is provided with sufficient outward stimulus. He sees people do things, and he tries to do them. But long before he utters his first word, he understands what is said to him (Lash, 1980, p. 57).

After that point, Anne Sullivan Macy spoke in full sentences into Helen's hand. She used gestures and signs to explain the extended meanings.

This is an example of learning language at a level of discussion. "Things" have symbols (words) that are used to describe them. A name is a word that is a linguistic sign which unites a sound–image, or a *signified* (concept) with a *signifier* (sound image) (Gadet, 1986, p. 29). For Helen Keller, this linkage was not a sound, but rather, a sensory cue left in her hand by her teacher and associated with the feeling of cold liquid over her hand. Rather than a sound acting as the bond that tied sound and concept together, it was her teacher, Anne Sullivan Macy, who became the silent "sound" producer.

The spelling in Helen Keller's hand by Anne Sullivan Macy was in English, an arbitrary system of signs unlike any other arbitrary system of signs such as German, Japanese, or Tagalog. Language structures are arbitrary conventions. They are *social structures*. But, unlike some social structures, they do not correspond to a given reality. Because they are essentially arbitrary, they change, or as Gadet (1986, p. 41) indicates, "There is nothing to prevent any series of sounds from being associated with any idea; any phonic element may correspond to any semantic element." There is no fixed status within language. Nothing can be held still and nothing can ever be considered "objective." Even if by consensus language could somehow be held still over time in order to fix some sort of meaning to words and sounds, the means of studying it, "the microscope as it were—would not be adequate to the purpose of scientific study, since *it too, as a metalanguage, is still nothing but language*" (Felperin, 1985, p. 63).

Perhaps Jack Solomon (1988) said it best: "We look upon our languages as objective reflections of reality, when they are actually codified systems of signs . . . Signs [words] are not windows through which the light of meaning innocently shines. They are screens that let through only those meanings that belong to the code" (pp. 2–3). There is no notation using language that is not free of ambiguity. Absolute meaning can therefore never be established. This state is called **indeterminancy,** a condition in the social sciences that provides an instructive backdrop to a real-life problem for Helen Keller and her teacher.

Helen Keller was accused of plagiarism on several occasions. She was also accused of being too "wordy." She knew only words, especially for colors, sounds, events, and abstract ideas. She was called a "dupe of words" by a French intellectual, and one interviewer for *The New Yorker* magazine said, "She talks bookishly. Never having heard a voice, she has never learned the easy vocabulary of ordinary discourse. To express her ideas, she falls back on the phrases she has learned from books, and uses words that sound stilted, poetical metaphors" (Lash, 1980, pp. 571, 573).

None other than Mark Twain defended Helen on her first charge of plagiarism. Twain roared:

> The kernel, the soul—let us go further and say the substance, the bulk, the actual and valuable material of *all* utterances—is plagiarism. For substantially all ideas are second-hand, consciously and unconsciously drawn from a million outside sources (Lash, 1980, p. 146).

Alexander Graham Bell also defended Helen Keller when he wrote:

> Our forms of expression are copied—verbatim et literatim—in our earlier years from the expressions of others which we have heard in childhood. It is difficult for us to trace the origins of our expressions because the language addressed to us in infancy has been given by word of mouth, and not permanently recorded in books so that investigators—being unable to examine the printed records of the language addressed to us in childhood—are unable to charge us with plagiarism (Lash, 1980, p. 291).

Many decades later, Michel Foucault (1972) echoed the comments by Twain and Bell when he similarly commented that, "The frontiers of a book are never clear-cut . . . it is caught up in a system of references to other books, other texts, other sentences; it is a node within a network" (p. 23). It is this network that forms a **discursive practice,** i.e., a tradition of texts, spoken and written, within a given historical period with its rules, written and unwritten, that govern what Foucault (1972) has called, "the enunciative function" in human affairs (p. 117).

The case of Helen Keller is especially important from the perspective of examining how one comes to acquire language and understand its *structure,* which later becomes a discursive practice. Helen was called upon to defend herself against criticism of either being a plagiarist or bookish, because her associations were derived from books rather than firsthand associations through her senses. Books *were* her experiences rather than the experiences themselves. As such, one could trace the acquisition of some of her words, phrases, and sentences to very specific sources.

This phenomenon happens to anyone using a language and thoughts expressed by others in that language. It is because of the fact that such "works" represent common and widely spread ideas and thoughts that many modern philosophers deny the whole idea of "authorship" (Derrida, 1976, p. 158).

> If sources and origins can never be fixed in the flux of discursive formations or the freeplay of infinite textuality, if the author himself is only an intersection of texts or discourses, the concept of author becomes meaningless (Felperin, 1988, p. 29).

It was this idea that both Twain and Bell were speaking about in defense of Helen Keller. The concept that speech and texts (writing) are all interconnected is called **intertextuality.**

Let us now move to an exemplar of discourse where the second level of language is used to engage in argumentation, without being conscious of exactly how the language itself shapes the argument, or of the system of thought which lies behind shaping the selection of words, but rather, where both are at work.

THE PLAY OF LANGUAGE: SOCRATES AND EUTHYPHRO

One of the earliest dialogues in Western writing regarding discourse in which at least two levels of language occur is a discussion between Socrates and Euthyphro. The latter is a professional priest, someone who is knowledgeable about the rules of conduct.

In this encounter, Plato provides a glimpse of a discussion involving what is pious behavior. Euthyphro has told Socrates that he is prosecuting his own father for the murder of a laborer who was himself a murderer. The astonished Socrates then engages Euthyphro in a discussion about the nature of piety (Grube, 1975).

Socrates: Is the pious loved by the gods because it is pious, or is it pious because it is loved by gods?

Euthyphro: I don't know what you mean, Socrates.

Socrates:	We speak of something . . . being led and something leading, of something being seen and something seeing, and you understand that these things are all different from one another and how they differ?
Euthyphro:	I think I do.
Socrates:	So there is something being loved and something loving, and the loving is a different thing.
Euthyphro:	Of course.
Socrates:	I want to say this, namely, that if anything comes to be, or is affected, it does not come to be because it is coming to be, but it is coming to be because it comes to be; nor is it affected because it is being affected but because something affects it. Or do you not agree?
Euthyphro:	I do.
Socrates:	So it is in the same case as the things just mentioned; it is not loved by those who love it because it is being loved, but it is being loved because they love it?
Euthyphro:	Necessarily.
Socrates:	What then do we say about the pious, Euthyphro? Surely, that it is loved by all the gods, according to what you say?
Euthyphro:	Yes.
Socrates:	Is it loved because it is pious, or for some other reason?
Euthyphro:	For no other reason.
Socrates:	It is loved then because it is pious, but it is pious because it is loved?
Euthyphro:	Apparently.
Socrates:	And because it is loved by the gods it is being loved and is dear to the gods?
Euthyphro:	Of course.
Socrates:	Now, if you will, do not hide things from me but tell me again from the beginning what piety is . . . be keen to tell me what the pious and the impious are.
Euthyphro:	But Socrates, I have no way of telling you what I have in mind, for whatever proposition we put forward goes around and refuses to stay put where we establish it.

Courtesy of Hackett Publishing Company, Inc., all rights reserved.

This discourse between Socrates and Euthyphro is beyond everyday talk, although the words are in the common Greek vocabulary of the day. The discourse takes place within understood cultural concepts. For example, the Greek concept of *hoison* means knowing the proper ritual for prayer and sacrifice. But the discourse extends this concept to the larger scope of general conduct which may be considered pious and how one comes to know what it is (Grube, 1975, p. 3).

The third level of discourse involves a related ideal beyond the discourse proper. That is, Plato asserted that the gods love the right because it is right, not because they love it. This point separated the gods and their behavior from *ultimate reality*. It meant that they too were accountable to this reality as humans were, and were created and had to exist within the same spectrum of values as humans did.

Another set of relationships at work in the Socrates and Euthyphro dialogue is a peculiar form of argument called **logic.** Logic is a kind of structured argumentative form of human communication created by the ancient Greeks (see Quine, 1982). While it has given Western thinking a distinctive form, in the mind of at least one provocative theorist—Edward de Bono (1972)—it has also been a great intellectual disaster.

Greek logic was a kind of **concept package** based on several unstated premises and set into a culture/time context far different from those of today. Says de Bono:

> The ancient Greeks lived in a static society. They directed their thinking to creating concepts and then refining them to such a point of perfection that they would never need changing. Instead of the uncertainty of experiment and observation, they preferred the certainty of logic to create truths. . . .New concepts were produced either by taking apart existing concepts in the process called analysis or by fitting them together to give bigger concepts. The result was a sharp, precise, and self-contained thinking system that examined the relationship between static and fixed concepts. This was a system that was not capable of evolution and not designed to cope with change" (p. 27).

de Bono has called Greek logic a "yes/no" system of thought. It is vertical. An argument proceeds by a kind of narrative examining only two possibilities. If "yes," then the train of thought is allowed to continue. If "no," then the narrative is concluded and returns to a former state. The problem with this form of argumentation is that it, "preserves ideas and is of no help in changing them—it has no creative ability whatsoever" (de Bono, 1972, p. 30).

Furthermore, the "concept package" of Greek logic produces

> box definitions. Something is either inside the box or outside it . . . but thinking does not need them, for rigid box definitions make the evolution of ideas impossible since an idea cannot drift in or out of a definition but must at all times be inside or outside" (de Bono, 1972, p. 31).

de Bono (1972) has contrasted vertical "yes/no" thinking systems with lateral ones. Vertical systems produce "right/wrong" distinctions. They are not useful in creating alternatives. "Lateral thinking" is required to create new ideas. An example of lateral thinking is the practice of **brainstorming,** a technique of free association not dependent upon "right answers" (see Osborn, 1965).

THE NATURE OF REALITY AND DISCOURSE

Discourse is the framework in which human perception is shaped by everyday language within a culture. Edward Hall (1981) defines the space into which a person is born and believes is his or her "identity" as:

> his culture, the total communication framework words, actions, postures, gestures, tones of voice, facial expressions, the way he handles time, space, and materials, and the way he works, plays, makes love, and defends himself (p. 42).

Human perception is not *outward*. Rather, **reality** is **inward,** simply because one never "sees" anything as it "is." Culture shapes perception from the moment of birth. One has to know what one is seeing in order to know what it is and to learn the language needed to identify it. Reality is therefore arbitrarily and inwardly defined. The outward boundaries of reality are defined by the context of time. It may be argued that context and time are synonymous because the nexus of dealing with time is the capability of engaging in differentiation/identification in the present.

Not only are the shifts of language occurring, but this same language must represent a kind of temporal space by which experience itself can be separated from the act of observing it. A speaker can be observing a sunset and experiencing it at the same time. However, when the speaker/viewer realizes that he or she is in the act of viewing a sunset, then he or she is not only experiencing, but is recognizing as well, the separateness of the act of experiencing it simultaneously. In this act, a human differentiates the act of sunset viewing from other kinds of acts, and in the process, identifies it using language. This kind of two-pronged act creates the concept of **time** (see Rapaport, 1991, p. 71).

Within this framework or discourse, language is both a product of, and a determiner of, temporal relationships. Language is both descriptive and prescriptive in this sense; it indicates "what is" as well as "what should or might be." Language cements the hierarchical nature of perceived relationships and of other "givens." Embedded in language are concealed hierarchies and power relationships. When human thought is reduced to a singular line of enunication, superior–subordinate relationships are frozen.

Language provides a somewhat false sense of "equality" within human communication. Rather than being perceived as artifacts of time, space, and culture, such relationships are viewed by those within a culture as "natural"—a point underscored by Hall (1966) when he said, "Culture hides much more than it reveals, and strangely enough what it hides, it hides most effectively from its own participants" (p. 39). Edward de Bono (1972) calls language, "our strongest patterning system" (p. 134). People using a language are often unaware of such patterns. Human thinking is shaped not by an independent reality which words represent, but by cultural metaphors without any inherent properties or fixed relations between them (Lakoff and Johnson, 1980, p. 210). A practice of exposing such patterns concealed in language is called **deconstruction** (Derrida, 1985, Rapaport, 1989).

THE SHIFTS OF MEANING IN LANGUAGE AND CULTURE

A generic example of how all of these concepts work in real life is provided in the social ritual of human courtship. Here, the relationships between the sexes are embedded in cultural, linguistic, and temporal webs that are constantly moving.

Rothman (1984) examined American courtship in four time periods beginning in 1770 and ending in 1980. She used love letters and diaries as her records of some 350 American women and men chronicling shifts in courtship and patterns of intimacy over 150 years. For more modern times, she used surveys, popular magazine articles, and scholarly sources such as books and papers.

The nature of the discourse about American courtship has changed substantially over time. Words, ideas, and practices have undergone alteration as attitudes and values respond to new and different conditions—largely economic and techno-logical. For example, the installation of telephones in homes brought an end to the formal letters of courtship and communication Rothman was able to utilize in her research from 1770 to 1920. Americans ceased writing to one another to communi-cate their views about love, duty, marriage, family views, and other matters.

Movies ushered forth new role models and examples of love and passion. They also provided a public place to hold hands and engage in surreptitious minor pet-ting. The automobile, however, provided young Americans with an instant getaway to private places for intimacies. These intimacies occurred in earlier times as well, but were harder to schedule.

Courtship can be considered a discursive practice—a kind of enveloping per-ceptual–cultural communicative totality that for a brief period of time was near consuming for men and women.

Practices considered "natural" today in the courtship ritual were not consid-ered so in earlier times. For example, 200 years ago, women were considered sexu-ally passionless, while men were considered "carnal creatures" who engaged in "licentious" acts whenever they could. The ideal of pleasure in the 1820s and 1830s was that women were above sexual passion, and men were to be in control and to be, "Christian gentlemen" (p. 51).

The concept of petting—i.e., physical relations between men and women with-out sexual intercourse, arose in the early nineteenth century (Rothman, 1987, p. 54). One female advisor writing in 1887 observed that, "We teach the girl *repression,* the boy *expression,* not simply by word and book, but the lessons are graven into their very being by all the traditions, prejudices, and customs of society" (p. 200). Petting or "spooning" has also been called "smooching, larking, sparking and even mugging," by the noted sexual historian and researcher Alfred Kinsey (Rothman, 1987, p. 289).

In Kinsey's work, he differentiated between *petting* and *heavy petting* and noted that about 80 percent of the women born just before 1900 had engaged in some sort of petting. The twenties through the fifties were times of "petting parties." Few Americans in the nineties would know that, "a snugglepup is a young man who attends petting parties" (Chicago Tribune, 1947).

By the sixties and seventies, petting parties had given way to actual sexual inter-course itself, so that in comparing the sexual behavior of the 1920s to that of the 1960s, Ira Reiss (1966) commented that, "What was done by a female in 1925 act-ing as a rebel and a deviant can be done by a female in 1965 as a conformist" (pp. 58–59). Clearly the discursive practice regarding courtship and sex had been altered. Some called it a "revolution" (Rothman, 1987, pp. 285-311).

One significant change during these years studied by Rothman was that of the honeymoon. The "idea" of a honeymoon was originally a "tour" of the important relatives' homes after a marriage had taken place. As such, the bridal or "nuptial trip," was accompanied by friends and relatives who acted as intermediaries in introducing families to new members. The bridal tour was a communal activity. Such tours were difficult to undertake because of poor physical transportation accommodations, and because of the fact that farmers could not leave their farms in the hands of friends or relatives for too many days.

However, by the 1870s, the bridal trip had been replaced by the emerging concept of the "honeymoon," with "an explicit sexual agenda" attached (p. 281). Instead of a journey in which family ties were joined and extended, the "honeymoon" became an activity of excluding relatives and friends for the purpose of initiating sexual bonding between the couple. Improved transportation facilities and changing work roles from the farm to the city made extended trips possible for a new bridge and groom. Honeymoons were planned around the menstruation cycle of the female. In the late nineteenth century, the ovulation specifics of menstruation were not even understood by medical authorities; they recommended that the honeymoon occur in the middle of the cycle, which was considered the safest period to avoid pregnancy. This period is actually the most likely time for conception to occur.

Within a changing discursive practice experienced by millions of Americans, the "honeymoon" was created, defined, and shaped into one of the "natural" events in the courtship cycle, supporting a $12.5 billion dollar a year wedding industry (Rothman, 1987, p. 311).

HEIDEGGER AND "DAS WORT"

The third level of language usage involves applying it as a reflective and philosophical tool. This application involves the previous two levels that have already been presented and discussed.

A good example of the reflective level of language used in both the arts and philosophy is presented in a work by Martin Heidegger in which the dialogue he entertains is with a poem by Stefan George called "Das Wort" (The Word) (Bernasconi, 1991, p. 49).

The poem is shown below:

Wonder from afar or dream
I brought to the border of my land

And tarried until the grey norn
Found the name in her bourn-

Thereupon I could grasp it tight and strong
Now it blossoms and gleams throughout the mark...

Once I arrived after a good journey
With a gem rich and frail

She sought long and gave me to know:
"Nothing sleeps here above deep ground"

Whereupon it escaped my hand
And my land never attained the treasure...

So sadly I learned renunciation:
Where the word is wanting no thing can be

Translated by Dorthea van Mucke.

George's poem is a translation from German (van Mucke, 1991). The word "mark" is a tract of land held in common by people living in a village, i.e., community land. A "norn" is a female fate derived from Scandinavian myths (Bernasconi, 1991, p. 63).

Stefan George's poem is language reflecting about language. Heidegger reads "Das Wort" as being about a poet who has an experience with words. That experience transforms him. The first part of the poem indicates that the poet is in command of the language itself. The poet is using the language to express his thoughts.

Then something happens. The poet fails to find a word he requires to express a thought. In this failure, he comes to recognize that in the silence of finding no word, he has discovered that there is a word for a word, but it is not a word at all. It is silence.

At that moment, the poet understands that he is not in control of language, but rather, it is in control of him. It speaks through him. And it is *nothing* and at once *something*. It is in this concept of *nothingness* that affirmation occurs. Heidegger calls this affirmation in nothingness **Being.** It is affirmation in the act of negation.

This is an extremely difficult concept for Westerners to understand—that *nothingness* is something. Westerners believe that nothingness means emptiness. Only the Japanese have a concept that nothingness is something. The word they use to describe such a positive space is **ma.** Hall (1969) notes that *ma* "is a basic building block in all Japanese spatial experience . . . a hidden consideration in the layout of all other spaces" (p. 153).

Hall's (1966), *The Silent Language,* is a work about how culture shapes and in turn, is shaped by language. Culture is essentially indeterministic, which is the reason why translation from one language to another is difficult. "Whenever people talk, they supply only part of the message. The rest is filled in by the listener. Much of what is *not* said is taken for granted. However, cultures vary in what is left unsaid" (Hall, 1969, p. 102).

Heidegger came to call what is actually said in the poem "Das Wort," and what is unsaid in what is said **rift.** "It means . . . silence is to be heard as silence and that the silence comes to permeate all speaking" (Bernasconi, 1991, p. 63).

The three levels of language combined into the idea of discourse relate *to the complexity and shifts in meaning itself* that occur within a language, and from language to language in translation. What is left unsaid is often impossible to communicate from culture to culture.

We have seen that language as a linear phenomenon submerges differences and relationships in its structure. Various views, images, concepts, and voices may be submerged and hidden in structure and meaning.

The person using language may not be aware of these hidden meanings. The person may also bring to language utilization his or her own bias in expressing thoughts and ideas. This bias or *agenda* usually involves the enhancement of the authority and power of the speaker. Let us see how it works.

THE CONCEPT OF POWER–KNOWLEDGE

Remember the example of the group that met to determine the future of your town, city, or region at the opening of the chapter? Inasmuch as you are a student in educational administration, you should be aware that there is such a group in this field. This group decides what issues will be discussed, who is qualified to discuss them, and what views will or will not have legitimacy. It isn't quite as closely knit geographically as our town group, but it does exist.

The right of our group to control the field was precedentially determined by a Papal decision in 1213 A.D. by Pope Innocent III. The Holy Father was presented with a dispute in which the professors of the University of Notre Dame in Paris were at loggerheads with the Chancellor. The issue was who should license teachers.

The practice to that point had been that bishops and other church officials were the ones who could grant a *licentia docendi* (a license to teach) in a specified geographical area. The professors were challenging this right on the basis of their expertise to determine qualifications based on an examination of a teacher's competence (Hoskin, 1991, pp. 45-46).

The professors argued that their expertise combined with the examination of competence was the only *proof* that a student could teach. At the heart of their claim was that even a talented layperson did not know how to read the sacred texts properly, in the spirit of *inquisitio,* or critical inquiry, because it required instruction to dicipher a new type of visual information system contained in the texts themselves (Hoskin, 1991, p. 45). The Pope, who had been a student at Bologna, determined that the professors were the ones, by right of expertise and examination, who should determine who was competent to teach.

Today, the professors in educational administration, and to some extent practitioners, are the ones who still determine what is to be studied in the field, who has a right to speak, who is qualified or not qualified, and who ascertains what issues and methods will be allowed to be utilized in the pursuit of new knowledge in the discipline.

The discussion among professors, practitioners and students is also a *discourse*. It is also exclusive because it only occurs within certain limitations, and it involves assumptions, written and unwritten rules, prior training, and specialized knowledge. In this sense, it is a bounded and structured discussion, and not truly an open forum for everyone who may have an opinion.

A person who is unstudied about the field and is unaware of how language and culture interact to produce a peculiar form of discourse may not be aware of these biases, cultural conditioning, or historical contexts. Such a person may believe he or she is really "open" to new knowledge and can actually see "with fresh eyes."

This kind of view of uncomplicated communication is naive because the communicator does not understand that language disguises, changes, reforms, and restructures thought in much the same way that a given computer program shapes, defines, and influences the kind of communication that is possible in expressing ideas and thought within it (see Pears, 1969, p. 55).

In reality, nobody ever really perceives or receives all the sensory stimuli that may exist in a field. Such stimuli are always filtered by the language of discourse, whether everyday language or scientific language. All human communication is therefore one or more "steps" removed from reality. Reality is never encountered directly or faced squarely. It is always obliquely perceived. A person who does not understand that his or her language is not "natural," or that his or her world is not as it may appear, is engaging in uncomplicated communication and is a **naive realist** (Lincoln and Guba, 1985, p. 83).

The idea that there is "one reality" out there waiting to be discovered through diligent pursuit of the "truth" is naive. It is oblivious to the context in which the pursuit itself is shaped *by that context*, its prior assumptions, biases, submerged or suppressed views and voices, unnoticed internal contradictions, and arbitrary language conventions which vary from culture to culture and from one time to another.

Famed husband and wife historians, Will and Ariel Durant (1968), co-authors of ten volumes of world history and civilization, put it bluntly, "total perspective is an optical illusion . . . Our knowledge of any past event is always incomplete, probably inaccurate, beclouded by ambivalent evidence and biased historians, perhaps distorted by our own patriotic or religious partisanship." (pp. 12–13). Even if it were possible for a historian to rise above these contextual contaminants, the Durants confessed that the historian, "betrays his secret predilection in his choice of materials, and in the nuances of his adjectives" (p. 12). The mere act of selection is itself an expression of bias. No scientist approaches scientific study with a blank mind. There can never be a purely "objective" study for this reason. All acts of science are fundamentally subjective in nature.

Scientific communities have developed their own discourse or *discursive practices*. Without understanding the nature of the discourse, one cannot communicate—either by listening and understanding, or by participating in a discussion beyond a very superficial level.

New knowledge is discovered *within* such discursive practices. In fact, the practices themselves limit what can be considered new knowledge and what cannot. The discourse exists in the form of implicit boundaries about what is important and what can be permitted to be debated.

Truth, as a concept, is relationally bound up *within a discourse*. It is never complete or unbiased because its categories within its discourse hide some things from being known (Lakoff and Johnson, 1980, p. 163). It is within these relations which Foucault (1972) envisions as existing between "institutions, economic and social process, behavioural patterns, systems of norms, techniques, types of classification, and modes of characterization," (p. 45), that truth as an objective state does not wait to be revealed. It does not pre-exist, nor is it independent of language. Instead, it waits to be seen as a *field of relations*.

Davidson (1986), quoting Foucault's thoughts (1980), has indicated the idea that truth is not a plane of pure objectivity, or even a state, but that:

> Truth is to be understood as a system of ordered procedures for the production, regulation, distribution, circulation and operation of statements. . .

> Truth is linked in a circular relation with systems of power which produce and sustain it, and to effects of power which induces it and which extends it (pp. 221-224).

Knowledge, truth, and inquiry are intimately connected to systems of power. These are supported by discursive practices which mutually reinforce the people and ideas in power. When a person seeks to discover or uncover the hidden relationships embedded in language and power, it is called **reflective discourse** or **critical discourse.** Critical discourse, sometimes called *critical theory*, is an attempt to expose the hidden sociopolitical relationships at work in the world—in scientific communities and in educational administration (see Foster, 1986).

For the education student, this view of knowledge and power may seem strange. At the bottom of this "strangeness" lies the concept that power and knowledge are separate things because some of their studies in sociology or anthropology presented knowledge in a culture as value-neutral and apolitical. This kind of "scientific rationality" defused the idea of truth, reality, and values from those involving arbitrary conveniences of authorities and the power of politicians, except as isolated societal phenomena (see Darder, 1991, p. 26).

This view of truth, reality, and values represents a bias and a distortion—a discursive practice that has passed itself off as "scientific" and "value–neutral," when it is anything but. It is part of the tradition of behaviorism, which divorced feelings, motivations, beliefs, and conscience–concern from studies. Such studies were considered "scientific" and therefore "objective" even as they rested on a set of assumptions *that were not* verified objectively. These "blinders" prevented behaviorists from seeing the unsubstantiated biases in their so-called "scientific" studies which depoliticized knowledge from the relationships of social and political power, even in fields that would otherwise have acknowledged them, such as sociology and anthropology.

THE DISCOURSE OF EDUCATIONAL ADMINISTRATION

Educational administration has long been influenced by the view of the behaviorists, because education professors became enamored by a peculiar concept of *theory,* and also because they adopted many of the "research practices" of the behavioral sciences (see Culbertson, 1965, p. 7). In fact, the word theory, has been appropriated by the behaviorists to mean an empirically verifiable set of neutral "facts," that have been inductively derived largely by observation alone. The behaviorists believe that only knowledge that is empirically verifiable can be considered scientific and therefore true. The concept of *discourse* is a direct challenge to this assumption. No discourse can be considered neutral or even "objective."

An example of how knowledge–power–politics come together in a discursive practice in educational administration is supplied by former United States Commissioner of Education, Ted Bell (1988) in his Reagan cabinet memoir, *The Thirteenth Man.* Bell describes his weak political base at the beginning of the David Stockman budget cuts. "He [Stockman] intended to reduce the federal role in education to rubble, take away crucial aid to needy college students, and slash financial assistance that supplemented the education of the disadvantaged and poor" (p. 67).

The political strategy selected by Bell was to consolidate federal programs into one law. The idea of the "block grant" was born on the shoals of the failed Nixon concept of special revenue sharing. What happened to Bell was that Stockman consolidated 44 unrelated federal programs into one pot. The conservatives liked it because it was simpler to abolish later. School administrators liked it because it weakened federal control over their use of the funds.

The consolidation put Chapter 1, a then $3.5 billion dollar program, into the same pot as bilingual education, which meant that bilingual education funding could be handsomely increased. Bell was opposed and knew Stockman would be as well.

Bell cornered Stockman in the Office of Management and Budget (OMB) with the question, "Dave, how would you like to increase the potential of having more federal money going to bilingual education by ten or twenty times?" Bell reminded Stockman that the right wing conservatives were afraid of Hispanics perpetuating their language. Stockman agreed to separate bilingual education from the federal block grant concept to avoid supporting an educational program that promoted Hispanic culture in which Hispanics—some 20 million Americans—have become the fastest growing minority in the country. At least one futurist indicates that the

Hispanic population will surpass the African-American population by the year 2010 (Dunn, 1991, p. 3A).

Political power uses knowledge to perpetuate its own existence. "Truth" functions to reinforce power relations. Truth is never politically neutral. It exists in a field of power configurations, hierarchies, and superior–subordinate socioeconomic positions.

THE RELATIONSHIP OF DISCOURSE AND THEORY

Theories are special kinds of explanations or narratives which emanate from peculiar discourses. No theory ever comes from "thin air." It has precedents, antecedents, and traces from many other ideas—all within a discourse which enables it to be envisioned, expanded, checked, debated, verified, criticized, changed, and ultimately, abandoned for another more promising narrative.

Discourses may be embedded in a web of common assumptions, accepted methods of inquiry, and frameworks of thought. Such frameworks of thought are called **paradigms** by the scientific historian Thomas Kuhn (1962).

Paradigms enclose any definition of truth used in science. Paradigms also exist in everyday discourse (see Polanyi, 1989). The use of a paradigm in science enables those working in a field to avoid spending unnecessary time on dealing with the problem of definition. The use of words to define other words leads to infinite regress, i.e., there is no satisfactory end to definition (see Albert, 1968).

Theories represent systems of power because no knowledge is ever neutral. Someone gains and someone loses. The true language of power is theory, because theory embraces both the structure of language (its langue), and its ability to describe things in order to communicate and influence others (its parole). Theories provide explanations and establish meanings of facts and events.

Theories work to reinforce existing power relationships. They do this by taking place within the existing mechanisms of social control in a society in which political control depends upon "a common social–moral language and in which one concept of reality is dominant, informing with its spirit all modes of thought and behavior." (Femia, 1987, p. 24). This type of control is called **hegemony.** Theory development therefore reinforces existing hegemonic sociopolitical relationships.

Heidegger's (1971) view of the primacy of language in discourse and theory is that:

> Language is, as world-moving Saying, the relation of all relations. It relates, maintains, proffers, and enriches the face-to-face encounter of the world's regions, holds and keeps them, in that it holds itself-Saying-in reserve (p. 107).

No discourse is language-free. A discourse is frozen in a language, a culture, and time–power relations. Theories emanate from such discourses and are part and parcel of them. They are no more objective—i.e., value-free or value-neutral—than political movements. Discourses, theories, and truth are relationally dependent and perceptually selective.

THE ENDURING LEGACY OF SCIENTIFIC MANAGEMENT

Perhaps the most powerful and longest lived discursive practice in educational administration has been that of **scientific management** or SM (Taylor, 1967). The tenets of scientific management were laid before the country in 1911 in the form of an essay that led to the establishment of a discursive practice, and in the words of Michel Foucault (1980), became a **regime of truth** (p. 133).

Frederick Taylor joined the labor force at Midvale Steel Company and became its chief engineer. He developed a procedure for work called "the task system," which later became famous as the Taylor System or "scientific management."

The premise of Taylor's scientific management was that inefficiency (waste) was everywhere, and that the solution to improved utilization of resources resided in "systematic management" instead of hiring or training unusual people. Finally, "systematic management" should be founded upon "true science" (p. 7).

This interrelated set of assertions framed the base for the application of Taylor's system of work task analysis which meant that:

> Management must take over and perform much of the work which is now left to the men; almost every act of the workman should be preceded by one or more preparatory acts of the management which enable him to do his work better and quicker than he otherwise could (p. 26).

And what precedents did Taylor have for his system? In his own words:

> There is absolutely nothing new in the task idea. Each one of us will remember that in his own case this idea was applied with good results in his schoolboy days. No efficient teacher would think of giving a class of students an indefinite lesson to learn. Each day a definite, clear-cut task is set by the teacher before each scholar, stating that he must learn just so much of the subject; and it is only by this means that proper, systematic progress can be made by the students. The average boy would go very slowly if, instead of being given a task, he were told to do as much as he could (p. 120).

Taylorism became the media event of the day. Newspapers and magazines of the time became missionaries searching for converts. Soon the intelligentsia were captivated by scientific management. Louis Brandeis, who later became a member of the U.S. Supreme Court, used the applications of scientific management to fight against giving the railroads fare increases for hauling freight on the grounds that they were not using SM in their operations (Strum, 1984, p. 160).

It was not long before the attention given to scientific management in business was turned to the nation's schools. Callahan (1962) noted that in 1911, J. George Becht, principal of the State Normal School in Pennsylvania, spoke before the Department of Superintendence (now the American Association of School Administrators—AASA) within the National Education Association (NEA) on the miracles of scientific management. In the summer of 1911 at the annual meeting of the NEA, the President of the National Council of Education urged the creation of a committee to examine "tests and the standards of efficiency of schools and school systems" (Callahan, 1962, p. 54).

Thereafter, with each meeting of the NEA, articles appeared in the *School Board Journal,* and speakers came forth to indict education for waste and inefficiency and to praise the concepts of Taylorism.

The role of the professoriate in controlling the curriculum and preparing superintendents was part of the establishment of this regime of truth. The key institutions and persons were Teachers College, Columbia University and the work of George Strayer, the work of Franklin Bobbitt at the University of Chicago, Edward Elliot at Wisconsin, Paul Hanus at Harvard, and Elwood P. Cubberley at Stanford. These academics became the interlocking people and institutions that came to dominate the curriculum. These men carried the doctrine of scientific management into dissertations (Schafer, 1990, p. 46). "The result was an emphasis upon the techniques and mechanics of administration" (Callahan, 1967, pp. 13–14).

Scientific management became within scholarly study, "the production of truth," or, in the words of Foucault (1980):

> 'Truth' is centered on the form of scientific discourse and the institutions which produce it; it is subject to constant economic and political incitement (the demand for truth, as much for economic production as for political power); it is the object, under diverse forms of immense diffusion and consumption (circulating through apparatuses of education and information whose extent is relatively broad in the social body . . .; it is produced and transmitted under the control, dominant if not exclusive, of a few great political and economic apparatuses (university, army, writing, media) (pp. 131–132).

Another catastrophic result of the regime of truth spawned by Taylorism was the reshaping of the American school superintendency from that of educational leader to that of chief executive officer along the lines of corporate presidents. This resulted in a shift in the university curriculum from a person concerned with instruction, curriculum and learning, to one concerned with personnel, law, finance, budgeting, planning, and management.

The metaphor that was applied to education in the nineteenth century was the school as a garden. In this garden, the child was a seed who was nourished by a teacher. With scientific management, the school became a factory. Children were raw materials to be changed into products that would be in demand within a consumer economy (see Eaton, 1991, pp. 18–19).

The American superintendency was an especially vulnerable public position to the legacy of scientific management because forces working against the person were many and became cumulative over time (Eaton, 1991, p. 19). The outcome was rapid turnover which has been endemic since its inception (see Burlingame, 1977).

In an AASA study in 1969–1970, the average number of years in the first superintendency was 6.4 with the median being 4.5 years (Knezevich, 1971, p. 13). A similar study in 1982 by AASA indicated that the average term for the superintendent was 5.6 years (see Cunningham and Hentges, 1982, p. 49).

In an effort to protract the period of employment, school superintendents are especially prone to adopt new "fads" such as scientific management and now total quality management in order to prolong their tenure; in the process, they turn attention away from strictly personality–political variables working against them by indicating they are responsive to criticisms of cost and inefficiencies. If such efforts fail, they can be blamed on an inadequate or ill-researched program instead of themselves or the systems they represent. Adoption of the business ethic and business ideologies rooted in factory models and metaphors such as scientific management was the result of the collaboration of professional associations, universities and professors of educational administration, the media, and the private sector which formed an **apparatus** (after Foucault) which transformed the superintendency into a corporate icon. This regime of truth continues into present times under different guises.

The so-called **effective schools** movement has ushered forth new indicators of Taylorism that emphasize routine instruction, tests, and standard curricula, as well as continued centralization of control within systems of education (see Cuban, 1984).

As late as 1991, a business task force in Cincinnati, Ohio, unleashed a new wave of scientific management by proposing to rename the office of superintendence to that of *president* because, "this position must function with more authority, and it must be refocused to concentrate on the 'product' of the system; i.e., *education*" (Buenger, 1991, p. 13). While "scientific management" as a term is outdated, it has been replaced by "quality management," or **total quality management** (**TQM**) and as before, has been embraced by the American Association of School Administrators which regularly features articles about it in its publications and sessions at its national conventions.

TQM AS CONTEMPORARY SCIENTIFIC MANAGEMENT

The new guru of scientific management is W. Edwards Deming, the American statistician consultant who is considered the mastermind who transformed bomb-stricken Japan into an economic superpower in less than three decades following Hiroshima and Nagaski.

Using many of the same notions as Frederick Taylor, including the idea that organizations are transformed individual by individual (English, 1992, p.284), Deming wants to "get inside" the head of the worker, but like Taylor, only after the proper framework has been established to run the system. Says Deming, "Without an aim, there is no system. The components of a system are necessary but not sufficient of themselves to accomplish the aim. They must be managed." (Rhodes, 1990, p. 34).

The framework for workers is "the same theoretical roadmap" that everybody must use. This roadmap is established by top management. "Management is prediction," says Deming (1993, p. 104). Prediction and control are the handmaidens of management. "In the absence of statistical control, no prediction is possible," warns Deming (1993, p. 180).

This same roadmap is what Frederick Taylor (1967) mentioned when he said, "Scientific management requires, first, a careful investigation of each of the many modifications of the same implement, developed under rule of thumb" (p. 118).

This investigation led to the creation of a standard (a roadmap). "This best method becomes standard, and remains standard, to be taught first to the teachers (or functional foremen) and by them to every workman in the establishment until it is superseded by a quicker and better series of movements. In this simple way one element after another of the science is developed" (p. 118). Deming's ideas are dependent on numbers, "quantifiable evidence of it [improvement]: percentages, numbers, lists of legitimate advantages" (Schmoker, 1992, p. 23).

It is remarkable how this neo-Taylorism about continuing to find quicker and better movements is echoed in the idea of *kaizen,* the Japanese word for "continuous improvement" (Schmoker, 1992, p.23) that is now rampant in discussions pertaining to Japanese manufacturing techniques (see Schonberger, 1982, pp. 52-53) and is applied to schools and education.

It is instructive to see that none of these ideas ever *change* the role of authority in organizations. From scientific management through effective schools and total quality management, educational administrators remain firmly in charge of traditional, hierarchical organizations. TQM, like scientific management, legitimates administrative authority under the guise of science. Rhodes (1990) says of total quality management in schools:

> The superintendent provides constancy and connections. He or she is responsible for the quality of the system . . . and the staff for the quality of the results. . . .Thus the staff works *in* the system, but leaders work *on* the system. Leaders must provide the connections to purpose, and to other interdependent functions that maintain systemic, systematic support (p. 33).

Both scientific management and total quality management as its modern-day phoenix assume what Stephen J. Ball indicates is the submersion of control and individual action in a technical metalanguage, "a view which contends that social life can be mastered scientifically and can be understood and organized according to lawlike generalizations" (p. 157). Ball notes that this was Max Weber's nightmare of *the iron cage* where, "specialists without spirit, sensualists without heart [are] caught in the delusion that [they] have achieved a level of development never before attained by mankind (Weber, 1948, p. 182).

One of the many ironies is that this discursive practice is passed off as neutral and objective, where its only purpose is to achieve improved quality (efficiency), instead of being recognized as a regime of truth—a view embedded in a series of circular relations in which opposition, dissent, and conflict are viewed as either deviant, aberrant responses or as psychological pathologies indicating personal unmet "needs,"—or, in the words of Deming, "Conflict and competition break connections to mutual purposes" (Rhodes, 1990, p. 31). Ball (1991) comments:

> Collective opposition is systematically misrecognized. Solutions are offered in terms of personal counselling or one-off adaptions of the system. The resister is cast as social deviant, and is normalized through coercive or therapeutic procedures (p. 158).

American educational administration was captured by the language and ideas of scientific management shortly into the beginning of the twentieth century. It remains firmly entrenched—if not in its theories, then in its *practice*. Scientific management is a discourse. It fosters a discursive practice that is normative—i.e., law-like.

One of the consequences of establishing a discursive practice is to answer the questions posed by Foucault (1972) when he asked, "Who is speaking? Who among the totality of speaking individuals, is accorded the right to use this sort of language?" (p. 50). Foucault wants to know, "Whose prestige is on the line in speaking, and from whom the speaker is then reinforced and assured that he or she is saying the truth?" (p. 50)

Scientific management and today's total quality managers not only reinforce existing systems of education, they legitimize the speakers as "experts" to engage in seeking to modify them as well. Their reassurance by administrators legitimizes their work and reduces other voices to "unscientific" or "uninformed" laypersons without a knowledge base of legitimacy from which to speak or protest. Protest in this scenario is simply the cacophony of the ignorant, the lazy, the malingerer, or the psychologically maladjusted—much like Taylor's pig iron workers who engaged in systematic "soldiering" unless someone coerced or co-opted them into working harder to increase productivity.

The ultimate purpose of a discursive practice is *exclusion*. "We know perfectly well that we are not free to say just anything, that we cannot simply speak of anything, when we like or where we like; not just anyone, finally, may speak of just anything," avers Michel Foucault (1977, p. 216).

The purpose of exclusion is to form a tight web and to confine discourse within it. In this practice, the public must not only concur, but must also endorse and support its own exclusion as being in its "best interest." All professions must eventually win this right in order to survive in a hierarchical society. As such, *truth,* is both the subject and the object of a profession. It is pursued and possessed only by those with a license to do so. It is very much a part of the circularity of those privy to the discursive practice itself.

SUMMARY

This chapter introduced the reader to the concept that at the root of any theoretical discussion regarding the field of educational administration lies the primacy of language and discourse framing both the formulation of theory and the discussion regarding it.

Language itself is an arbitrary set of signs which vary in time, space, and culture and can be seen as functioning at three levels: the naming of things by words, the structure (i.e., sequence and rules) of the language itself, and a recognition of the limitations of words and language in dealing with human experience and perception. The idea of a word that stands for a word but isn't one is a form of thought advanced by Martin Heidegger, a German philosopher who called the unsaid in what is said *rift*.

Theory and practice are tied together within a *discursive practice* which is shaped by and supports an interlocking series of persons and agencies in the larger society. These form Foucault's concept of "apparatuses." It is within these apparatuses that discourse concerning knowledge and truth takes place. A search for knowledge occurs within a set of power relationships which reinforce existing social arrangements. Truth, therefore, cannot be considered outside these arrangements since the search for truth is shaped by such arrangements and exists within them. Truth is therefore circular and relational, particularly in the social sciences.

Current notions of "truth" in educational administration exist within a network or web of relationships involving professional associations, university professors, university curricula, research conventions, sanctioned methods, court decisions, and state/federal laws. They are sanctioned by the public who is led to believe that expertise is the result of professionalism in a designated field.

Educational administration has been thoroughly captured by the discursive practice of scientific management as technique. This discursive practice is rooted on the false concept of objective knowledge. While some of the techniques of scientific management have been discarded, the fundamental tenets of its approach remain interlocked within the conceptual framework of both professors and practitioners in the field. The infatuation with Deming's "quality" is simply a continuation of the same discourse with a different technique. Centering a discipline on technique results in reinforcing the status quo, as no fundamental shifts are required to adopt them.

Perception Check and Applications

1. The Instability of Language

Take any passage in the Old or New Testament of the *Bible.* According to biblical scholars (Eiselen, Lewis, and Downey, 1957) a reader must understand four things to translate biblical passages with any comprehension. They are: (1) history, (2) geography, (3) religious development and (4) context (p. 5). Try to establish the meaning of the passage. See if you can identify the three levels of language usage described in the chapter. Indicate how your understanding of history, geography, religious development and context help you interpret what you have read.

2. The Nature of Discursive Practices

The chapter identifies scientific management, effective schools, and total quality management as *discursive practices* in educational administration. Identify other discursive practices in education.

Check the definition of a *paradigm* and compare it to the idea of a discursive practice. What are the differences?

At what point would a paradigm shift signal a change in a discursive practice?

3. Linguistic and Conceptual Packages

Edward de Bono (1991) has identified Greek logic as a kind of conceptual package that defines thinking. It is best applied in a search for the "right answer." However, if one is searching to generate alternatives, "lateral thinking" is preferred. One technique of lateral thinking is "brainstorming" (see Osborn, 1965). Review some of the various techniques common in management circles and group them into either (a) examples of vertical, yes/no thinking, or (b) examples of lateral thinking. For starters, try collective bargaining, flowcharting, strategic planning, and force-field analysis.

4. Power and Knowledge: Conflict in South Carolina

Knowledge is never neutral. It is pursued within a given socioeconomic–political reality. For example, in May of 1993, the chairperson of the Department of Educational Leadership and Policy Development in the College of Education at the University of South Carolina, Columbia, sent out over 1000 letters announcing a new course centered around the theme of combating the challenge of Christian fundamentalism to public education in a secular democracy. When severe protests were registered by state politicians and evangelical preachers, the University President, John Palms, said, "It looks like there was an agenda here. The university's position is to seek truth and enlightenment." Palms then indicated that the dean of the college of education had "taken corrective action" to readvertise the course which "addresses the issues from an academic standpoint and doesn't have an agenda or a position" (Associated Press, 1993, May 30, p. 5A). The chairperson of the Department then sent out a second letter in which he indicated that the first letter, "did not appropriately reflect the intended objectivity" of the course.

Discuss this situation. Where is objectivity? Was any position objective in the South Carolina bruhaha? How do the events demonstrate the concept of "power–knowledge"?

5. Bias and Reality

Take the quote from the historians Will and Ariel Durant that the historian, "betrays his secret predilection in his choice of materials, and in the nuances of his adjectives," and apply it to explain the following cases:

- The L.A. riots of 1992 following the Rodney King verdict

- The Gulf War and the portrayal of Saddam Hussein in the Western press

- The Clarence Thomas/Anita Hill confrontation over his appointment to the U.S. Supreme Court

- The resignation of Mikhael Gorbachev and the dissolution of the USSR

- The continuing debate as to whether there was a conspiracy to assassinate JFK

6. Scientific Management and TQM

Based on a close reading of Frederick Taylor and W. Edwards Deming, build a case either pro or con that the latter is simply a modern expression of the former. In this account, take cognizance of the place of management, the role of the worker in shaping the work, reward systems, data collection and utilization, and overt and covert meanings of words used by both advocates.

7. The Production of Truth

Examine the function of the production of truth in dissertation research in your own department of educational administration. Check out the last five dissertations in your department of educational administration. Compare and contrast them to one another. What is similar or dissimilar? Are the sources, meanings, and terms the same? Are the methodologies employed to conduct research similar? If yes, what do these comparisons reveal about what your professors believe to be the way "truth" is discovered in educational research?

8. The Vulnerability Thesis of the American School Superintendent

It was Raymond Callahan (1962) who first advanced the idea called "the vulnerability thesis" of the American school superintendent. In what ways does this idea explain Callahan's central premise that the superintendency has been completely captured by business management concepts?

Key Chapter Concepts and Terms

apparatus

The organizations and agencies that make an interlocking set of beliefs, practices, or theories into a web leading to a regime of truth.

axiology

A combination of two Greek words—*axios* (of like value, worthy) and *logos* (account, theory) (Runes, 1984, p. 47). A pursuit of the question, "What is good or of greatest value?"

Being

Reality, totality, God in a nonanthropomorphic sense.

brainstorming

A technique developed by Alex Osborne (1963) in his book, *Applied Imagination,* in which a group of people are encouraged to "think out loud" without judgments being made about whether what they are thinking is valuable, practical or applicable.

concept package

Refers to a descriptive practice by Edward de Bono (1972) to indicate how thoughts are collected by the human brain—i.e., in "packages." Logic is a kind of "conceptual package" in the way thoughts are brought together in argumentative form.

deconstruction

A technique of reflective discourse which attempts to reveal the hidden suppressions in language. Language is linear and sequential. Opposition and differences are submerged in this linearity. Deconstruction "destroys" the linearity of language so that other meanings and voices appear. It also reduces the differences between words and categories and binary distinctions by showing that the boundaries which separate them are not firm.

discourse

What is said and what is written in a given area, occupation, role, or discipline (the unit of analysis may vary). In educational administration, *discourse* consists of textbooks, laws, term papers, exams, requirements, customs, rules, traditions, speeches, and even information conversation at professional meetings and conventions.

discursive practice

A body of rules which establish how actions (practice) is to be carried out, conceptualized, discussed, explained, and perpetuated. Initially, discursive practices are usually attached to theories. Over time, the theories may become lost, but the practices may be continued by tradition.

effective schools movement

A set of beliefs, often tautological, that describe "good schools." Based on the research of Ronald Edmonds of Harvard following in the footsteps of the 1966 Coleman Report. In many instances, effective schools have become recipes to be laid on schools like templates.

epistemology

A word combined from two Greek words, *episteme* (knowledge) and *logos* (theory). A branch of philosophy which inquires as to the nature of knowledge, or to the question, "What is true?"

hegemony

A monopoly of power or authority garnered by a group or groups which act to perpetuate their control of a given situation or human condition. In intellectual work, the group that "owns" particular theories and benefits from their continuance through grants, promotions, and other forms of prestige and emoluments.

indeterminism

The idea that a search for stable precedents that are causative of individual actions is futile, or that individual actions are free from a predetermined cause such as fate. Similarly applied on a political scale, no nation is selected by history to rule over others.

intertextuality

The relating of one text to another without regard for the author. The idea that there is no author of a text because human thought and expression are continuous and cumulative in nature. No one person thinks alone. Language itself has a life of its own and speaks through people. The only important thing, it is thought, is the text and not the author.

logic

A peculiar form of argument to determine if some statements are true or false based on a series of linear "yes" or "no" decisions. Used by the ancient Greeks, notably Socrates' discourses written down by Plato.

ma

A Japanese word for "space," or what some Westerners would call "nothing" or "emptiness." Considered a "positive" concept instead of a negative one. Used in the construction of Japanese gardens and interior design.

naive realist

The view that one merely has to look "out there," and "that" (what is seen) is reality. A view that what one sees, one "gets." This idea fails to recognize that "seeing" is selective and is "biased" from the beginning by the identification of objects and concepts prior to the act of perception itself.

ontology

A branch of philosophy that deals with the question, "What is real?" This is based on a discussion of being or "the essence of things" (Runes, 1984, p. 235).

paradigm

A collection of beliefs organized around a set of common problems, procedures, and solutions which act as a short cut for those conducting inquiry using the same beliefs or assumptions. Quantum physics is a paradigm. Investigators working in this area all accept a number of premises and definitions as they go about their work. Paradigms act to enable the researcher to avoid the quagmire of the problem of linguistic definition and the shifts in language and hence, meaning (see Chapter 2).

philosophy

A combination of two Greek words—*philein* (to love) and *sophia* (wisdom) (Runes, 1984, p. 251). Used to refer to the explanation of all things, or technically, the science of sciences.

power–knowledge

A relationship based on the inquiry of Michel Foucault which indicates that knowledge is based on systems of relationships in the larger social world. Knowledge is never neutral. It is embedded in hierarchical relationships that are usually reinforced with "new" knowledge.

reality as inward

The idea that "reality" is not "out there," but rather, "in there"—i.e., inside the head, culture, context, and language of the perceiver.

reflective or critical discourse

A discussion that examines the hidden assumptions and biases upon which text and speech are based. Critical discourse searches for the sociopolitical–economic biases inherent in the discussion and attempts to answer the question posed by Michel Foucault (1972), "Who is allowed to speak?"

regime of truth

The triumph of a point of view embedded in a series of thoughts, theories, ideas, or practices that are considered "true," and those outside false. Usually involves more than one person or agency. Regimes of truth are politically repressive to all other possibilities.

rift

The word given to a word which is unsaid within another word or expression. Created by the German philosopher Martin Heidegger.

scientific management

An approach to organizing work involving a "conceptual package" that values breaking it into smaller pieces to gain increasing control over the work from the worker. Created by Frederick Taylor after his experience in the Midvale Steel Company. The premise for engaging in "scientific management" is that undesigned and unspecified work (also uncontrolled) is inherently inefficient and haphazard, and hence, "unscientific." The process is supposed to be "scientific" by accretion, i.e., timed steps lead to more timed steps which eventually becomes "scientific," and therefore faster, measurable, and replicable.

theory

A story or narrative that tries to describe and explain, and on occasion predict, what is related to what, and what may occur under certain conditions. Theories give meaning to data and help a researcher or investigator sort, label, prioritize, sift, and weigh what would otherwise be a hopeless enterprise.

thesis of vulnerability

A premise advanced by Raymond Callahan (1962) based on the idea that the public school superintendent was extremely vulnerable to community pressure groups and sought ways to buffer himself/herself against the politics of the office. This was accomplished by adopting business techniques under the umbrella of efficiency. One outcome was the reconfiguration of the role of superintendent itself into a corporate officer instead of a genuine educational leader.

time

That point at which a perceiving person recognizes the difference between the act of perception and the perceiver in the act of perception. Modern philosophers acknowledge only time in the present and reject Aristotelian time which defines a past, present, and future.

total quality management (TQM)

Attributed to the managerial approach developed by W. Edwards Deming, the American guru who is said to have propelled the Japanese to world dominance in some areas of manufacturing. TQM involves creating common objectives and shared purposes among workers without the use of cash incentives. TQM does not advocate redistributing power within an organization, but it does use shared data with a "human relations" format. Work units are rewarded for looking for new forms of "efficiency." TQM reinforces both bureaucracy and hegemony of those already in control of the organization.

truth

Believed to be some objective, finite, and stable state that exists somewhere and is unsullied by human bias and perception/cultural filters. Meaning does not depend upon human perception which is subject to distortion and error.

References

Albert, H. (1968). *Traktat uber kritische Vernunft* as cited in Boudon, R. (1986), *The Analysis of Ideology*. Chicago: University of Chicago Press, p. 143.

Associated Press (May 30, 1993). "USC Alters Course Description," *The Beaufort Gazette*, p. 5A.

Ball, S. J. (1991). "Management as Moral Technology," in S. J. Ball (Ed.), *Foucault and Education*. London: Routledge, pp. 153–166.

Bell, T. H. (1988). *The Thirteenth Man*. New York: The Free Press.

Bernasconi, R. (1991). *The Question of Language in Heidegger's History of Being*. Atlantic Highlands, New Jersey: Humanities Press International, Inc.

Boudon, R. (1986). *The Analysis of Ideology*. Chicago: University of Chicago Press.

Buenger, C. L. (1991, September 5). *The Cincinnati Business Committee Task Force on Public Schools: Report and Recommendations*.

Burlingame, M. (1977). *An Exploratory Study of Turnover and Career Mobility of Public School District Superintendents in the State of Illinois from 1960–1976*. Springfield, Illinois: Office of Education.

Callahan, R. E. (1956). *An Introduction to Education in American Society*. New York: Alfred A. Knopf.

Callahan, R. E. (1962). *Education and the Cult of Efficiency*. Chicago: University of Chicago Press.

Canguilhem, G. (1988). *Ideology and Rationality in the History of the Life Sciences*. Cambridge: Massachusetts: MIT Press.

Cherryholmes, C. C. (1988). *Power and Criticism*. New York: Teachers College Press.

Chicago Tribune (1947, December 11), pp. 3–6 as cited in M. M. Mathews (Ed.)(1951), *A Dictionary of Americanisms*. Chicago: University of Chicago Press, p. 1228.

Cuban, L. (1984, May). "Transforming the Frog into a Prince: Effective Schools Research, Policy, and Practice at the District Level," *Harvard Educational Review*, 54:2, pp.129–151.

Culbertson, J. A. (1965). "Trends and Issues in the Development of a Science of Administration," in *Perspectives on Educational Administration and the Behavioral Sciences*. Eugene, Oregon: The Center for the Advanced Study of Educational Administration.

Cunningham, L. V., and Hentges, J. (Eds.) (1982). *The American School Superintendency, 1982: The Full Report*. Arlington, Virginia: AASA.

Darder, A. (1991). *Culture and Power in the Classroom*. New York: Bergin & Garvey.

Davidson, A. (1986). "Archaeology, Genealogy, Ethics," in D. C. Hoy (Ed.), *Foucault: A Critical Reader*. Oxford: Blackwell.

de Bono, E. (1972). *Po: Beyond Yes and No*. New York: Penguin Books.

de Bono, E. (1991). "Lateral and Vertical Thinking," in J. Henry (Ed.), *Creative Management*. London: Sage, pp. 16–23.

Deming, W. E. (1991). *Out of the Crisis.* Cambridge, MA: Massachusetts Institute of Technology.

Deming, W. E. (1993). *The New Economics.* Cambridge, MA: Massachusetts Institute of Technology.

Derrida, J. (1985). "Deconstruction in America." From an interview that appeared in *Society for Critical Exchange,* 17 (Winter).

Dunn, W. (1991, April 11). "Survey Shows Hispanic Diversity," *USA Today,* p. 3A.

Durant, W., and Durant, A. (1968). *The Lessons of History.* New York: Simon and Schuster.

Eaton, W. E. (1991). "The Vulnerability of School Superintendents: The Thesis Reconsidered," in W. E. Eaton (Ed.), *Shaping the Superintendency: A Reexamination of Callahan and The Cult of Efficiency.* New York: Teachers College Press, pp. 11–35.

Eiselen, F. C., Lewis, E., and Downey, D. G. (1957). *The Abindgon Bible Commentary.* New York: Doubleday & Company.

English, F. W. (1992). *Educational Administration: The Human Science.* New York: HarperCollins.

Felperin, H. (1988). *Beyond Deconstruction.* Oxford: Clarendon Press.

Femia, J. V. (1987). *Gramsci's Political Thought.* Oxford: Clarendon Press.

Foster, W. (1986). *Paradigms and Promises.* Buffalo, New York: Prometheus Books.

Foucault, M. (1972). *The Archaeology of Knowledge.* New York: Pantheon Books.

Foucault, M. (1980). *Power/Knowledge.* New York: Pantheon Books.

Gadet, F. (1986). *Saussure and Contemporary Culture.* London, England: Hutchinson Radius.

Grube, G. M. A. (1975). *The Trial and Death of Socrates.* Indianapolis: Hackett Publishing Company, Inc.

Hall, E. T. (1966). *The Silent Language.* New York: Doubleday and Co.

Hall, E. T. (1969). *The Hidden Dimension.* New York: Anchor Books.

Hall, E. T. (1977). *Beyond Culture.* New York: Anchor Books.

Heidegger, M. (1971). *On the Way to Language.* New York: Harper and Row.

Hoskin, K. (1990). "Foucault Under Examination: The Crypto-Educationalist Unmasked," in S. J. Ball (Ed.), *Foucault and Education.* London: Routledge.

Knezevich, S. J. (Ed.). *The American School Superintendent.* Arlington, Virginia: AASA.

Kuhn, T. S. (1962). *The Structure of Scientific Revolutions.* Chicago: University of Chicago Press.

Lakoff, G., and Johnson, M. (1980). *Metaphors We Live By.* Chicago: University of Chicago Press.

Lash, J. P. (1980). *Helen and Teacher.* New York: Delacorte Press.

Lincoln, Y. S. and Guba, E. G. (1985). *Naturalistic Inquiry.* Beverly Hills, CA: SAGE Publications.

Osborn, A. F. (1965). *Applied Imagination.* New York: Charles Scribner's Sons.

Palmer B. D. (1990). *Descent into Discourse.* Philadelphia, Pennsylvania: Temple University Press.

Pears, D. (1969). *Ludwig Wittgenstein.* New York: The Viking Press.

Polanyi, L. (1989). *Telling the American Story.* Cambridge, MA: MIT Press.

Popper, K. R. (1934). "The Empirical Basis," in D. Miller (Ed.), *Popper Selections.* Princeton, New Jersey: Princeton University Press, pp. 152–170.

Popper, K. R. (1960). "Knowledge without Authority," in D. Miller, (Ed.), *Popper Selections.* Princeton, New Jersey: Princeton University Press, pp. 46–57.

Quine, W. V. (1982). *Methods of Logic.* Cambridge, MA: Harvard University Press.

Rapaport, H. (1989). *Heidegger and Derrida*. Lincoln, Nebraska: University of Nebraska Press.

Reiss, I. (1966). "Sexual Codes," *JSI* [44] pp. 58–59, as cited in Rothman, E. J. (1987), p. 360.

Rhodes, L. A. (November, 1990). "Why Quality is Within Our Grasp . . . If We Reach," *AASA School Administrator,* 10:47, pp. 31–34.

Rothman, E. K. (1987). *Hands and Hearts: A History of Courtship in America*. Cambridge, MA: Harvard University Press.

Runes, D. D. (1984). *Dictionary of Philosophy*. Totowa, New Jersey: Rowman & Allanheld.

Schafer, R. J. (1991). "Footnotes on Callahan's Teachers College," in W. E. Eaton (Ed.), *Shaping the Superintendency: A Reexamination of Callahan and The Cult of Efficiency*. New York: Teachers College Press, pp. 36–66.

Schmoker, M. (1992, May 13). "What Schools Can Learn From Toyota of America," *Education Week,* 11:34, pp. 23, 25.

Schonberger, R. J. (1982). *Japanese Manufacturing Techniques*. New York: The Free Press.

Shumway, D. R. (1992). *Michel Foucault*. Charlottesville, Virginia: The University Press of Virginia.

Solomon, J. (1988). *The Signs of the Times*. Los Angeles: Jeremy P. Tarcher, Inc.

Strum, P. (1984). *Louis D. Brandeis: Justice for the People*. New York: Schocken Books.

Taylor, F. W. (1967). *The Principles of Scientific Management*. New York: W. W. Norton and Company, Inc.

van Mucke, D. (1991). Translated "Das Wort" for Bernasconi (1991), p. 63.

Weber, M. (1948). *The Protestant Ethic and the Spirit of Capitalism*. New York: Scribners and Sons.

Chapter 2

THEORY AND IDEOLOGY

Theories are the **metanarratives** that direct scientific inquiry. A metanarrative is a "privileged story or discourse" based on claims that it is "better suited" to frame scientific study (Cherryholmes, 1988, p. 11).

A metanarrative can function within a larger paradigm. A paradigm is an interlocking set of beliefs, rules, and procedures based on the solution to a larger problem on which scientists may be working at any given time. A paradigm can generate several competing theories simultaneously. It may be years before they are all weeded out.

Western science presents itself as the pursuit of truth by "value-free" or "value-neutral" methods (Lakoff and Johnson, 1980, p. 159). However, scientific work is much more creative, volatile, and subjective than most researchers would care to admit publicly. In fact, scientists often shield their subjectivities and create myths about their own work in order to hide these elements from the public (see Beveridge, 1950). Part of the privileged position that scientists enjoy is based on shrouding their work in a cloak of mysterious activities.

Truthful and "objective" scientific work is supposed to be "above" the garden variety intuitions, thoughts, whims, and subjectivities of common people. Scientists have created myths of their own to perpetuate the belief that only the privileged can engage in "true science." The scientists who work in universities, think-tanks, or corporate laboratories are not subject to the rules of everyday life. Scientific researchers are supposedly "above the laws" and govern the rest of humanity. For this reason, stories that surface about "scientific fraud" and occasionally bubble into public consciousness are very disturbing, even though many concede the problem is more widespread than admitted (see Wheeler, 1992, p. 1).

Publicity about squabbles between academics on highly personal grounds mar the image of reasoned debate about how ideas are supposed to be evaluated. Inevitably, the concept of the "objective pursuit of truth" in academe as the norm is shown to be a myth.

One example was the case of Columbia professor Carolyn G. Heilbrun who announced her departure from the English Department with the bitter note, "I've lost the spirit to continue. The atmosphere became impossible. Quite literally, no one in the department spoke to me all year." Professor Heilbrun was referring to the "old-boy network" that ran her department and which she referred to as, "the tree house gang. They're like boys in a treehouse: No girls allowed." One of Dr. Heilbrun's colleagues said of her, "We've lost one of the women who helped create American feminism." (Heller, 1992, p. A13).

In addition to the frailties that becloud most human endeavors, science is locked into a process in which it is often exceptionally difficult to separate what is *true* from what is *false*. Furthermore, science often pursues the false for a very long time before it is abandoned. What is false is often considered true, and much work is expended on advancing a false claim that is later exposed as **pseudoscience,** or as an **ideology.**

This sobering fact ought to indicate that in every area where researchers are pursuing a scientific agenda, there are beliefs, premises, metanarratives, and paradigms that are false, but which we now believe are true. The more we invest in them, teach them, expand and expound on them, the more difficult it is to abandon them when they are exposed as ideologies instead of theories. This predictable dilemma means that there are powerful vested interests in pursuing that which is not theoretical and which is patently, but not obviously, false.

The matter is made more complicated by the fact that some ideologies can generate extremely fruitful explanations even though they may be false at their core. When false leads are the pet perspectives of a field's leading gurus, a discipline may be stunted or led astray. For example, British Mayan expert Eric Thompson's cherished belief that the ancient Mayan stelae scriptures were nothing more than symbolic pictures held up true decipherment for nearly 40 years. Thompson's position as an expert and his public ridicule of competing theories that were essentially correct scared off scholars who refused to tangle with his barbed tongue and poison pen (see Coe, 1992, p. 260).

AN EXAMPLE OF PSEUDOSCIENCE IN ACTION: WILHEIM FLIESS

For 15 years, Wilhelm Fliess was a confidant and major co-worker of Sigmund Freud and helped in the development of psychoanalysis in Germany. Fliess' theories regarding periodicity were supported by thousands of medical observations of his time. His work was demonstrative of avant-garde thinking and statistical manipulations which were quite sophisticated. At one point in his work, he was so confident of his theories that he declared he had banished "chance" from the sphere of events he was observing (Sulloway, 1979, p. 170). His work was very fashionable for over 20 years. Today it even enjoys lingering flickers of popularity in the idea of "biorhythms."

Wilhelm Fliess' metanarratives brought together several related ideas—all firmly rooted in clinical medicine and biology. First, Fliess believed that the human nose was linked to the sex organs, and that it was the cause of some psychosexual problems of the times. Fliess' conclusions were supported by emerging medical evidence of the times (and still considered true) that indicated that nasal tissue swells during menstruation. Furthermore, nasal bleeding is frequent during menstruation and pregnancy, and in some males during puberty. Nose tissue is anatomically similar to that of an erect penis; such "erectile tissue" exists only in the genitalia, the nipples, and the nose. In some cases of arrested development of the sexual organs, there was a simultaneous absence of olfactory lobes and nerves (Sulloway, 1979, p. 148). Some of these observations and thoughts were as old as Pliny (Sulloway, 1979, p. 149). [Most likely Plinius Valerianus, a physician in the court of the Emperor Constantine] (Fruend and Andrews, 1854, p. 1153). The link to Darwin was supplied by the belief that in less-advanced animals, there was a connection between sex and smell. The development of certain psychosocial-sexual problems affiliated with the nose led to the medical technique of nose cocaine application and nasal cauterization to "cure" certain neuroses.

Sigmund Freud allowed Wilhelm Fliess to operate repeatedly on his own nose and sinuses to cure some of his neuroses (Sulloway, 1979, p. 143). The nasal genital theory of Fliess is generally conceded to be a kind of "crackpot" idea in the medical community today, despite the fact that the use of cocaine in nasal surgery is exceptionally widespread among otolaryngologists (Sulloway, 1979, p. 152). The theory of evolution by Charles Darwin provided the idea of not only linking the nose to the sex organs for Fliess, but also provided him with the idea of *periodicity*.

Periodicity is the time of the lunar periods, generally 28 days. It was within this period that cycles of reproduction and evolution may have occurred. This observation by Darwin was followed by the research of other scientists of Darwin's time who documented the cycles of egg laying and reproduction of hundreds of birds and other mammals.

It was not long before the menstruation period became the area of investigation, and was linked to the lunar tides and electrical periodicities. For example, Svante Arrhenius (1859–1927), a Nobel prize winner in 1903, linked the average length of the menstrual cycle in his city (26.68 days) to two electrical periodicities which were quite close in length.

Wilhelm Fliess and other leading scientists believed that the average 23-day period of the human menstrual cycle, in various combinations and re-combinations, explained much of human growth and development. The usual length of human gestation (between 276 and 280 days) was simply 12 times the length of the average ovulation cycle (between 23 and 23 1/3 days).

From biological research in less-advanced animals, Fliess surmised that humans were bisexual in nature and therefore, men had to have a sexual cycle similar to women's. Data concerning the 23-day cycle in men and women was supplied by ratio figures of the determination of sex in human embryos. It showed the normal ratio between the sexes at birth as nearly 105 or 106 males to every 100 females.

Extrapolating data from a definitive study conducted in 1884 based on a figure of 10 million stillborn fetuses, Fliess then calculated the number of stillborn fetuses as 129 males to 100 females. When 129 stillborn males is divided by 106 live-born males, the ratio is 1.217 or 28/23! Fliess argued that the number 23 was supported by the research derived data of his time. These data convinced Fliess that all human sexual chemistry could be explained by 23- and 28-day periods or rhythms. Later Fliess' findings were converted into "biorhythms" so one could predict when certain golfers would win or lose major golf tournaments. Although Fliess' numerologies enjoy popularity today in Japan, Germany, Switzerland, and the United States, they are not considered indicative of any larger scientific theory or idea other than interesting statistical meanderings (Sulloway, 1979, p. 142).

Fliess' findings were supported by thousands of observations. How could they have been wrong? Even in modern science there is a belief that the number of observations is critical to supporting a finding, or even more basic, that from observations, findings are derived. This approach to science has been called the **inductive method** or simply, *induction* (see Oskamp, 1972). Modern science has even taken up the idea that one does not engage in any presuppositions, but rather, builds from these "raw data" the stuff upon which findings, conclusions, constructs, and eventually whole theories are spun. This so-called procedure has been called by some, "the scientific method" (see Van Dalen, 1979, pp. 17–32).

The problem with the inductive method is that it is highly susceptible to beliefs guiding what the data are then supposed to show; there is no way around this problem. All data gathering must assume certain things, or the researcher would not know what data to gather in the first place. This dilemma means that there is already a series of beliefs in place to help point the researcher in the direction of where to look and what to look for in the initial collection of data. On this matter, Highwater (1990) notes, "If even 'objectified' science is a construction based upon a belief system, then it too must be understood as an aspect of mythology" (p. 151).

In the case of Wilhelm Fliess, he was so convinced that his theory of periodicity was correct, that he gathered his data to support his theory instead of using the data to determine if his theory was correct or incorrect, or in the words of Gould (1981), "Theories are built upon the interpretation of numbers, and interpreters are often trapped by their own rhetoric. They believe in their own objectivity, and fail to discern the prejudice that leads them to one interpretation among many consistent with their numbers" (p. 341). The philosopher Bertrand Russell (1946) was even stronger in his criticism, "every attempt to arrive at general scientific laws from particular observations is fallacious" (p. 698).

MORE PSEUDOSCIENCE: THE PRACTICE OF VENESECTION

Another practice attached to a belief was that of *venesection* (bloodletting by opening a vein) by medical doctors. Venesection enjoyed wide popularity in Europe and the United States. As late as 1913 doctors were still arguing for bloodletting in medical practice (Duffy, 1979, p. 233). The historical roots of bloodletting can be traced to the ancient Greeks who bled men and expected them to return to a healthy life after observing the "salutary effects" of menstruation in women. Bleeding was a kind of "therapeutic menstruation" (Highwater, 1990, p. 165).

Bleeding was believed necessary in colonial times because nearly all physicians subscribed to the theory that the body was governed by various "humors" being in balance. This "humoral theory" was advanced by the English physician Dr. Thomas Sydenham. According to humoral theory, a person became sick when gloomy, sinful, or evil matter entered the body via the air and began to ferment and putrefy within it. Bleeding, vomiting, sweating, and purging were believed necessary to remove these putrifying elements from the body. Such damaging matter was particularly virulent and airborn at night. Colonial windows were kept shut to avoid disease. Colonial beds through the late nineteenth century were constructed so that people slept sitting up instead of lying down. This prevented them from being totally captured by disease in a prone position (see two photos on next page). This "disease theory" is why beds were shorter and the headboards so much heavier than modern-day beds. Bleeding a patient was also thought necessary to relieve pressure on the arteries and heart in the case of fever (Duffy, 1979, p. 100).

Pre-modern medicine did not distinguish between moral and nonmoral afflictions. Disease was believed to be attributed to guilt and sin, along with foul

Many people are not aware of the theory behind the construction of their beds. When disease was considered to be the product of night air inhalation, it was believed to be more healthy to sleep sitting up. This resulted in shorter beds and stronger headboards. When this theory of disease was abandoned, beds became longer and the size and strength of headboards was reduced. Practices are often continued long after the theories that produced them have been discarded.

smelling matter that entered the body involuntarily. Mental diseases were believed to be caused by the clogging of the arteries or "thick blood." The "cure" was purification achieved by blood transfusion. Evil internal fermentations were also relieved via the injection of bitters, including eating soap which was believed to "dissolve" these maladies, or eating even stronger doses of soluable tartar (a kind of sediment mixed with yeast from the bottom of wine casks) to deal with forms of melancholia (Foucault, 1973, p. 165).

The nineteenth century medical profession extolled the idea of "herioc practice," which meant that the use of bleeding, purgatives, and emetics to induce frequent vomiting were pushed to the point of being life threatening to the patient. The metanarrative behind this form of medicine was that the cure should be as violent as the disease in order to "match" its effects on the patient (Duffy, 1979, p. 100) and thus restore the body to "balance." Eventually it was this form of practicing medicine that brought such a strong reaction from the public against medical doctors and that caused medical practice to be questioned by the doctors themselves.

The case of venesection is one in which doctors treated patients in ways that not only endangered them, but killed them by the scores as well. Doctors believed that they were doing good for their patients. Their practices were derived from the theories that supported them. Data gathered on the effects of bleeding reinforced rather than negated the continuation of the practices themselves because:

> The enterprise did not proceed from observation to the construction of explanatory images; that on the contrary, the images assured the initial role of synthesis, that their organizing force made possible a structure of perception, in which at last the symptoms could attain their significant value and be organized as the visible presence of truth (Foucault, 1973, p. 135).

Feyerabend (1991) adds that the Western definition of medicine precludes the physician from healing the patient within the patient's own definition of health. Rather, Western medicine insists that a physician work from a theory that, "views the patient through the spectacles of some abstract theory; depending on the theory the patient becomes a sewer system, or a molecular aggregate, or a sack full of humours" (p. 118). The irony of this approach is illustrated in a comment by the editor of a nationally prominent medical journal, "although people still die in our hospitals, very few die undiagnosed" (Feyerabend, 1991, pp. 119–120).

The "Teach My Kid" cartoon that began this chapter is a good example of running schools from a theory, without enabling them to be more effective or humane in the process.

The opposite of the inductive method is the **deductive method.** It refers to the practice of formulating principles or laws, and then gathering data to ascertain if they are accurate or predictive (Beveridge, 1950, p. 113). Deductive science has some spectacular success stories, though in some cases the researchers take pains to "cover up" their essentially deductive lines of inquiry within the acceptable traditions of induction. We shall examine one example in the next section.

DEDUCTIVE GIANTS IN THE SCIENTIFIC COMMUNITY

We shall examine two giants in the scientific community who utilized deductive lines of inquiry: Albert Einstein and Sigmund Freud.

In the case of Einstein, he openly eschewed inductive approaches:

There is no inductive method which could lead to the fundamental concepts of physics. Failure to understand this fact constituted the basic philosophical error of so many investigators of the nineteenth century. . . .We now realize with special clarity, how much in error are those theorists who believe that theory comes inductively from experience (Beveridge, 1950, p. 183).

Einstein worked from his own special feelings and perceptions. "There is no logical way to the discovery of these elemental laws. There is only the way of intuition, which is helped by a feeling for the order lying behind the appearance" (Einstein, 1933). Einstein's perception is underscored by Karl Popper (1986): "There is no such thing as a logical method of having new ideas, or a logical reconstruction of this process . . . every discovery contains 'an irrational element', or 'a creative intuition'" (p. 32). Sulloway (1979) also commented on this aspect when he noted that, "The mythology of science goes to great lengths to mask both the theory-laden nature of its achievements and the role that creative inspiration so often plays in them" (p. 502). Because of the disparity between science as lived and science as written about, Feyerabend (1991) has called most scientific papers "fairy tales" (p. 9).

During the time period 1911–1921, Einstein was hard at work on the general theory of relativity. This theory deals with what happens to gravity when it encounters curved space near massive objects. Einstein's theory predicted that time would move more slowly near the enormous clumping of huge stars in the universe. Supposedly, when asked how he would feel if experiments did not confirm his theory, Einstein is said to have commented, "I would feel sorry for the dear Lord—my theory is correct" (Wilford, 1992, p. B5).

Einstein's deductive theory was never directly tested; few theories can be tested at all. Instead, they must be reduced to statements that can be tested, or that are at least testable in principle (Popper, 1968, p. 47).

This is precisely what happened with Einstein and his theory of general relativity. Several experiments were devised to see if Einstein's theory could predict observed phenomena. Einstein never performed the observations necessary to provide support for his theory. Instead, Dr. Erwin Freundlich, an astronomer in Berlin, mounted several efforts to show that the theory of general relativity was correct (Wilford, 1992, p. B5).

One of the first attempts was to detect if starlight turned red near massive objects. This would demonstrate that space was compressed near the object. Dr. Freundlich found that when attempting to measure light around the planet Jupiter, he was not able to discern the reddening effect. Einstein remarked, "If only we had a considerably larger planet than Jupiter. . . .But nature has not made it a priority to make it easy for us to discover its laws" (Wilford, 1992, p. B5).

Based on studies conducted with a telescope between 1911 and 1913, Dr. Freundlich was successful in showing that Einstein's theory of relativity was much more accurate in predicting Mercury's orbital quirks than Newton's concept of gravity. Thus, the superiority of Einstein's theory began to take shape. A new theory's superiority to an old one—in this case Einstein's over Newton's—is determined by the fact that the new one "corrects the old theory, so that it actually contradicts the old theory; it contains the old theory, but only as an approximation" (Popper, 1979, p. 16).

In 1919, a British astronomer confirmed one of Einstein's predictions of observing an eclipse and the displacement of starlight. Einstein's ideas were confirmed as late as the 1960s by early communication problems between spacecraft radio signals deflected by the sun. These aspects of Einstein's theory of relativity were being confirmed some 50 years after its basic conceptualization.

The Einstein example is a case refuting the idea of *induction* as the "way of science." In fact, Karl Popper (1968) says, "there is no such thing as induction. . . . Inference to theories, from singular statements which are 'verified by experience' . . . is logically inadmissible. Theories are, therefore, *never* empirically verifiable" (p. 40). Popper concludes that theories cannot be verified, but only corroborated. He rejects the idea that theories are *true* or *false* (the utilization of Greek logic), to posit that theories are, "more or less *probable*" (p. 251). This does not mean that statements derived from a theory are not falsifiable, but that a theory *in its totality* is not true or false. We shall return to this point later in the chapter.

SIGMUND FREUD AND DARWINIAN DREAMS

Sigmund Freud's work has left a lasting and profound impact on the human mind. The popular "cocktail party circuit" is sprinkled with terms from Freud's theories. Millions have been exposed to glimpses of Freud, the latest being the Academy award winning psycho-thriller, *The Silence of the Lambs* starring Jodie Foster.

Sigmund Freud borrowed key concepts from the work of Charles Darwin. These concepts were never derived empirically as the scientific method or induction would describe, but rather, were utilized and then covered up by Freud himself for fear that his work would not be accepted by the scientific community of his time as "science."

Frank Sulloway (1979) puts it bluntly:

> Freud, like most successful scientists, employed a highly hypothetico-deductive methodology in his researches. Nonetheless, what has so often shielded this methodology, and accompanying biological premises, from public recognition is the traditional form of argumentation in which scientific research is cast. The historian, in particular, must constantly be aware that the structure of Freud's published arguments is often the exact reverse of the actual genesis of his ideas (p. 421).

Freud was particularly sensitive to the criticism that his work was "mere speculation" and not science at all. He indicated to a friend that, "If only one could get the better people to realize that all our theories are based on experience and not just fabricated out of thin air or thought up over the writing desk. *But the latter is what they all really assume*" (Sulloway, 1979, p. 421).

So Sigmund Freud had a reason to disguise, even lie about his work and its actual orgins in order to ensure its acceptance at the time. Freud accepted the biological premise that, *ontogeny recapitulates phylogeny,* which means that each developing human child manifests the same cycle of creation as the entire human race in its evolutionary development. If this were so, then each developing human also went through the same sexual development as the human species in its evolution (Sulloway, 1979, p. 259). On this assertion, most of Freud's work in child psychology rests. The idea of evolution—the gradual development of more sophisticated and adaptable organisms responding to challenge and contextual change— spawned the notion of stages and with it, of neurotic *fixations* and *regressions* along the way. A human being could encounter psychosexual problems because of trauma encountered at a particular stage. From this theory came the necessary therapy, as in the case of humoral theory and the concept of venesection.

If psychosexual problems were due to fixation at a stage of development, or even a regression to an earlier developmental rung on the phylogenetic ladder, then the doctor had to devise a method of enabling the patient to "get back to" that rung and recognize what had occurred. The patient could then "cure" himself/herself with this recognition. The process was called a *catharsis* (Sulloway, 1979, p. 55).

At first, cocaine was used to put a patient "in the mood," and later, for hypnosis. The method finally used for a catharsis was called "free association," where the patient could say anything and start anywhere she or he preferred. The reason for using free association was that it was drug-free, and because hypnosis did not always work on every patient.

Freud did not worry about "free association" as a method because his underlying belief was the idea that sexual–psychological development was *absolutely predetermined,* and therefore starting anywhere would eventually get him to the place of difficulty in the development of a human being. As Sulloway notes, "Freud. . .did not believe that anything at all was truly 'free' in the life of the mind" (p. 95). This is another example of a professional practice that is always embedded in the theory or belief system that surrounds it.

FREUD'S DREAM THEORY

Freud's most provocative, robust, and boldly applied theoretical work was *The Interpretation of Dreams,* first released in 1899. The book is still in print (Freud, 1978). Freud's position on dreams is only today beginning to be challenged by modern theoretical research on dream–sleep (Blakeslee, 1992).

To understand Freud's theory and his views on dreams, one must reconstruct the critical assumptions underlying his work. First, Freud was a **determinist;** he believed that there was no human "free will." All psychic responses were shaped by causes if one could take enough time to discover them (Runes, 1984, p. 94). This assumption was comingled with his belief that all causes can be reduced to single ones. This process is called *reductionism.*

In Freud's work, his single causative factor of neurosis was aborted—normal psychosexual development. Freud believed that all neuroses were caused by the psychosexual development of a human being. The developmental cycle of a human was anchored by an acceptance of Darwin's concepts of evolution, and by the ideas of Jean-Baptiste Lamarck (1744–1829) that specific genetic tendencies and abilities were directly passed on from parents to offspring via the desire to satisfy internal psychic needs. This doctrine would drive evolution in a much more discernible manner than Darwin's "natural selection" view. Freud held this view long after others had abandoned most of Lamarck's work (Sulloway, 1979, p. 274).

Because Freud was a convinced determinist, he could attack the trivial and link it to something much larger. He wrote books on jokes and speech errors (Freudian slips) that most people and scientists had up to that point considered harmless. Freud, however, saw nothing frivolous about them. He looked upon "the sexual function. . .as the foundation of hysteria and of the psychoneuroses in general" (Sulloway, 1979, p. 90).

Thus, Freud's indispensable metanarrative to all of his work was the sexual function. He focused on this area because he believed: (a) all things could be reduced to single causes, and (b) causes could be explained if one understood their potential impact on normal human evolutionary development which were, (c) established by psychic forces within humans and which drove their responses in everyday life.

Neuroses represented a maladjustment to a situation which caused a breakdown in this normal evolutionary process. Because humans developed predictably, one simply had to trace back to the moment in the conscious mind where the problem manifested itself, and the person could then understand and transform himself/herself into the normal evolutionary channel toward "normality."

Freud took this set of beliefs, with his mainstay metanarrative of the sexual etiology of all neuroses, into his study of human dreams. First, he dismissed the view that dreams were simply the eccentricities of the somatic process. This view has reasserted itself in modern dream–sleep research. Freud, however, did not accept this perspective because his metanarrative precluded this explanation of human psychic activity. Instead, Freud developed his own "theory" or story about how dreams work and what they meant.

According to Freud, all dreams represented a wish; they were the mental manifestations of human desires. These psychic urges were the same forces that drove Lamarckian progeny to replicate their parents' psychic needs in the whole of human evolution.

Human wishes emerged in sleep. The wishes were mixed with the events of the day. The content of the dream had to be interpreted, but "the theme to which these dreams point is, of course, always the history of the malady that is responsible for the neurosis" (Freud, 1978, p. 16).

Freud conjured that the primary cause of dreams were "two psychic forces (tendencies or systems). The first forms the wish expressed by the dream. The second exercises a censorship over this dream-wish, thereby enforcing on it a distortion" (Freud, 1978, p. 52).

Even in sleep, consciousness requires that as wishes pass into the second "agency of the mind" to become recognized, they be approved by that same "agency." In order to obtain approval, the first agency disguises the wishes which he/she knows the second will find disagreeable. In this way, the dream content is transfigured to be able to pass through to consciousness (represented by being able to remember a dream). The transfiguration represents a distortion, but it is an ingenious distortion.

Dreams are highly compacted—i.e., condensations of the past day's experiences, people, actions, and feelings. They are filled with images. Freud insisted that these images not be thought of as pictures, but rather, as *symbols* (Freud, 1978, p. 175). The great challenge before the psychoanalyst was deciphering the symbols in dreams, and helping the patient understand their meaning and importance. This was the process of translating the "latent content" of a dream and bringing it to the waking consciousness of the patient, thereby engaging them in catharsis.

Now, if the underlying etiology of all neuroses is sexual, then it would stand to reason that most, if not all, of the symbols in dreams would be sexual ones. Freud does not disappoint us. He tells us that, "All elongated objects, sticks, tree trunks, umbrellas (on account of the opening, which might be likened to an erection), all sharp and elongated weapons, knives, daggers, and pikes, represent the male member" (Freud, 1978, p. 242).

The female organ is represented by "small boxes, chests, cupboards and ovens . . . also cavities, ships, and all kinds of vessels—A room in a dream generally represents a woman" (Freud, 1987, p. 242). The symbols for the sexual act are, according to Freud, going up and down steep inclines, ladders, and stairs (p. 243).

Freud added to his list of symbols that a female's hat was a male sex organ, and the necktie was as well. Castration is represented by "baldness, hair-cutting, the loss of teeth and beheading" (p. 244). Freud's determinism is clearly revealed in his comment about this, "It may be said that there is no class of ideas which cannot be enlisted in the representation of sexual facts and wishes" (p. 253).

Sulloway (1979) reports that in the eighth and revised edition of *The Interpretation of Dreams,* fully one-fourth ($n=47$) of the 226 dreams reported were Freud's (p. 345). Freud never reported fully on any of his own dreams, fearing that public disclosure would do him harm. Here, we have a metanarrative, largely supported by the theorist's own, very personal recollections which are not fully revealed as support for the theory itself. Echoing comments earlier by Russell, no amount of data can establish or prove anything inductively. One of Freud's most universally accepted concepts had an n (number) of exactly one (1). That was the idea of the Oedipal complex, which Freud recalled as a sexual longing for his mother and a jealousy of his father (Sulloway, 1979, p. 209). In fact, Freud's major reductionist premise—that all neuroses were caused by sexual maladjustment—was based on 18 cases of hysteria ($n=18$) (Sulloway, 1979, p. 91).

MODERN DREAM–SLEEP RESEARCH: A NEW METANARRATIVE

Modern-day dream–sleep research has rejected the Freudian determinism idea that unlocking dream symbolism paved the way to breaking the chains of neuroses in which a person may be trapped. Modern dream–sleep metanarratives have re-established the physiological importance of understanding sleep through electro-chemical analyses.

The contemporary view of sleep is that the brain is engaged in a continuous struggle between two primary circuits—one that requires sleep and another that results in waking. These states are produced by chemicals.

Sleep is believed to consist of four periods. One period occurs about 90 minutes after sleep has begun and reoccurs about 30 minutes before waking up. These two periods are marked with unusually rapid eye movements behind the closed lids. It is called REM (rapid eye movement) sleep.

REM sleep is the result of nervous impulses traveling to the section of the brain that deals with visual data from the spinal cord. For this reason, REM sleep results in highly visual remembrances—the imagery of dreams. Sleep researchers believe that during REM sleep, the brain is even more active than it is when it is awake, even though the body is inert.

REM sleep and dreams appear to some researchers as the brain's way of consolidating memory. In this model, dreams are what happens when some memories acquired during the day are saved and some are jettisoned. Memories to be saved are removed from short-term memory banks, broken into fragments and stored in long-term memory circuits. When one of the circuits is stimulated in REM sleep, the entire memory, and related memories, can flood into dreams (see Blakeslee, 1992, p. B8).

This mixing of memories within the brain's circuits also explains why recent events, anxieties, and tensions flow over into some dream content. As problems are solved, they cease to be part of dreams.

THEORY AND THE PROBLEM OF DEFINITION

These two metanarratives about sleep and dreams bring forth a host of questions about discerning which one is true. Both classical Freudian dream theory and modern-day metanarratives help explain certain data and phenomena.

Yet one view is receding in popularity and another is advancing. One view is considered more "scientific" than the other. In time, it is possible that the classical Freudian dream theory will become a pseudoscience itself, just as Wilhelm Fliess' periodicity and biorhythms were once thought to be "cutting edge science" (see Torrey, 1992).

Popper (1968) has indicated that what is considered "scientific" is a matter of convention—of rules—not of some absolute pure state like "truth" waiting to be discovered (p. 53). For this reason, "science undoubtedly helps in creating and spreading true ideas, it also plays an important role in confirming and propagating false ideas" (Boudon, 1989, p. 5).

One of the major dilemmas facing science is the problem of using language to communicate its workings. Language is not stable. Languages change over time. Words within languages never stake out clear-cut boundaries. There are paronomastic slippages between words in the same language and from language to language. This situation creates a continuous problem of instability and blurring in using language as the basis of precise communication, or in science to denote categories that differentiate between phenomena being investigated.

An example of such "slippage" is provided by Boudon (1989) when he relates a story by Thomas Kuhn (1962) that the latter had been deeply puzzled by the paradox in some of Aristotle's work. The great Greek philosopher had developed such provocative outlines in areas such as logic, rhetoric, ethics, and politics that they are still in use today. Aristotle's view on physics, however, was very "ho hum," so much so that contemporary physicists do not take his ideas seriously. Kuhn was puzzled. How could such a brilliant mind have been so far off in physics?

It was not until viewing a tree and thinking about Aristotle's concepts of physics that Kuhn discovered the answer to the puzzle. He suddenly recalled that modern-day physicists have a very different concept of movement than did Aristotle. Modern physicists view movement by "extrapolating from the nature of the body, for an Aristotlian physicist the movement is conceived as a property of the body itself" (Boudon, 1989, p. 90). These two very different views of movement enabled Aristotle to view a tree growing in the same way as a ball moving down an inclined plane, a view not shared by contemporary physicists.

The meaning of language shifts for researchers is this:

> A research scientist is located within a linguistic framework which tradition provides, and which as a general rule the scientist does not question. . . it is not only a lexical corpus which is inherited, but also a syntax, and at a still higher level of abstraction, might be called theoretical and methodological perspectives. . .paradigms (Boudon, 1989, p. 90).

Pursuing lines of inquiry using everyday language sometimes results in linguistic paradoxes in which the rules of the language cancel the logic out in certain situations. One of the most famous examples is *the liar's paradox* or variants. One variant of this classical language dilemma is called **Epimenides Paradox.** Epimenides was a Cretan who said that all Cretans were liars. Now, if all Cretans were liars, then Epimenides, who was a Cretan, told you the truth. (He didn't lie to you. What he told you was true, but he lied to you.) Therefore, it is false (from Haack, 1978, p. 136).

This is an example of linguistic rules within languages that prevent logical lines of inquiry from unraveling. If meanings within languages based upon the slippages of words within languages also cause communication problems and result in what linguists call *aporias* (uncertainties), then any person pursuing the rules of scientific methodologies will encounter problems in knowing what is true from what is false. (We shall take this issue up in the next chapter when we consider theories of truth.)

THREE CLASSIC PROBLEMS OF DEFINITION IN RESEARCH

In facing the fundamental problem of definition, a researcher confronts three classical problems: (1) infinite regress, (2) arbitrary closure (dogmatism) and (3) a return to the vicious cycle of infinite regress at some point because of a breakdown in set logic (Boudon, 1989, p. 143).

Infinite regress refers to the problem that one definition always leads to another, and that one to another, because no definition is ultimately, completely closed. An example might be with the word "love," which one dictionary defines as, "affection based on admiration or benevolence," or, "a warm attachment, enthusiasm or devotion," or, "attraction based on sexual desire" (Webster's, 1972, p. 501).

One could ask, "What is affection?" This question could lead to a plurality of meanings such as, "a moderate feeling or emotion," or "tender attachment" (p. 15). And then, "What is a feeling?" could lead to, "the undifferentiated background of one's awareness considered apart from any identifiable sensation, perception, or thought" (p. 306). There is no end to this regression, which is why it is called *infinite*. A researcher is caught up in the same web of linguistic mazes as anyone else.

A second problem is simply arbitrarily selecting one definition as final and absolute, and not permitting any deviation or questions to be raised about it. It means pretending that language can be fixated at a certain point and with it, the meaning of words. The result is **dogmatism.**

Linguist E. D. Hirsch, Jr. (1988) argues for linguistic fixation in his book, *Cultural Literacy.* Hirsch concedes that the development of national language is the outcome of an arbitrary decision to "freeze" language development at one state of evolution through imposed standardization. He also admits that "it is a self-conscious political and educational arrangement" (p. 71), and that, "fixed national languages are deliberate constructs" (p. 77). When language is frozen in form, and with it the inherent grammar and usage as well, "The choice of forms and conventions of word order and grammar must all be taken from currently accepted forms, whether or not these have any inherent symmetry or efficiency" (p. 79). We might add here, whether or not the changes in language forms would permit a discourse that would enable a researcher to pursue the question of what was true *or truer* than something else, is also frozen as well.

E. D. Hirsch admits that the freezing of language is a political and arbitrary act. Yet, he fails to see that oral changes in language which would "correct" the phrase, "I am, " and would rule incorrect the phrase, "I be," would place millions of children immediately at odds with their schools, even when he admits that the use of "I be," "is a far more effective and rational pattern," than "I am" (p. 80).

A political system that has frozen its language, its phrasing, and its conceptual schema in a structure that displaces children in its schools cannot be politically neutral. When those who control the schools have children in classes that do the best, and those who are disenfranchised and poor continue to be failed by the system, "schooling" is not a neutral activity. Building a so-called "cultural literacy" from this concept is "cultural elitism" and is a form of social oppression. It is also an example of Foucault's (1980) "power–knowledge" dyad replete with its dominant political overtones in establishing a *regime of truth* perpetuated in the schools.

The third problem in dealing with linguistic definition is to pursue definition up to a point, but to have it embedded in a circular definition of the larger whole. This results in nondefinition and nonelimination, and a vicious cycle "of self-dependence" (Haack, 1978, p. 151).

One of the most controversial moments in American education came when Arthur R. Jensen (1969) of the University of California at Berkeley argued in his article, "How Much Can We Boost IQ and Scholastic Achievement" in the *Harvard Educational Review* that the failure of Title I to improve school achievement was more genetic than it was environmental. Historic charges that such tests were racist were immediately raised in the national uproar following the article's publication. Jensen never defined intelligence in his article. He averred that an adequate definition was not possible, therefore, one could never know what intelligence *really* was (p. 6).

A way out of this dilemma for Jensen was to shift gears, and say that although he could not define it, he *could* measure it. Borrowing from Professor Edwin Boring, Jensen indicated that "intelligence, by definition, is what intelligence tests measure" (p. 8).

Defining intelligence by a subset of the definition of *intelligence* (which was not defined) is an example of "the vicious circle principle" or (V.C.P.). Bertrand Russell attributed this fallacy as the root cause of all fallacies—namely that, "a collection mustn't involve or be definable only in terms of itself" (see Haack, 1978, p. 141).

Here is Russell's (1908) explanation of the fallacy in the Jensenian definition of intelligence:

> 'Whatever involves *all* of a collection must not be one of the collection'; or, conversely, 'If provided a certain collection had a total, it would have members only definable in terms of that total, then the said collection has no total . . . I mean that statements about all its members are nonsense' (p. 63).

The imposition of V.C.P. means that no statement can be eliminated as not appropriate because by definition, it is already part of the whole, and therefore, cannot be a member of the whole. An intelligence test is therefore not a definition of intelligence.

Jensen's work also suffers from the problem of **reification** (Gould, 1981, p. 239), i.e., when an abstraction or a statistical concept becomes a thing. Jensen's work is an example of intelligence—never defined—being wrangled from mathematical patterns alone, then arranged on a ladder using implied worth. In this case, Jensen arranges living creatures by intelligence of g factors. Gould (1981) calls the idea one of the oldest cultural prejudices of the Western world (p. 318).

Gould (1981) summarizes the use of statistics as employed by Jensen (and Fliess):

> Much of the fascination of statistics lies embedded in our gut feeling—and never trust a gut feeling—that abstract measures summarizing large tables of data must express something more real and fundamental than the data themselves (p. 239).

Reams of numerical data cannot make a flawed theory any less flawed. Numbers can be used to support almost any view or cause, or in the words of Darrell Huff (1954), author of the book *How to Lie With Statistics,* "Many a statistic is false on its face. It gets by only because the magic of numbers brings about a suspension of common sense" (p. 138).

SPREADING IDEOLOGY IN THE NAME OF SCIENCE

Those working in science resolve the problem of definition by claiming that their assertions are obvious or "manifest" and do not need any further elaboration. They may refuse to engage in definitions at all, for as Popper (1979) reminds us, "I am not interested in definitions; since all definitions must use undefined terms, it does not, as a rule, matter whether we use a term as a primitive term or as a defined term" (p. 58).

The third way those working in science bypass the problem of definition is to work within a *paradigm* (Kuhn, 1962). A paradigm involves researchers working around a common problem, or a generally accepted methodology for solving problems. Paradigms enclose any definition of truth used in science. Paradigms also exist in everyday discourse (see Polanyi, 1989). The use of a paradigm in science enables those working in a field to avoid spending unnecessary time wrestling with definitions.

In this sense, a paradigm represents a partial closure, at least in the matter of definitions. In the words of Popper (1934), "Every test of a theory, whether resulting in its corroboration or falsification, must stop at some basic statement or other which we *decide to accept*" (p. 159). Popper indicates that this problem has no natural end. Those working on a problem simply decide to stop at some juncture. This notion of scientific inquiry reinforces the idea that truth is locked into a system of words, assumptions, contexts, and arbitrary decisions. Truth is a captive of the conceptual metaphorical structure in which it is embedded. Actions taken will be congruent with that structure, and come to serve as self-fulfilling prophecies (Lakoff and Johnson, 1980, p. 156).

A theory that cannot be debated, attacked, criticized, and ultimately exposed on its most basic premises and assumptions is called an *ideology*. One definition of ideologies is that they are, "reassuring fables, unconsciously complicit in a judgment determined by self-interest" (Canguilheim, 1988, p. 31).

Ideologies are metanarratives about things that cannot be completely open about their assumptions. The lack of openness occurs either because their advocates do not permit it, or because they are unconsciously accepted or hidden from view. Ideologies often rest on "self-evident" or "unexamined" truths.

Diagram 2 is a schematic of how, in the pursuit of truth, working within a generally accepted paradigm, researchers can end up with an ideology or pseudoscience believing that in fact it is science and do what Boudon (1989) indicated, spreading that which was false in the name of science itself.

Paradigms are frameworks of thoughts. They rest upon some scientific data and facts. In the case of Wilhelm Fliess, his assertions regarding periodicity rested on a scientific base. He was working within the same paradigm as Freud, using the same assumptions and facts. Some of the assumptions were garnered from Darwin, others from leading biologists and researchers of his time.

Fliess spun off his metanarrative from these webs of thoughts and networks of interlocking facts and assumptions. His work was considered scientific. It was validated statistically. Yet today, Fliess' work is an ideology, and the larger Freudian paradigm from which the ideology was derived is highly suspect itself.

Diagram 2   THE DEVELOPMENT OF IDEOLOGY WORKING WITHIN A GENERALLY
ACCEPTED PARADIGM

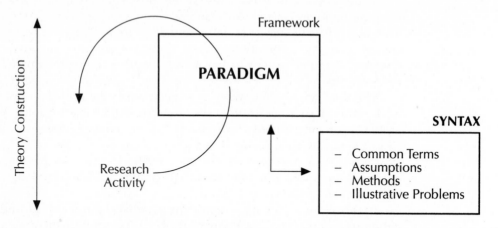

Boudon (1989) believes that the development of ideologies is part and parcel of normal scientific work, particularly in the social sciences. The reason is that the words and ideas utilized in the social sciences have no counterpart in reality. They cannot be directly verified or checked (p. 91). Ideas such as Freud's "unconscious" do not stand for anything in reality.

Paradigms in the social sciences (education is one and is grounded in others such as sociology, anthropology, psychology, political science, and history) are highly susceptible to "E effects." These refer to "epistemological effects" and cluster within paradigms as unstated or unverified abstractions or mental processes that cannot be checked against reality. As a result, social science paradigms are highly likely to spin off metanarratives that are ideologies rather than scientific theories. Collections of facts can be supported by any number of theories, and all of them may be false (see Beveridge, 1950, p. 113).

Boudon (1989) provides the historical context for understanding how the work of Wilhelm Fliess and many others working in social scientific fields was once considered "scientific" and how it is now is viewed as "pseudoscientific," when he explains that:

> Before there are serious questions raised about a paradigm, it will often have had time to produce theories which will be widely accepted by the scientific community, which will have unquestioned scientific authority and which consequently might well exert considerable social and political influence (p. 92).

Research in the social sciences is therefore likely to produce many pseudoscientific metanarratives that, in time, prove to be fallacious, like periodicity and perhaps even psychoanalyses and its deterministic foundations centered in reductionism as well.

Paradigms spin off theories rather naturally in the development of stories or metanarratives in science. Knowing how to verify such theories as reliable constructs and even in learning to view paradigm truthfulness itself is the subject of the next chapter.

PSEUDOSCIENCE IN EDUCATIONAL ADMINISTRATION

As a field, educational administration began as a pseudoscience since it was grounded in Taylor's scientific management concepts. Early university doctoral programs were all devoted to making the field of educational administration like engineering based on "value neutral" concepts linked to objectivistic science (see Callahan, 1962, and Eaton, 1990). Later, the field's dominant metanarrative became organizational theory. The result of this transformation has been that educational administration has been epitomized by Thomas Sergiovanni (1993) as "characterless" with "little or no identity of its own . . . little or no sense of what it is, what it means, where it is going, or even why it exists" (p. 1).

One example of recent pseudoscientific activity has been the so-called "effective schools" research. The "effective schools" research is most likely an ideology passed off as scientific doctrine.

The derivation of the effective schools research was staked out by examining statistical outliers of high-scoring schools on standardized tests. Within the "normal" distribution of scores, the outliers were treated as special causes (exceptions to the rules) instead of as common causes (within the rules).

Because the schools were created by common cause variations and therefore within the norms, the characteristics of these schools yielded only correlates. The list of the "effective" correlates such as a strong principal, a learner-oriented faculty who believe all children can learn, a disciplined environment, a program centered on academics, and a structured system of feedback to students (Edmonds, 1982) will not predict success on standardized tests. It stands to reason that common causes would not predict, but would be correlative. Due to the fact that studies which show no significant difference in the application of the correlates are rarely reported in research or professional journals (called "publication bias" by Light and Pillemer, 1984, p. 35), it is difficult to gauge whether they are simply the result of random variables functioning within normal fluctuations of a bell-shaped distribution where chance would be at work, or whether they are really more causal (and hence, controllable) in nature. Some studies have shown no significant difference in achievement when applying the effective school correlates (see Grady, Wayson and Zirkel, 1989).

The effective schools research may also be an example of the "blind spot" of most Western scientific reasoning, i.e., a refusal to consider that its "objectivity" is a myth, a kind of transparent, self-deception that is easily deluded into accepting one world view as true over another possible world view. It is also a case where correlates (descriptors) are passed off as axioms (givens), and where principles are disguised as laws instead of being considered propositions to be tested (see McGowan, 1991, p. 102). Deming's (1991) 14 points of quality are a prime example of hypotheses stated as laws. One consequence is that Western science has been troubled with producing tautologies (self-evident "truths") supported by statistical data that fail to predict. The litmus test is prediction. Tautologies cannot predict. Their prediction power is zero, although their descriptive fecundity may be profound.

Another problem with the effective schools research is that as "objectivist science," it fits neatly into the status quo, reinforcing existing notions of bureaucratic authority and control. Administrative positions are seen as being justified by "research" as necessary, particularly the role of the principal as rule giver and interpretor of norms. The research of so-called "effective schools" buttresses conventional administrative hierarchies at a time when they are severely being called into question by school reformers across the nation (see Steffy, 1993, pp. 257–278). Conventional science is grounded in control over both man and nature. It is aptly represented in the "power–knowledge" concept.

SUMMARY

Both theories and ideologies emanate from paradigms. Paradigms in the social sciences are laced with assumptions and concepts that do not refer directly to reality, but rather, to mental processes.

This situation means that researchers working within a common paradigm are susceptible to developing metanarratives that, although appearing to be "scientific," eventually prove to be pseudoscientific. Pseudoscience contains some scientific data and is rooted in scientific ideas, concepts, or accepted positions. However, as a totality, a pseudoscientific metanarrative or theory is *false*.

Scientific theories can be developed with inductive or deductive methods. The mythology of science insists that nearly all accepted theories or "breakthroughs" were derived inductively using the so-called scientific method. Many scientists are very uncomfortable admitting how patently subjective and intuitive scientific work really is.

Since nearly all scientific studies begin with a point of view, none of them can truly be considered objective. Nearly all are subjective, and nearly all utilize deductive methods—i.e., proceeding from premises, assumptions, laws, or theories to "dig" for data that can refute or sustain such positions.

Reductionism in science is the search for one causative factor that lies behind all "effects." Determinism is the belief that all effects in science are causal in nature and simply need to be "discovered."

Theories are embedded in language. The use of language and with it, words, present researchers with the dilemma of using definitions that are inherently unstable. Upon close examination, the findings, classifications, categories, and all distinctions revealed in research may collapse.

The use of definitions in science presents the researcher with several dilemmas. Among them is the problem of infinite regress, or endless definitions that are never truly closed. Another is an arbitrary stopping that raises the issue of dogmatism. Finally, the matter of Russell's vicious circle principle (or V.C.P.) presents the dilemma of definition within set theory, which indicates that in some situations, the use of some words or terms results in ineliminability, which negates a definition based on a word because it is still part of the word and is not different. An example was provided in the case of Jensen's definition of intelligence in the continuing controversy over whether I.Q. is chiefly hereditary or environmental.

We also have the example of a practice being thoroughly discredited, and with it, the theory that has supported it in the case of venesection. Surprisingly, blood-letting as a practice may reappear in medical circles supported by a new theory. A Finnish medical study of 1900 men in the age range of 42 to 60 years reported in 1992 that high levels of iron in the blood increased the risk of heart attack. One way of reducing the iron levels was to bleed patients to remove excess iron and prevent heart disease (Altman, 1992, p. A1, A6). The Finnish study also demonstrates that practices are always the captive of some theory.

Perception Check and Applications

1. Pseudoscience in Education

As an applied social science field, education has had its share of pseudoscientific theories. Trace the creation of the metanarratives of Arnold Gesell and G. Stanley Hall in American education. What were the larger paradigms in which their theories emerged? What has happened to their ideas today and what, if any, legacies did they leave in the field?

2. Intelligence and the Problem of Definition

The chapter dealt with the problem of definition and used the example of "intelligence." One of the other problems with intelligence is that it has been *reified,* i.e., made into a concrete "thing" from an abstraction. Read Stephen Jay Gould's, (1981) *The Mismeasure of Man,* specifically chapter six, "The Real Error of Cyril Burt," pp. 234–320, for an account of how intelligence has been misnamed and how statistics have been used to justify the views of those with predetermined beliefs. Find other words in education that have similar problems with definitions and have had to resort to statistical patterns for "proof."

3. Contemporary Metanarratives in Education

Identify at least five metanarratives that are at work in schools and are rarely questioned by teachers or administrators. To help trigger your response, you may wish to review one or more of the following works: Basil Bernstein (1990), *The Structuring of Pedagogic Discourse* (London: Routledge); Peter McLaren (1986), *Schooling as a Ritual Performance* (London: Routledge & Kegan Paul); Larry Cuban (1984), *How Teachers Taught* (New York: Longman); or Henry Giroux (1983), *Theory and Resistance in Education* (South Hadley, Massachusetts: Bergin and Garvey).

4. Controversial Metanarratives and Educational Conflict

One of the most controversial areas of public education has been that of sex education. What are the overt and covert issues with including sex education in public schools? You may wish to read or review Mary Breasted's (1970) classic book, *Oh! Sex Education* (New York: Signet Book) to assist you in identifying the major issues. Who benefits from including sex education in the curriculum? What are the actual reasons for supporting or resisting sex education in public schools?

5. America's Elite Boarding Schools: Power–Knowledge from Birth to Death

Michel Foucault's concept of "power–knowledge" is no more apparently at work than in the curriculum and methods of America's elite boarding schools. Read Peter W. Cookson, Jr. and Caroline H. Persell's (1985) book, *Preparing for Power* (New York: Basic Books, Inc.) and identify the ways that children of the people from privileged sectors of America are prepared for entrance to corporate networks and webs of influence in American society. Engage in a discussion as to how or if public schools could incorporate some of the same strategies and what the forms of resistance might be if they were so incorporated in public schools.

Key Chapter Concepts and Terms

deductive method

From the Latin *deductio* which means "a leading down" (Runes, 1984, p. 90). Refers to the method of generalizing from very broad principles or laws to specific instances or events based on predictions from them. In logic, a conclusion that follows from the premise.

determinism

The concept that all facts in the universe are the result of laws or causes. Unlocking human behavior or psychological problems meant that one had to come to understand the causative factors which produced the mental effects observed or experienced. According to Runes (1984), it was "contained as a theory in the atomism of Democritus of Abdera" (p. 94).

dogmatism

A point of view that is insufficiently grounded in fact, empirical data, or rationale to support a premise, assumption, or conclusion. From the Greek word *dogma*, i.e., opinion (Runes, 1984, p. 99).

Epimenides paradox (the liar's paradox)

A very ancient riddle in which the rules of language turn in on themselves, producing a standing contradiction, a surprise, or a situation contrary to all expectations (Freund and Andrews, 1854, p. 1077).

ideology

A false metanarrative that is considered true, also pseudoscience (see above). Originally, it referred to a term by Destutt de Tracy for the analyses of ideas emanating from sensory inputs (see Runes, 1984, p. 156). Later, the term was applied by Napoleon to all political philosophies that he disliked.

inductive method

Sometimes called the "Baconian method" after Francis Bacon (1561–1626) in which specific data or facts are accumulated and formulated into laws or principles. This procedure enabled man to master nature (Runes, 1984, p. 49). Also refers to the idea of generalizing about a class of objects based on an analysis of only a few of them.

infinite regress

The problem of definition in the social sciences using natural language. Linguistic definitions rarely close a word completely, leaving no room for ambiguity. Defined words must use undefined words to explain or border them. There is no end to this problem except to resort to the use of nonnatural languages.

metanarrative

An idea, position, or theory, that enjoys a privileged position of unquestioned supremacy in research or inquiry because it is viewed as the "truth," or the exemplary way of thinking about or performing scientific research. Often rests upon assumptions and premises that are not scientific, or have not been subject to serious criticism.

pseudoscience

A metanarrative that "looks like" science but is not. Ultimately, pseudoscience is exposed because it cannot really be tested or criticized, or because it fails to pass a number of scientific tests. Pseudoscience often includes some truly scientific factoids, or rests on some actual scientific premises. However, the total metanarrative is completely false.

reductionism

A process of eliminating most possible causes except one or two for all observed effects. Often related to the *principle of parsimony* in statistics in which the greatest number of explanations is subsumed under the most universal heading or formula in which the least number of assumptions have been made. This idea is sometimes called *Ockham's razor* after William of Ockham (Runes, 1984, p. 242).

reification

The process of making abstractions into "real things," forgetting that they are not actually reality. Some examples are the I.Q. as advanced by Arthur Jensen or Cyril Burt, and the concept of the unconscious of Sigmund Freud.

the scientific method

A procedure derived by logicians of the last century that describes a step-by-step approach to applying scientific reasoning. The "method" is a representative of the logical positivistic approach to science, sometimes called scientific empiricism or logical empiricism (Runes, 1984, p. 302). The scientific method is an example of one paradigm in science, and is representative of it, i.e., *logical positivism*.

References

Altman, L. K. (1992, September 8). "High Levels of Iron Promote Heart Attacks Finnish Study Finds," *Lexington Herald-Leader,* pp. A1, A6.

Beveridge, W. I. B. (1950). *The Art of Scientific Investigation.* New York: Vintage Books.

Blakeslee, S. (1992, January 7). "Scientists Unraveling Chemistry of Dreams," *New York Times,* p. B5.

Boudin, R. (1989). *The Analysis of Ideology.* Chicago: University of Chicago Press.

Callahan, R. E. (1962). *Education and the Cult of Efficiency.* Chicago: University of Chicago Press.

Canguilhem, G. (1988). *Ideology and Rationality in the History of the Life Sciences.* Cambridge, MA: MIT Press.

Cherryholmes, C. H. (1988). *Power and Criticism.* New York: Teachers College Press.

Coe, M. D. (1991). *Breaking the Maya Code.* New York: Thames and Hudson, Inc.

Deming, W. E. (1991). *Out of the Crisis.* Cambridge, MA: MIT Press.

Duffy, J. (1979). *The Healers: A History of American Medicine.* Urbana, Illinois: University of Illinois Press.

Eaton, W. E. (Ed.) (1990). *Shaping the Superintendency.* New York: Teachers College Press.

Edmonds, R. R. (1982). "Programs of School Improvement: An Overview," *Educational Leadership,* 40, pp. 4–11.

Einstein, A. (1933). Preface in *Where is Science Going?* by Max Planck. Trans. by James Murphy. London: George Allen Unwin Ltd.

Feyerabend, P. (1991). *Three Dialogues on Knowledge.* Oxford, England: Basil Blackwell Ltd.

Freud, S. (1978). *The Interpretation of Dreams.* Trans. by A. A. Brill. New York: Random House.

Freund, W., and Andrews, E. A. (1854). *A Copius and Critical Latin–English Lexicon.* New York: Harper and Brothers Publishers.

Foucault, M. (1973). *Madness and Civilization.* New York: Random House.

Foucault, M. (1980). *Power/Knowledge.* New York: Pantheon Books.

Gould, S. J. (1981). *The Mismeasure of Man.* New York: W. W. Norton and Company.

Grady, M. L., Wayson, W. W., and Zirkel, P. A. (1989). "A Review of Effective Schools Research as it Relates to Effective Principals." Tempe, Arizona: University Council for Educational Administration.

Haack, S. (1978). *Philosophy of Logics.* Cambridge, England: Cambridge University Press.

Heller, S. (1992, May 20). "A Leading Feminist Literary Critic Quits Post at Columbia, Citing 'Impossible' Atmosphere," *The Chronicle of Higher Education,* 38:37, pp. A13–14.

Highwater, J. (1990). *Myth and Sexuality.* New York: Penguin Books.

Hirsch, E. D., Jr. (1988). *Cultural Literacy.* New York: Random House.

Huff, D. (1954). *How to Lie With Statistics.* New York: W. W. Norton and Company.

Jensen, A. R. (1969, Winter). "How Much Can We Boost IQ and Scholastic Achievement," *Harvard Educational Review,* 39:1, pp. 1–123.

Kuhn, T. S. (1962). *The Structure of Scientific Revolutions.* Chicago: University of Chicago Press.

Lakoff, G., and Johnson, M. (1980). *Metaphors We Live By.* Chicago: University of Chicago Press.

Light, R. J., and Pillemer, D. B. (1984). *Summing Up: The Science of Reviewing Research.* Cambridge, MA: Harvard University Press.

McGowan, J. (1991). *Postmodernism and Its Critics.* Ithaca, New York: Cornell University Press.

Oskamp, S. (1972). "Methods of Studying Human Behavior," in L. S. Wrightsman (Ed.), *Social Psychology in the Seventies.* Monterey, California: Brooks/Cole, pp. 30–67.

Polanyi, L. (1989). *Telling the American Story.* Cambridge, MA: MIT Press.

Popper, K. (1934). "The Empirical Basis," in D. Miller (Ed.), *Popper Selections.* Princeton, New Jersey: Princeton University Press, pp. 152–170.

Popper, K. (1968). *The Logic of Scientific Discovery.* New York: Harper and Row.

Popper, K. (1979). *Objective Knowledge: An Evolutionary Approach.* Oxford, England: Clarendon Press.

Runes, D. D. (1984). *Dictionary of Philosophy.* Totowa, New Jersey: Rowman & Allanheld.

Russell, B. (1908). "Mathematical Logic as Based on The Theory of Types," *American Journal of Mathematics,* 30, as cited in Haack, p. 263.

Russell, B. (1945). *A History of Western Philosophy.* New York: Simon and Schuster.

Sergiovanni, T. J. (1993, April 13). "Organizations or Communities? Changing the Metaphor Changes the Theory" Invited address of Division A, American Educational Research Association, Annual Meeting, unpublished paper, 27 pp.

Steffy, B. E. (1993). *The Kentucky Education Reform: Lessons for America.* Lancaster, PA: Technomic.

Sulloway, F. J. (1979). *Freud: Biologist of the Mind.* New York: Basic Books.

Torrey, E. F. (1992). *Freudian Fraud.* New York: HarperCollins Publishers.

Van Dalen, D. B. (1979). *Understanding Educational Research.* New York: McGraw Hill Book Company.

Webster's Seventh New Collegiate Dictionary (1972). Springfield, MA: G. & C. Merriam Company.

Wheeler, D. L. (1992, April 29). "Scientists Begin to Question Confidentiality of Fraud Investigations," *The Chronicle of Higher Education,* 38:34, pp. 1 and A8.

Wilford, J. N. (1992, March 24). "Letters to a Supporter Record Einstein's Search for Proof," *New York Times* p. B5.

Chapter
3

THEORIES OF TRUTH

The purpose of science is to discern what is true from what is not. Those engaged in the enterprise of science are not supposed to be satisfied with anything less than understanding the universe, the nature of existence and the reasons behind what humans perceive to be true, and the procedures for discerning the nature of things.

Science, as an activity, is a fairly recent one in human affairs. Long before what we call the kind of scientific work that occurs in contemporary society in universities, corporate laboratories, and public and privately funded think-tanks, humans were wondering and probing about reality, about the nature of human actions, and about developing customs, traditions, and practices loosely called *knowledge* about such matters. The repository of human knowledge became the arts and the humanities. "A really comprehensive world view absolutely cannot do without the poets," says philosopher Paul Feyerabend (1991, p. 148). Before the development of writing, such things were passed on by oral tradition.

The development of science is dependent upon the capability of people to depict human thought processes, namely, ideas. The development of writing is the cornerstone of scientific endeavors, as well as religion, literature, and drama.

The other crucial activity for science was the creation of systems of numeration or numbers to communicate amounts and mass. From these two sources, such applied activities as road and building construction, astronomical observations, and systems of warfare were begun.

Very primitive forms of both objects and numeration are found in native Indian populations, notably the Maoris of New Zealand. They used tally sticks for making various notations regarding genealogy and for detailing financial transactions. "Tallies seem to be distributed all over the world," comments writing scholar Hans Jensen (1969, p. 25).

The development of true script which would qualify as human writing depends upon the production of some sort of drawing or symbol that is used for communication. Rock drawings on mountain ledges or in caves is a kind of subject writing that may involve a simple story line. From these evolved the use of more or less conventional symbols (word-pictures). Once symbols had become stylized, all that remained was the connection to the human voice and speech.

There are several systems in which the voice and speech were attached to writing schemes. Coe (1992) has identified three such basic writing systems. The first was logographic such as Chinese or ancient Egyptian, in which a single morpheme or a whole word was attached to a written sign (p. 27). The second is classified as *syllabic*. This type of system would be represented in Mycenaean writing, or the modern Cherokee Indian text (p. 28). The third would be alphabetical, originating with the Greeks in the ninth century B.C., based on an earlier Phoenician model that they had adopted (p. 29).

Very early in human development, political leaders keenly understood the intimate linkage between writing and ethnic or national unity. Writing generates a level of consciousness among its users. Kablai Khan, the great Mongol warrior, used national Mongolian script to consolidate his political holdings. Likewise, when the Spaniards entered Mexico in 1520 under Hernando Cortez, they sacked and burned the great Aztec libraries in order to destroy that culture. Book burning is an assault on a culture, whether performed by the Chinese dictator Shi Huang-ti in 213 B.C. or Adolf Hitler in the 1930s in Germany (see Jensen, 1969, p. 18).

When the tools of human communication, as represented in the press and in magazine publishing, are considered in twentieth century America, the use of script constitutes a monopoly. It represents systematic propaganda to perpetuate the existing political arrangements and privilege (see Herman and Chomsky, 1988). Texts are the way humans "reproduce the world to a manageable format" says Umberto Eco (1990). However, he adds that they, "are open to an intersubjective interpretive discourse" (p. 21).

SCIENCE AS A DISTINCTIVE TEXT

Scientific work utilizing script and a set of procedures based on implicit and explicit belief systems can be considered a *text*. The analysis of texts is called *hermeneutics*. It involves interpreting the meaning of script. No text has a single meaning that is stamped by someone in authority. The act of interpretation, "is a dialectic between openness and form, initiative on the part of the interpreter and contextual pressure" (Eco, 1990, p. 21).

German philosopher Wilhelm Dilthey (1833–1911) was one of the first serious, modern scholars to reinstate the hermeneutical interpretation of texts beyond Bible studies and ancient scripts. Dilthey applied hermeneutical methods to larger social phenomena in order to gain greater understanding of their meaning. In this effort, he was greatly influenced by Friedrich Schleiermacher (Palmer, 1969). He called his method **the hermeneutical circle** (Rickman, 1976, pp. 10–11).

Dilthey's idea was that interpreting a text can really only be understood within a language and a culture. To understand a culture, one had to treat it as a text itself. Science can also be treated as a text. The advantage in doing so expands the frame of reference for the investigator and his or her comprehension of the impact of what is being studied.

The hermeneutical circle plunged the researcher right into the middle of things. It was the recognition that truth was never self-contained or walled-off from its relationships with larger social agencies and mores. The same is true of science. Science is not an activity that is divorced from the rest of human endeavors and problems. By considering it a text and applying certain methods to it as a whole, we can come to a better understanding of its strengths and weaknesses.

A good example of the hermeneutical circle is an examination of the *Darwinian Revolution* by Michael Ruse (1979) in Great Britain between the years 1830 and 1875. Ruse indicates that, "The Darwinian Revolution cannot be considered a single thing . . . often it is portrayed as a triumph of science over religion . . . it had different sides, difference causes, and different effects" (p. 273). Without using the hermeneutical circle, a researcher would underestimate the causes and conflict produced by Darwin's ideas in England.

Behind science and virtually all human communication lies *language*.

The phenomenon of understanding, then, shows the universality of human linguisticality as a limitless medium that carries everything within it—not only the 'culture' that has been handed down to us through language, but absolutely everything—everything (in the world and out of it) is included in the realm of 'understandings' and understandability in which we move (Gadamer, 1976, p. 25).

Gadamer (1976) reiterates that language is not simply a mirror. Rather, it is a game of constant interpretation that each of us plays every day. "In this game, nobody is above and before all the others," he concludes (p. 32).

Present-day hermeneutics includes the influence of a living language, complete with its own biases which are linked to political and social power relationships in a social context. Language itself is authoritarian in this sense and Gadamer (1976) reminds us that, "Reality does not happen 'behind the back' of language . . . reality happens precisely *within* language" (p. 35).

So the very language science uses is itself fraught with subjectivities and prejudice. We have learned to "see" with prejudice and we were blinded by it. Even though we thought we were "open" to truth and were actively pursuing it, the very words we were using to think about it, closed our eyes to the possibilities that were before us. It is only through "hermeneutical reflection" that these distinctions and contradictions can be broached and recognized (Gadamer, 1976, p. 38). Such reflection means coming into conscious realization of the ways that perception is preshaped by one's culture and the language habits of the group into which a person was born and reared (see Sapir, 1949, p. 160).

The interaction between language and culture and cultural stereotypes was brilliantly illustrated by Professor Shelley Fisher Fishkin in her research into the origins of Mark Twain's character, Huckleberry Finn. Fishkin's research has discovered a strong possibility that Huckleberry Finn was African American.

In her research, Fishkin came across an article in *The New York Times* in 1874 in which Samuel Clemens (Mark Twain) described a "sociable Jimmy"—an African-American teenager who fascinated him with his language patterns. By tracing the language patterns from the article to those used by Twain in *The Adventures of Huckleberry Finn*, Fishkin developed a strong argument that Huck was African American. The importance of the finding concedes Fishkin, is that,

> Literary criticism has been segregated. The assumption has been that white texts grew out of a white tradition, black texts out of a black tradition. I'm suggesting that African-American voices have helped shape what we have thought of as mainstream American literature. (Winkler, 1992, p. A6).

The finding also de-centers the current arguments about multiculturalism. Those in favor of multiculturalism want to include "minority" works in the curriculum. Those opposed want to keep "great" literary works separate. Neither side is correct if *The Adventures of Huckleberry Finn*, the great American novel, was a product of multicultural voices embodied in its main character.

The shocking nature of the revelation that Huck Finn was African American has taken scholars aback at their own racism and classifications. Why was the great American novel not considered multicultural? The evidence from the article was known to other Twain scholars. Even people who are aware of language prejudice can be blind to the obvious.

THE SEARCH FOR TRUTH

The popular image of a scientist struggling for truth in the laboratory, overcoming the odds, and battling against the skeptics who doubt his or her theory about "X" is the stuff of Hollywood and pulp novels. We owe this image of the pursuit of truth to Plato, and to his idealistic conception of truth as a state or condition above all others that was "real." Plato's truth was stable and for all time. Words stood for fixed properties and things in the world, and these were related to each other. The "truth" merely had to be teased out from the confusion of mortal homo sapien by logical thought processes (see Lakoff and Johnson, 1980, p. 204).

It was this concept of truth that George Howland (1896), Superintendent of Schools of Chicago, spoke of under the title, "How The School Develops Character":

> The pupil must know what is true and beautiful ere the conception of truth and beauty can dawn upon his mental vision, must learn of the good and the right if ever goodness and righteousness shall be to him more than empty words (p. 114).

With the rise of science in the seventeenth century and its accompanying doctrines and methods of "objectivity," many people became convinced that it (science) was supposed to be the golden road to this intellectual nirvana. Paul Feyerabend (1991) denies that understanding science can be approached logically. Instead, "you have to approach science. . . by tracing. . .life stories. . . .analogies there are—but no permanent structures" (p. 156). Science itself has many false roads, and is easily prejudiced by linguistic bias and statistical manipulation. As a result, what is believed to be true today may not be so tomorrow. What then is truth?

The modern notion of **truth** is that few things are ever really true, and if they appear to be, they will not endure over time and will eventually become false. What appears to be "true" is simply a statement or proposition that cannot be shown to be false *for the moment*. This is the "game" of science, and it has no end. There is no final verification possible, so there are no ultimate truths (Popper, 1968, p. 53).

CONTEMPORARY OBSERVATIONS ABOUT TRUTH

What we know about truth can be derived from these observations:

1.   Truth Is Linguistically and Culturally Defined.

Truth is neither absolute nor universal. It is embedded and relative to linguistic conceptual systems, part and parcel of everyday discourse and specific cultures (see Lakoff and Johnson, 1980, p. 159). Because of these temporal and specific cultural conditions, "all observers are not led by the same physical evidence to the same picture of the universe" [called **the Sapir-Whorf hypothesis**] (Whorf, 1956, p. 214). For example, the Eskimo language has four words for *snow*, the Hopi language uses the same word for *insect, pilot,* and *plane,* and some Arabic languages have nearly 100 words for *camel*. Some Native American languages have no noun/verb distinctions, and others have no word for *time*. English makes the words *flame, storm, lightning,* and *spark* nouns, while Hopi represents them with verbs (Palmer, 1986, p. 45). The ancient Egyptians used a 24-letter alphabet, but all the letters were consonant signs only (Jensen, 1969, p. 62). What is true is culturally constructed. Truth is therefore invented and not discovered (Eco, 1990, p. 67).

The invention of truth was forcibly illustrated in July of 1992 when the Yokohama Rubber Company in Tokyo, Japan apologized to its Arabic customers for making tires with treads that resembled the word for Allah, the Islamic God. The Yokohama Rubber Company indicated that the tread design (called Y-814) was generated by a computer which was searching for maximization of driver safety and was not intended as a blasphemy against the Islamic Supreme Diety. The company also apologized for its ignorance of Islam (Associated Press, July 25, 1992, p. A3).

In some languages, it is impossible to separate the meaning between a written sentence and an utterance. English is one of these languages (Palmer, 1986, p. 154). A model is provided by Matthews (1965) in which the North American Hidatsa Indian language contains six examples of the meaning of a sentence being determined by the mood imparted by the speaker in uttering it. In Hidatsa, if the speaker knows the sentence he relates is true, it is spoken with great emphasis. If this emphatic mood is questionable, the speaker is considered a liar. If the same sentence is delivered in the indefinite mood, it means that he/she does not really know whether it is true. If the sentence ends with a period mood, it means that the speaker believes it to be true. However, if it does not, then he/she did not lie, but was simply mistaken (Palmer, 1986, p. 152).

Political relationships are part of all texts since they are,"products or inscriptions of the discursive formations of institutions or ideologies" (Felperin, 1988, p. 32). Such ideologies are usually submerged in the requirements for linearity and sequencing in speech and script. They are therefore "hidden" to those using them, and to those who may believe that they are "open" and nonprejudiced in their observations. This blindness leads to ethnocentrism, a view that holds that people who are not like you are inherently inferior. Says Paul Feyerabend (1991), "Many people make the mistake of assuming that the world that arose as a response to their actions, or their history, underlies all other cultures, only the others are too stupid to notice" (p. 43). Lakoff and Johnson, (1980) indicated that, "Absolute objective truth is not only mistaken, but socially and politically dangerous" (p. 159).

Each human culture acts upon reality, and in turn is shaped by the actions and interactions with it. More than one response works. To survive, human cultures must find sustenance (response) from that reality or "Being." They are successful or they perish. This observation means that, "there is no way of connecting the reactions with universal substance or universal laws" (Feyerabend, 1991, p. 43). The full implication of this observation is that *truth is contextually dependent* rather than contextually independent.

The necessity of knowing the context to understand if a sentence is true is established by trying to ascertain a sentence's meaning, independent of context. Usually, a second sentence is required—normally, a paraphrase. But how is one to know which sentence is true, or even if the two are similar *without knowing the context* in which both would be used? (Palmer, 1986, p.48)

In history, one of the most fundamental lessons of context in establishing meaning occurred with the discovery of the Rosetta stone in Egypt (which is recounted in some detail in the next section). It was only by assuming that all three texts on the Rosetta stone referenced the *same* event, that translation was possible—an example that meaning is contextually dependent.

Eco (1990) affirms Charles Sanders Peirce's principle of contextuality that, "something can be truly asserted within a given universe of discourse and under a given description, but his assertion does not exhaust all the other, and potentially infinite, determinations of that object" (p. 37). The case of the Rosetta stone certainly underscores Peirce's principle.

2.   Truth Is Relational and Circular.

"To learn a language is to learn the meaning of its sentences, and hence to learn what observations to count as evidence for and against them," says philosopher W. V. Quine (1974, p. 38). The meaning of truth depends upon a statement's relations with other statements. The meaning of "red" is established in a network of relationships. A red cloud has no particular meaning in weather systems. However, a red traffic signal does have a specific meaning *within* a communication system (from Palmer, 1986, p. 3). The fact that "red" means "stop" is purely contained within that notational/communication system. It is relational and circular—i.e., other signs and colors are dependent upon "red" to establish their meanings, as "red" is counterdependent upon them for the same reason.

A true statement is positioned in a "web" of statements and assertations. True statements are linked to others and within larger frameworks or paradigms. These are circular in nature—i.e., all definitions lead back to assumptions upon which the paradigm rests and also to undefined words, like spokes in a wheel. For this reason, Popper (1988) has indicated that most theories contain their own "truth" and are therefore unable to predict any situation which involves their own rejection (p. 67).

However, when undefined words are used to indicate meaning in the act of definition (and there is no end to this process called infinite regress), boundaries are created for what is considered true to be indexed, like a dictionary within a language. But, since there is no end to the shifting from one word to another undefined one, there can be no final or authoritative, transcendental meaning possible, because such a meaning is infinitely postponed (see Eco, 1990, p. 27).

Truth is confined to language syntax and its content-meaning will vary *from language to language.* This circularity to "boxed" and circular meanings within languages (not always translatable to others) is reinforced by the fact that languages are indeterminate in categorizing "reality" to the point where, "there is no absolute line . . . between what is in the world and what is in language" (Palmer, 1986, p. 32). This concept was reinforced by Dick Littlebear, a North American Cheyenne (1992):

We need our land and we need our language. The two are inseparable. . . . There are references to the land that can be articulated only in the Cheyenne language. I believe that once those sacred references can no longer be expressed . . . These vital links will no longer exist in the tribal consciousness (Crawford, p. B5).

Language indeterminacy shrouds truth in tentativeness, and denies anything resembling a stable "objectivity" within one language or across other languages. It negates the search for causation because decisions are independent of one another and are not connected. The idea of a "free will" and the arbitrariness of all linguistic conventions is underscored and affirmed by linguistic scholarship.

Perhaps one of the most famous examples of language indeterminancy might be the case of the Rosetta stone—that famous chunk of black basalt found in 1799 at the mouth of the Nile River in Egypt by a French engineer with Napoleon's army. The broken tablet contained three separate scripts: Egyptian hieroglyphs, demotic (a kind of secular and condensed form of hieroglyphs), and Greek. Inasmuch as the Greek script was describing a royal event (the reign of King Ptolmey Epiphanes, 204–181 B.C.), it was assumed that all three texts were similar (Jensen, 1969, p. 74).

The Rosetta stone promised a way to "break the hieroglyphic code" of the ancient Egyptians which up to that point appeared impenetrable to analysts. The translation was a lot more difficult, and took longer than anyone imagined. The definitive dictionary of hieroglyphics was not published until 1926—120 years after the Rosetta stone discovery in the land of the sphinx (Jensen, 1969, p. 78).

The first attempt to translate the Rosetta stone obviously moved from the Greek to the second script, the demotic. This involved changing proper names in Greek to proper names in demotic. But this translator incorrectly assumed that demotic was an alphabetical text when it was not. The next move by a subsequent translator occurred in 1815 when a demotic alphabet was created. After this, the move to hieroglyphics was attempted. Again, the proper names were deciphered in ancient Egyptian which yielded only six hieroglyphic letters with phonetic equivalents. All work then came to a halt. No one could go any further.

The person credited with the breakthrough was a young Frenchman named J. F. Champollion (1790–1832). His diligence and hard work eventually paid off. Champollion's strategy was based on an intensive study of Coptic, one form of a linguistic evolution from ancient Egyptian. By comparing forms of Coptic to demotic, and an even earlier type of hieroglyph called hieratic, he could trace the development of the language.

In the deciphering process, Champollion noticed something that contradicted a previous assumption he had made about the Egyptian hieroglyphs. Initially, Champollion thought the hieroglyphs were pure picture script. Then, he discovered that this portion of the Rosetta stone contained three times as many signs as the Greek words contained. It was apparent to him that each hieroglyphic sign could not be a whole word. He worked from Greek to demotic to hieratic and into the hieroglyphs, and then found the name of the king, p,t,o,l,m,i,s. This insight eventually unlocked the secret of ancient Egyptian writing, but even the details eluded Champollion's exacting mind (Jensen, 1969, pp. 76–77).

It was not until 1867 that further scholarly work unveiled the place of *determinatives* in ancient Egyptian texts. These were certain picture–sign extensions with written phonetic additives that indicated a generic sphere of concepts to which a word belonged. This graphic–phonetic combination limited the meaning to only one of many possibilities.

Ancient Egyptian texts therefore contained around 700 different kinds of signs. These consisted of word–picture signs and from some of these determinatives, double-consonant signs for phonetic groups labeled syllable–signs. Others were single-consonant signs or letters.

The dramatic story of the unlocking of ancient Egyptian texts from the Rosetta stone underscores the arbitrariness of language development. It also illustrates the patent difficulties in attempting a language-to-language translation based on the many assumptions of parallelism in human experience, perception of reality, or oral and written expressions and conventions.

Another bit of history regarding the Rosetta stone is supplied by Asante (1990). Because of the prejudice and ignorance of the European historians and archeaologists regarding Africa, the Rosetta stone was believed to unlock the key to ancient Egyptian writing which was classified in England as an "Oriental" language rather than an African one. Africans were not believed to have developed a written language. Because the Arabs had conquered Egypt by the time Europeans had arrived on their military expeditions, they saw hieroglyphics as Eastern rather than African, even though this ancient language predated Arab conquest (pp. 59–68). The belief that African civilizations were not as advanced as European civilizations in the development of writing is still a prevalent myth, even among educated people.

As a final comment, when languages are translated, some small points upon which arguments may hinge can be lost. In 1925, in the famous *Scopes* Trial in Dayton, Tennessee, when Darwin's evolution theory tangled with the Biblical version of Genesis and classroom teaching, the defense team tried to raise the issue of linguistic distortion (English and Zirkel, 1989–1990).

The original Hebrew translation of Genesis did not read, "In the beginning God created the heaven and earth." Instead, the *literal* words read, " When the gods began to set in motion the heavens and earth" (DeCamp, 1968, p. 178). The difference is significant. In the first translation, it is God who is fusing the materials to fashion a heaven and an earth. In the second, the heavens and earth already exist, and the gods (plural instead of singular) are merely putting them into place. Darwin's theory of evolution clashes with the first translation of Genesis. Presumably, the second perspective regarding evolution could have been the way the gods, "set into motion" the heavens and earth—the exact translation of Genesis in Hebrew.

The difference between the two texts was the result of a power shift in ancient Hebrew society (refer to Foucault's power–knowledge concept in Chapter 1). The Hebrew priests of the storm god Yahveh (Jehovah) became the dominant group around the sixth century B.C., and suppressed the worship of all other gods. Hebrew society at this point was polytheistic. With this transition, it became monotheistic. The texts of the times were rewritten into the *Book of Law* in the reign of Josiah in 621 B.C. (Eiselen, Lewis, and Downey, 1957, p. 92). The texts were changed to shift "gods" to "God" to show that the Hebrews were monotheists all along. In southern Israel, God was named *Jehovah*. In northern Israel, texts show

God to be called *Elohim* (Eiselen, Lewis, and Downey, 1957, p. 218).

The Hebrew language is a difficult one to translate. It has 22 letters, all consonants, and "some of these can scarcely be represented by our English letters, or spoken by our vocal organs" (Eiselen, Lewis, and Downey, 1957, p. 100). Furthermore, Hebrew uses few particles and compounds and eschews independent pronouns and tenses. Acts are either completed or incompleted, without any reference to time: "it is not always easy for the modern interpreter to put himself in the place of the ancient writer" (Eiselen, Lewis, and Downey, 1957, p. 99).

3.   Truth Is Theory-Embedded.

True statements are linked to a theory, either explicitly or implicitly. All assertions are linked to some larger story and become "stories within stories" (Cherryholmes, 1988, p. 156). Those dealing with true statements may not fully understand what theory a true statement represents because, as Feyerabend (1991) indicates, "theories very often contain hidden assumptions one is not even aware of" (p. 20), or they may have selected the wrong theory.

Such was the case in the American Civil War when medical doctors treated the wounded. While doctors understood that infection that could eventually kill patients developed, they ascribed these problems to foul air or to some sort of contagion. The concept of asepsis or sterilization to prevent bacterial infection was unknown. Some observed medical conditions were simply misread. For example, a preliminary infection in which pus was produced near a wound was labeled, "laudable pus," and was believed to be a sign that the patient was recovering (Duffy, 1979, p. 222).

When gangrene was discovered among 50 patients after the battle of Antietam in 1862 (the bloodiest battle in American military history—Sears, 1983), doctors were ordered to wash their hands after treating such cases. Many were outraged at this command. Even though no new cases were reported after extensive hand washing, no orders were given extending the procedure to other types of wounds or patients (Tschanz, 1992, p. 37). This is an example of where a true statement (pertaining to hand washing) was not understood, was resisted, and was not continued because no medical theory of the day accounted for its therapeutic results. The role of germs or bacteria in wound infection—the true theory that would eventually revolutionize medical practice—was unknown. It was always embedded in the nature of infection. Yet medical doctors who believed that disease was a product of the sum of symptoms instead of an entity were utterly incapable of comprehending the nature of infection (Peirce, 1955, p. 51)

As late as July 2, 1881, when U.S. President James A. Garfield was shot in his third rib by an assassin, doctors probed the bullet wound with their fingers (insuring infection), and noted "laudable pus" developing on July 5. As the infection spread to abdominal peritonitis, they were still not worried. The President died on September 19 from infection (Duffy, 1979, p. 249).

4.   Truth Jump-Starts New Stories Which May Not Be True.

Some true statements can be linked to any number of theories, as in the case of Darwin's notion of natural selection–adaptation being used to support and promote a variety of social doctrines, including shady business practices in the name of competition, and even religious ones: "God picks out a select few" (see Ruse, 1979, p. 264). In the words of Feyerabend (1991), "But ideas, [such as true statements], like butterflies, do not merely exist; they develop, they enter into relations with other ideas and they have effects" (p. 163). Nowhere was this more amply illustrated than the effects of Darwin's ideas on all aspects of British life, from its political system to its economic base (see Ruse, 1979).

Darwin's ideas generated a host of fallacious theories in other fields, notably the false "truth" of *recapitulation* (Gould, 1981, p. 114). The idea embodied in recapitulation was that "ontogeny recapitulates phylogeny," or that growth of a human retraces the growth of the species itself. Thus, the true observation that, at a certain point in time, a human embryo possessed slits in the head like fish gills, provided "evidence" that humans were passing through the fish stage in their evolution to the current level of development.

With recapitulation, all animals could be ranked on the same scale. Humans could be ordered into groups which were "higher" or "lower." The American paleontologist E. D. Cope was a recapitulationist. He theorized that humans could be sorted into four lower classes *beneath* Nordic white males: nonwhite races, all women, southern European males, and lower classes within superior races such as the Irish (Gould, 1981, p. 115).

The influence of the recapitulationists was widespread. Both Freud and Yung were recapitulationists (Gould, 1981, p. 114). The classification of the human family by race on a scale of development was endorsed by the founder of anthropology, J. F. Blumenbach, who devised a scheme of sorting the races into groups on the basis of intelligence and perceived "civilization" (Gould, 1981, p. 32).

Blumenbach's ideas entered school books, among them an 1881 geography text, *Appleton's Standard Higher Geography,* which displayed the five racial categories, noting that the Caucasian was, "the most intellectual and civilized race, and embraces the leading nations of the earth" (p. 14). As "proof" of the premise, three human skulls are shown with the most developed being the Caucasian, followed by the Monogolian and then the Ethiopian. The use of skulls to demonstrate intellectual capacity emanates from a defunct school of thought called crainiometry based on Darwin's theory of evolution, and within it, the related concept of recapitulation, which was supposed to be one of the undergirding "truths" supporting it.

Paul Broca (1824–1880) was a professor of clinical surgery on the faculty of medicine in Paris. Through meticulous calculation of the size of human skulls, Broca would lay claim to the classification of races, and stake out the superiority of white males and the white race on his observations.

Broca's "hidden assumption," which he never challenged, was that human variation was linear and hierarchical (see the previous section about truth for theory embeddedness).

Gould (1981) carefully researched Broca's experiments in measuring human skulls. He found no statistical differences in one of Broca's key samples (p. 95), while Broca claimed the sample "proved" his observations. Broca worked from predetermined perspectives toward evidence that supported his conclusions, all the while denying he was doing so (Gadamer's "double hermeneutic," see Outhwaite,

1991, p. 34). His collection of statistical data was enormous. All of it pointed to his conclusions, yet all of it was fallacious in supporting a theory that was patently false.

As was the case with Wilhelm Fliess, Paul Broca's statistics were applied with a hidden prejudice. In summing up Broca's mistaken concept, Gould (1981) warns, "Broca was an exemplary scientist; no one has ever surpassed him in meticulous care and accuracy of measurement. By what right . . . can we identify his prejudice and hold that science now operates independently of culture and class?" (p. 74).

Because of Broca's "research," American history books such as Ridpath's (1874), *History of the United States* could open their texts with this statement, "The western continent was first seen by white men in A.D. 986" (p. 13). This statement ignores the fact that native Americans were *already* on the contintent and had "seen" it thousands of years earlier. The "ladder" of the ranking of the races on "scientific racism" did much to influence the American mindset about racial inferiority. Reformers in the first half of the twentieth century couched their educational aims for centralized control in order to "elevate the inferior race" (Apple, 1991, p. 18). Once established by supposed facts, false theories and statements often die hard, and they leave vestiges of intellectual debris scattered across many generations that may not perish until the civilization itself dies.

5.   Truth Is a Temporary Truce with Reality.

Truth is regarded as a statement or proposition that no one has been able to prove to be false. No statement is forever "true," in this sense. It is merely accepted as a temporary truce in the neverending struggle to find a test which will eventually show that it is false.

This premise, encapsulated in a procedure, is Popper's (1979) concept of **the critical method.** He describes it as, "a method of trial and the elimination of errors, or proposing theories and submitting them to the severest tests we can design" (p. 16). In the same passage, Popper concedes that in a case where an infinite number of theories is possible, *no method* can deduce which theory is true. The researcher is then faced with the situation in which any number of theories may be true or false. In such a situation, there can be no mystical entity labeled, "objective reality" which will finally be "discovered" and revealed for all time as true (Feyerabend, 1991, p. 140) because reality, like a culture, is invented—not discovered. Reality is a **synechism,** i.e., a situation in which no person or group can ever exhaust the possibilities of determination, or as Peirce concludes, "Reality is a continuum which swims in indeterminancy" (1934: 6. 171).

It is due to this indeterminancy that Newton's theories still work. They still predict. They don't explain some of the phenomena that Einstein's theories do, yet Newton's theories are not false. They are simply not as "true" as Einstein's. In time, Einstein's theories may be similarly pushed aside.

Some theories are totally false, even though they may contain some true facts or accurate data measurements, as in the cases of Wilhelm Fliess and Paul Broca. False theories may have a few kernels of truth within their orbits, but in the main, they point to conclusions that were false.

It is often difficult for scientists to differentiate between theories and to assess their overall truth content. In fact, theories or paradigms are never in themselves "testable." They simply contain too many possibilities to test, and for some statements, there is no way test them directly. It was because of this dilemma that Popper (1968) commented, "I do not demand that every scientific statement must *have in fact been tested* before it is accepted. I only demand that every such statement must be *capable* of being tested." (p. 48). Devising appropriately rigorous tests of statements derived from a theory may be exceptionally difficult.

One example in current research has surfaced in the study of AIDS (Acquired Immune Deficiency Syndrome). Because of a lack of progress in finding an antidote for AIDS, some scientists are reappraising an early assumption, namely that one virus—HIV—causes AIDS (DeLoughry, 1991, p. A9).

Prodded by a single dissenter in the AIDS research community, Dr. Peter Duesberg, a professor of molecular and cell biology at the University of California at Berkeley, who has been creating a rumpus since 1987 by denying that HIV even causes AIDS at all, the research community is thus reexamining its initial premise. Duesberg's position is that HIV infects too few cells of the body's immune system te cause a person to become seriously ill. He has championed the idea that certain cofactors with HIV are mainly responsible for a patient finally getting AIDS. This "cofactor" theory has been gaining ground within the AIDS research community, though many totally reject Dr. Duesberg's premise that HIV has no role in causing AIDS.

Duesberg has been critical of the "right science," representing certain views that are adopted by the NIH (National Institute of Health of the U.S. Government) and that come to be the major criterion for promoting certain scientific work at the expense of others. "Academic freedom has become a victim of centralization and mega-grants," avers Duesberg (DeLoughry, 1991, p. A9), and, "The peer review system tries to keep you in a pack, or maybe running behind it. If you run too far ahead of it, then you're threatening their livelihood" (p. A15).

Duesberg's views, while unpopular, are conceded by other researchers to have been the fulcrum for reappraisal of the idea that the HIV theory alone was considered the major and singular causative agent for AIDS. "We closed the door too soon," admits Robert S. Root-Bernstein, a professor of physiology at Michigan State University, "it would have been a lot healthier to try a variety of ideas and find out that some of them don't work" (DeLoughry, 1991, p. A9).

A recent example of a well-accepted theory that is not able to account for all of the phenomena under its aegis, is the study of the pink lady slip orchid that grows wild in Virginia's great Shenandoah Valley. Professor of Zoology Douglas E. Gill, an evolutionary biologist at the University of Maryland, has been systematically gathering data about this plant that baffles traditional Darwinian natural selection propositions (McDonald, 1991, p. A6).

Darwin's premise—that organisms survive and reproduce in proportion to their adaptability to their environments—does not explain how the pink lady slip orchid manages to survive in the Shenendoah Valley. Professor Gill found that none of the 1200 orchids he studied in a one-acre plot had been pollinated. Over

14 years of observation, Dr. Gill found that of 3300 plants, only 1000 flowered and only 23 had been pollinated. The mystery was how this plant reproduces itself in order to survive in its environment. Its incapacity to do so would reject Darwin's natural selection thesis.

At first, Professor Gill thought that the flowers were in some way not attracting bees for pollination purposes. This proved correct. How then does the orchid attain pollination? Many orchids self-pollinate. The type of pink lady slip orchid studied by Gill is not one of them. He says, "There is no way I can show in this orchid a significant pattern of natural selection for certain flower morphologies" (McDonald, 1991, p. A8).

Gill and most of his biology colleagues still accept Darwin's main premise in his seminal 1859 work, *On The Origin of Species by Natural Selection*. Even Darwin himself, who wrote a book about orchids in 1862, was stumped by some orchids who defied his theory.

The inability of a theory to account for every possible variable does not necessarily invalidate it or lead to its abandonment. "Every scientific theory, interpreted in a literal way, is in conflict with numerous facts!" says Paul Feyerabend (1991). As a result:

> You will no longer think of a theory as a well defined entity that says exactly what difficulties will make it disappear; you will think of it as a vague promise whose meaning is constantly being changed and refined by the difficulties one decides to accept (p. 41).

It seems clear that theories or metanarratives must be dissembled into special kinds of statements or propositions to be tested. The dissembling takes the form of "deducing from them statements of a lesser level of universality. These statements in their turn, since they are to be intersubjectively testable, must be testable in like manner—and so *ad infinitum*" (Popper, 1968, p. 47).

At the same time, the manner in which various tests are devised to assess whether statements or propositions are true is at least partly determined by theories about truth and its nature. It is to this matter that attention is now given.

THEORIES OF TRUTH

If science is concerned with determining if some statements, derived from theories embedded in paradigms, are true or false, then those pursuing this quest should know what *truth* is. If not, how can they recognize it when it is discerned, revealed, deduced, or constructed?

The question, *what is truth?* has been taken up by scores of philosophers over the ages. The answer is, "it all depends." Aristotle defined truth in this way:

> To say of what is that it is not, or of what is not that it is, is false, while to say of what is that it is, or of what is not that it is not, is true. (from Haack, 1988, p. 88).

In attempting this definition, Aristotle was caught in a definite language quandary. "To say of what is [to speak about something] that it is not [that is not true] or of what is not [to say something that is not true] that it is [but which is true] is false [is not true], while to say of what is that it is [to speak about something which is true and it is true, and therefore true] or what is not that is not [or is false and therefore false] is true [is really false and therefore true]." This explanation is reminiscent of the very famous language problem, *the liar's paradox,* a version of which (Epimenides paradox) was discussed in Chapter Two.

The liar's paradox occurs if one person should say to another, "Everything I tell you is a lie." If, however, this is true, then the person has not lied to you. On the other hand, if the person tells the truth, he has lied to you, but he has told you the truth. Aristotle's definition contradicts the liar's paradox, yet by saying, "truth is what is true and therefore not false," he has not explained very much.

This transparency of language, and the inability to explore reality through it, was discussed by Ludwig Wittgenstein (1889–1951) in *Tractatus Logico-Philosophicus* (1921, 1961). In this work, Wittgenstein declared that,"What finds its reflection in language, language cannot represent. What expresses itself in language, we cannot express by means of language" (p. 26).

The inability of language to describe itself was not due to the rules of language, but to "the linguistic inaccessibility of the relation of a true sentence to the fact that makes it true" (Hintikka and Hintikka, 1989, p. 18). In this sense, Wittgenstein was attempting to deal with Russell's paradox described earlier in dealing with the definition of intelligence by Arthur Jensen (see Chapter 2)— i.e., "whatever involves all of a collection must not be one of the collection" (Haack, 1988, p. 141 after Russell, 1908, p. 63). There are five theories of truth. They are (1) correspondence theories, (2) semantic theories, (3) pragmatist theories, (4) coherence theories, and (5) redundancy theories (after Haack, 1988, p. 87).

Correspondence Theories of Truth

The **correspondence theory of truth** holds that what is "true" (a propositional statement) corresponds to or approximates the "facts." In order for the statement, "Abraham Lincoln had a beard," to be considered "true," it would have to be verified by: (1) verbal descriptions of the sixteenth President of the United States, (2) drawings, paintings, or photographs, or (3) other referential material that contained data regarding his facial features. These would reveal that although Abraham Lincoln did grow a beard, he was not always hirsute. Of the 118 known photographs of Lincoln, 39 show him without whiskers, and the remainder indicate a beard (Kunhardt, 1983, p. 212).

The correspondence theory is nearly universal in its simple and straightforward appeal. Is something true? Go and observe for yourself! The correspondence theory is widely used in educational research. It is bound up with a logical positivistic view or outlook regarding causes, and is a favorite of those pursuing behavioristic studies (see Schrag, 1992).

True statements are ones that can be verified. Verification consists of finding sensory data, or experiential information that will support or not support a propositional statement. The idea behind science utilizing the correspondence theory is that of empiricism. Empiricism holds that there is no knowledge possible (or worthwhile) outside of the human senses. Empiricism denies that there is any such thing as inborn, innate, or a priori knowledge. It rejects the idea "that there are universal or necessary truths" (Runes, 1984, p. 105).

House (1991) has delineated the traditional, largely positivistic tenets involved in defining educational research linked to the correspondence theory of truth as (paraphrased):

1. all scientific propositions are founded on data and facts, in which hypotheses are verified against the facts;
2. scientific theories are those using hypothetical–deductive methods which assume their meaning via linkages to observations and definitions stated in performance terms;
3. the activity of research is itself *atheoretical;* the most important aspect of a theory is its ability to predict events, occurrences, or results;
4. causality is that which links events with contingencies;
5. explanation and prediction are considered parallel forms (pp. 2–3).

The correspondence theory of truth has a number of problems, chiefly the ambiguous nature of "facts." It also has problems with human language in conveying "facts." Finally, the unreliability and subjectivity of human experience in "verifying" truth is also a problem.

Karl Popper (1968) comments on the instability of the scientific enterprise in words that ought to create doubt that what is "scientific" is permanent and lasting:

> Science does not rest upon solid bedrock. The bold structure of its theories rises, as it were, above a swamp. It is like a building erected on piles . . . and if we stop driving the piles deeper, it is not because we have reached firm ground . . . we are satisfied that the piles are firm enough to carry the structure (p. 111).

There are no granite substructures upon which to build science, and experience is a mercurial substructure at best. To illustrate the problems with the correspondence theory, we shall review an academic "flap" that erupted over the research conducted on date rape on American college and university campuses in the winter of 1992.

Mary Koss, a professor of psychology at the University of Arizona, conducted a survey study of 6159 college students in 1985. Professor Koss published her results which indicated that 15 percent of the women indicated they had been raped at some time in their lives. Within this sample, 27 percent said they had been raped, 16 percent said they did not know it was a crime, and 46 percent said they thought the problem was primarily one of miscommunication; 11 percent indicated they did not believe a crime had been committed (Collison, 1992, p. A35).

Koss' survey results were criticized publicly by Neil Gilbert, a professor of social welfare at the University of California at Berkeley. Gilbert indicated that the results were blown all out of proportion for the purpose of "imposing new norms governing intimacy between the sexes" by radical feminists. Gilbert postulated that the feminists were, "playing fast and loose with the numbers" to create a fraudulent "epidemic" (Collison, 1992, p. A37).

Among the problems with Koss' data, Gilbert points out that 73 percent of the women who said they had been raped did not report it. He comments, "How can you say college-educated women don't know they've been raped? That description infantilizes women. When you're raped, you feel violated. That's saying it's such a complex crime that these women could not know they have been raped." Gilbert says Koss' data indicated that approximately 40 percent of the women who said they were raped slept with their rapists again. Gilbert postulates, "Rape is a brutal crime. If you were raped, why would you sleep with your rapist again?" (Collison, 1992, p. A37).

Gilbert points out the federal statistics on rape, which indicate that only one woman in 1000 has been the victim of rape. Even if these data are flawed and underreported, it cannot be as high as Koss is reporting, avers the Berkeley professor. In an article he authored on the Koss data, Gilbert accused the radical feminists of ruling out as possible causes of the data, "passion, emotional turmoil, entreaties, flirtation, provocation, demureness." In its place they want, "cool-headed contractual sex. 'Will you do it, yes or no? Please sign on the line below'" (Collison, 1992, p. A37).

Gilbert's feminist critics are quick to retort that as a male, he doesn't know what he is talking about, has never done research in the field, and does not understand the situation many collegiate women confront. Professor Koss rebuts Gilbert's criticism by saying, "He is saying to women, 'This experience is not real, you have misperceived your experience.' The failure to embrace the correct legal label for one's victimization does not mean that the victimization did not occur" (p. A37).

Another riposte to Gilbert's naysaying is that of Andrea Parrot, assistant professor at Cornell University, "No one has a problem with a stranger who jumps out of the bushes, beats his victim to a pulp, and brutally rapes her. But when a woman knows her accuser, when she may have been drinking, people have a lot more trouble with that. Most people, including victims of rape, don't call it rape."

Gilbert agrees. "Maybe she had too much to drink, lost her inhibitions, and had sex with him. The next morning she was sorry. And a large part of it is miscommunication. The problem with men and women is insensitivity and miscommunication, but you can't call that rape" (Collison, 1992, p. A37).

This rancorous academic debate over date rape epitomizes the problems with the classical correspondence theory. What is true is rooted in human sensory experience. That is the only possible way to verify something. Yet human experience does not provide an unequivocal *foundational cornerstone* upon which to validate the "truth." As the date-rape controversy indicates, human experience is neither universal, objective, nor theory-free, and it hardly provides an unambiguous framework within which to discern something as elusive as the truth. The reason is supplied by the American philosopher Charles Sanders Peirce (1955):

> Direct experience is neither certain nor uncertain because it affirms nothing—it just is. There are delusions, hallucinations, dreams. But there is no mistake that such things really do appear, and direct experience means simply the appearance. It involves no error, because it testifies to nothing but its own appearance. For the same reason, it affords no

certainty. It is not exact, because it leaves much vague; though it is not inexact either; that is, it has no false exactitude (pp. 57–58).

Rape, like other human experiences, is a cultural artifact, i.e., a human construct (Foucault, 1990a) made possible as Reay Tannahill (1982) notes because of frontal sex, where the prospect of running away from undesired coitus was severely reduced. "In the living world, only one species of spider appears to share with humanity the ability to conclude a mating against the will of the female" (p. 17).

There is no word in Arabic that is the equivalent of the English word *rape* (Hall, 1969, p. 158). One of the reasons is that Arabs have a different concept of the private zones outside of the body. While touching someone in the Western world can amount to an assault on that person (consider the definitions of sexual harassment as unwanted touching by one person or another in American–European cultures), in the Arab world, the real person is located deeper in the human body, beyond the skin. Arabs therefore stand closer to other people than most Americans find comfortable. The idea of where the *real person* is located is centered differently in these two cultures.

Gender differences and gender polarities are taught within cultures. "Sexuality is shaped by social forces," notes Jamke Highwater (1990) in his book, *Myth and Sexuality*, "Far from being the most natural force of our lives, it is, in fact, the most susceptible to cultural influences. . . . We constantly construct boundaries that have no basis in 'Nature'" (p. 6)

In American culture, there are clear, conceptual differences between male and female, heterosexual and homosexual sex. These concepts are considered *binary opposites* (polarized on the same continuum). Yet other cultures often have no such demarcations. The ancient Greeks made no such distinctions. It was possible for an ordinary Greek male to love a boy and a woman without being considered a homosexual, bisexual, or "confused."

Highwater (1990) indicates that in Mombasa, a person's sex is assigned on the basis of biology, so a lesbian is always considered a woman. In neighboring Oman, it is the sexual act and not biology that defines a person's sex. In this case, a male homosexual may become a woman (p. 17). As far as sexuality is concerned, there is no reality (or experience) that is ultimately definitive.

Now consider the problem that even within cultures, gender differences change perception and hence, experience. In ancient Greece, a man was punished more severely for seduction than for rape. A violation of a woman was a crime against the man who had authority over her. Seduction was considered worse because it involved changing the affections of the woman toward the man who possessed her. Rape was a violation that did not trespass the authoritative man in the same way (Foucault, 1990b, p. 146).

Within the same culture, men and women are taught to view their bodies differently. In previous eras of American culture, sex was a commodity. Females were taught to fashion themselves as sex objects, to appear "desirable" to males. Women were taught to worry about how they looked, fussing over their hair and bodily attractiveness to the point where between 20 and 30 percent experienced health related complications trying to change their body shape or weight. Between 5 and

20 percent with anorexia nervosa will die of complications of this self-inflicted disease, including suicide (Ogden and Germinario, 1988, p. 141). Highwater (1990) indicates that the body has become equated with money, power, and desire (p. 171). In the age of commercialized sex and violence, the male body has become a weapon. When used against women, it is an agent of fear and personal/political terrorism. Sex has become more than an erotic act. It has become a tool of political repression in which one side gains superiority over the other. This is an act of domination. Rape is an act of aggression, not of passion.

Part of the agenda of the radical feminists is to redefine for women and men the act of rape, from misplaced passion to that of physical aggression. What is happening is the process of redefining experience to fit a different point of view about what the experience is and what it means. If women couldn't tell that they had been raped, but it actually did happen, why did they not perceive it as rape? One reason is that their cultural framework regarding the act of rape did not include the experience they encountered. When redefined, the experience becomes rape.

So Professor Gilbert is right and wrong. Women had a real experience. Many did not define it as rape until the concept was placed into a context or situation that could be identified as rape. Experience does not define reality, it follows it. Experience does not verify the "facts" independent of a concept of what the "facts" are within an overall framework of meaning.

This process invalidates one of the principles of the correspondence theory, namely that experience is atheoretical. As Popper (1979) remarks, "All knowledge is theory-impregnated, including our observations" (p. 71). The idea that observation as a form of experience verification is really just another point of view often hidden to the observer, is one of the major problems in sustaining logical positivism, behaviorism, and the concept that only observable "facts," are allowed to be used to ascertain what is true. This naive assumption that observation can be "theory-free," is one of the blind spots of positivistic science because it represents an *unsupported belief* that cannot be supported by experience itself, or, in the words of Evers and Lakomski (1991), "our knowledge of how we know the class of epistemically privileged items is not itself epistemically privileged" (p. 228). While positivistic science consists of correspondence to the facts, its hidden premises are unsupportable by any "facts." This blind spot is positivism's implicit conceit. This means that positivism is oblivious to its own "double hermeneutic" context. It also explains why positivism is susceptible to tautologies.

Much of educational research methodology rests on applying the correspondence theory of truth. One way of shoring up some of the deficiencies of determining the "facts" is to use a variety of methodologies.

For example, Denzin (1978) indicates that research methodologies, "represent different means of acting on the environment of the scientist. Surveys, for example, dictate a stance toward the invariant and stable features of this reality, while participant observation assumes a reality continually in change and flux . . . Each research method reveals peculiar elements of symbolic reality" (p. 292). So the concept of *triangulation,* i.e., using many different methods to verify a "fact" is better than relying on only one. However, set within a generally positivistic framework, the shortcomings of the correspondence theory itself are still manifest.

Semantic Theories of Truth

Semantic theories of truth are the descendents of Aristotle's version of the nature of truth. Semantic theories have to take into account two major problems in discerning what is true from what is not. The first problem is that natural languages (English, French, German, etc.) are "semantically closed," meaning that even with correct use one can fall into the trap of *antinomy.*

Antinomy is the condition where two correct inferences can be equally and validly drawn from the same passage resulting in contradictions such as the infamous liar's paradox. Alfred Tarski (1956) indicates that, "natural languages contain their own metalanguages, so that truth cannot be defined without running into paradox" (from Haack, 1988, p. 120).

The second problem facing those using natural languages is that they must be formally specifiable, i.e., follow patterns of logic. Few natural languages are capable of behaving in this manner simply because logical truth is very independent to the world of experience (Palmer, 1986, p. 190). Natural languages convey the world of experience. It is this gap (between experience and logic) which accounts for the problem of paradox. Furthermore, logicians are not interested in the way the world is, but rather, the way the world might possibly be, i.e., **modal logic** (Palmer, 1986, p. 192).

The difference between these two worlds produces two kinds of truth. The first kind is analytical. The second is synthetic. Analytical truth is dependent upon logic and not upon experience. The example provided by Palmer of an analytical truth is the statement, "All bachelors are unmarried" (p. 204). This statement would be true on Mars, the moon, or on Earth. It is not dependent upon experience.

Synthetic truth is world dependent. Again, Palmer (1986) provides an example with, "All bachelors are happy" (p. 204). While logical analysis would be used to support the first statement, observation and other data gathering would have to be used to determine the veracity of the second statement. The truthfulness of the second statement is contextual and conditional, since happiness on earth does not insure happiness anywhere else. Theories of semantic truth have to deal with the dilemma of **disambiguated** (logical) **language.** They are concerned with logical language and logical truth derivations, which are not experience dependent.

Tarski (1956) begins defining the creation of a disambiguated language by providing for *adequacy conditions* that a definition of truth must meet, and then he indicates a definition of truth which would satisfy those same conditions (Haack, 1988, p. 99). Tarski indicates that *any acceptable definition of truth should have as a consequence all instances of a (T) schema:*

(T) S is true if (if and only if) p

The p can be replaced by any language sentence for which truth is being defined. The S is replaced by a name of the sentence which replaces p, and the sentence on the right is referenced by its quotation-mark name on the left.

'The sky is blue' is true if and only if the sky is blue.

Diagram 3   STEPS IN THE PROCESS OF WORKING IN AN OBJECT
AND METALANGUAGE

Object Language	Metalanguage
1. Selection of English as the language of expression	Specify the syntactical structure of English
2. English contains expressions or translations of truth	English must contain the appropriate syntactical vocabulary including the symbols of truth
3. Use specific language logic	Define satisfactory conditions
4. Define truth	Be sure all conditions are met
"True in O"	"Satisfied in O"

Extrapolated from Susan Haack (1988, p. 105).

As Haack (1988, p. 100) explains, the statement is not a definition of truth. It is a statement of the conditions of adequacy for truth. For something to be true, all statements about it must be contained within it. Thus, "all bachelors are unmarried," is true if and only if all bachelors are not married.

Theories of semantic truth rely on the use of a metalanguage (the language used to talk about language), and an object language (the language in which the nature of truth is being expressed). In explaining how a statement is to be judged as true, one has to work back and forth between the two languages as shown in Diagram 3. Truth in the object language (called truth in O) and the conditions within that language that must be reflected in the metalanguage (satisfying conditions in O as determined in the metalanguage or satisfied in O).

A true statement is satisfied by objects, actually any object within a complete sentence. For example,

"_____is a dog."

1. Fido is a dog.
2. Lassie is a dog.
3. Queenie is a dog.
4. Hector is a dog.
   etc.

These sentences are not true or false in an empirical (synthetic) world. They are correct "objects" in an analytical one. It is possible, however, for one of the statements to be logically true, but empirically false, i.e., if there was not a dog named Hector.

These same object sentences would all be false as follows:

1. Napoleon is a dog.
2. Jesse James is a dog.

3. Mati Hari is a dog.

4. Cleopatra is a dog.

5. Pat Garrett is a dog.

Alfred Tarski (1956) asserts that a true sentence is "satisfied by all sequences and is false if it is satisfied by none" (from Haack, 1988, p. 107). Sentence sequence propriety also moves back and forth from the synthetic to the analytical worlds. For example, the statement "San Francisco is north of Los Angeles" is analytically correct, but empirically false.

Obviously, Tarsky's approach requires a special type of utterance translated into writing. All utterances are not so clear or unambiguous. For example, a more difficult sentence to translate would be:

"The principal is an instructional leader."

Here we have a problem with the word *principal,* and the word *leader.* A school principal is not the same as a specific person with a discrete identity unique to itself. A "leader" is much more opaque than a "dog." A dog is a simple, nearly universal, easily recognizable creature. A leader is not in the same category. While the statement is analytically true, it is not true because it could not satisfy all sequences (possibilities) in the actual world.

In order to be true it must include all cases (sequences) or none. Now change the sentence to:

"Harry Jones is a school principal."

If there is a Harry Jones ($n=1$) who occupies a position called "school principal" ($n=1$), then the statement includes all possibilities and excludes none, and if in the actual world, then it is true. Tarski's approach requires a very small vocabulary and the use of "atomic sentences" or "semantic primitives."

Truth Problems with the "Frontier Hypothesis"

There have been few theories as influential as Frederick Jackson Turner's "frontier thesis" which was first delivered in 1893 at the Chicago World's Fair. Since this hot July afternoon when he read his paper to a small and bored group, the frontier thesis came to dominate all explanations of how America developed, how American character was shaped, and how American attitudes about democracy and life were forged in the anvil of westward expansion. Turner was highly influenced by the two prevailing metanarratives of his time—geographical determinism as embodied in Darwin's evolutionary ideas, and Lamarck's notions of the carrying of genetic influences in hereditary patterns from generation to generation (Billington, 1973, p. 114).

Turner's hypothesis was that the American character was fundamentally shaped in the westward expansion movement through geography and free land. The frontier was a place where the old social order was not established. There was social fluidity. The raw environment dictated that people stay close to the land, and remain practical and inventive as new challenges arose. Turner saw the westward flow of population expansion as contributing to the development of social democracy, independence, and nationalism. As the frontier expanded, American society was continually reborn and redefined. Americans remained coarse but strong, curious, and materialistic people as well. Three centuries of westward movement had bred these traits into Americans (in the Lamarckian sense) which distinguished them from Easterners or Europeans (see Billington, 1973, p. 128).

To this day, Turner's thesis remains a part of interpreting what makes America and an American. The important point for the discussion regarding Turner's concept was that it was never empirically validated. It was a grand story, a metanarrative that arose to help explain trends, data, and observations made by others.

Even Turner's kindest critic and biographer, Ray Billington, noted that, "he advanced not a shred of evidence to substantiate his statements. Unfortunately, Turner's frontiersmen did not always behave as he reasoned they should behave" (p. 199).

Turner was not able to adequately frame what he meant by the "frontier." His writings attest to a variety of definitions: a process, a place, and a population. His last try in 1914 was, "the temporary boundary of an expanding society at the edge of substantial free lands . . . that zone of settlement nearest the wilderness, wherein society and government are loosely or incompletely organized" (Billington, 1974, p. 452).

Even though Frederick Jackson Turner understood that a historian is influenced by his times, his experience, his class, and his nationality, and therefore was never free to objectively look at data (Billington, 1974, p. 179), he nonetheless cast a theory that included all of the traits he could not avoid.

For example, the American Indian was seen as a blocking force against the march of civilization from East to West (Billington, 1974, p. 454). In this attitude, Turner was a man of his times, who saw no civilization where the Indian had trod or hunted before the white migration from the East began. The governmentally endorsed genocide against the Indian that resulted in the death of thousands of native people in the process of "shaping the American character" was not a theme he pursued (see also Davidson and Lytle, 1986, p. 105). Turner's anti-nativism bias hidden in his proffered "objectivity" has been thoroughly flipped on its head by UC–Berkeley Professor Ronald Takaki's book, A Different Mirror. In this very different history text of America, Professor Takaki begins the story with Newfoundland's scared Indians who encountered Leif Erickson's brother, Thorvald, on the beach. By beginning history with the Indians, Takaki acknowledges that America was already peopled when Europeans landed. America was never a "virgin" land; it was already civilized (see Coughlan, 1993, p. A9).

One of Turner's own students, Thomas Perkins Abernethy, used his mentor's methods to substantiate his frontier thesis, only to find that his data contradicted Turner's in a study of the development of Tennessee (Davidson and Lytle, 1986, p. 96). Abernethy found that greedy land speculators, including some state legislators in North Carolina, made a fat profit on lands they later sold to the "pioneers." Instead of the hardy pioneers carving out niches of land, toiling to bring their piece of America to fruition, Abernethy found that, "America was run largely by speculators in real estate" (Davidson and Lytle, 1986, p. 98).

Frederick Jackson Turner's "frontier thesis" was immersed in the ideas of its times—ideas that have since been abandoned. Among them were strong tides of Darwinian determinism and Lamarckian genetic transference, intermingled with the ethnocentrism of the European outlook on the native cultures that existed in the North American continent before the Vikings, Columbus, or the Puritans supposedly "discovered" them.

In this outlook, the semantic theory of truth is as contextually bound as the correspondence theory that it attempted to supplant. Languages are contextually sensitive and time sensitive and even Tarski noted that what was true in one language may be false or inconsequential in another. The only "truth" that exists may be in the metalanguage. Truth is therefore relative (Haack, 1988, p. 114).

Critics of the semantic theory of truth also attack it as another form of correspondence theory. If one insists that what is true is simply what is perceived as true, then the truth is actually what *corresponds* to what is perceived as true. Other critics aver that the use of semantic theory as presented by Tarski is an example of "physicalism," i.e., a movement to reduce all phenomena to that of concrete, physical objects and their relations. Such a scheme is utterly useless in describing a nonphysical object like the "frontier."

Willard Van Orman Quine (1980) has disputed the whole idea that there is analytical truth and synthetic truth. Quine posits that the phrase, "No bachelor is married," is nothing like a truth statement grounded in some ulterior factual or logical world. To use language as Tarski employs it simply is the result of "language synonymy," i.e., replacing synonyms for synonyms (pp. 20–23). This kind of language game is rooted in common observations within the same language. Finally, "the old champions of a verification theory of meaning went wrong in speaking too blithely of the meaning of individual sentences. Most sentences do not admit separately of observational evidence. Sentences interlock" (Quine, 1974, p. 38). The interlocking of sentences means that when considering what is true based on some sort of observation, the researcher has to decide which sentences are false and which ones should be considered to remain as true. Quine (1980) insists that "the unit of empirical significance is the whole of science, "and not individual sentences, one by one. To this matter he adds, "it is nonsense . . . to speak of a linguistic component and a factual component in the truth of any individual statement" (p. 42).

A larger view of the matter is of a theory itself and its value. Turner's "frontier theory" may have been false, but its value was in directing studies that found a more accurate account of the development of America. In this respect, the value of Turner's theory was that it shaped subsequent studies to pointedly refute it by denying that the West was developed as Turner predicted. The value of the metanarrative was that it pointed the researcher in a direction to sort out the "facts" as a matter of refutation. Even a false theory has great value in science in the long run, as long as it does not come to be enshrined as an absolute answer. In this case it has ceased to be science and becomes dogma.

Pragmatist Theories of Truth

The pragmatist theory of truth was enunciated by Charles Sanders Peirce (1955) as, "a method of ascertaining the meanings of hard words and of abstract concepts" (p. 271). The term *pragmatism* comes from the Greek word meaning *action* from which the English words *practice* and *practical* are derived. The *pragmatic method* is an approach to truth that determines it by defining, "what conduct it is fitted to produce: that conduct is for us its sole significance" (James, 1991, p. 23). Having defined pragmatism, James then indicates that, "Theories thus become instruments, not answers to enigmas" (p. 26).

The great pragmatists of science were John Dewey, Charles Sanders Peirce, and William James. Pragmatism is a form of correspondence, but it is a form of the idea that insists the meaning of a concept is that it ultimately makes a difference in the real world. If there is no difference, then there is no meaning. This idea was Peirce's concept of the *theory of inquiry* which formulated a scientific method that was superior over others such as authority or a priori beliefs. Such a method ultimately led to "stable beliefs, beliefs which will not be thrown into doubt" (Haack, 198, p. 97).

The notion of *correspondence* in the pragmatic theory of truth is that the scientific method will be constrained by reality, and therefore what it produces will *correspond* to that reality. The definition of truth is very much a part of the method of discerning it. It was regarding this problem that Karl Popper (1965) commented that the search for theories which were simply powerful instruments [methodologies] may be quite well supported by false theories as well as true ones (p. 226). The theories of Wilhelm Fliess and Paul Broca come to mind in this regard.

None of the pragmatists believed in absolute truth. Dewey described truth as "warranted assertibility," (1938, p. 345), and like Peirce, believed it to be stable, i.e., safe from doubt. Peirce (1955) proffered that knowledge was never absolute and existed in a state of uncertainty and indeterminancy, in fact "all things so swim in continua" (p. 356).

Coherence Theories of Truth

A coherentist perspective on the theory of truth takes a position on two views: (1) the truthfulness of a statement or theory can only be judged in a context of other statements (a kind of contextual set) and (2) trying to return to an experiential base of verification to discern the matter of truthfulness will neither be productive nor definitive. The criteria for determining a superior theory are those that Evers and Lakomski (1991) indicate are "extra-empirical" (p. 37). A superior theory is one that is more consistent, comprehensive, simple, conservative, fecund, and possesses greater explanatory unity than others. This is an adaptation of correspondence. A superior theory is one that "corresponds" to these requirements better than others. It is assumed in turn that superior theories are world descriptive as well, and can be verified empirically (adhere to the facts).

The problem with coherency theories is, according to Popper (1979), that they confuse consistency with truth, i.e., a statement is considered true if it corresponds to other statements we have accepted as true. This procedure is a very conservative one, "entrenched knowledge can hardly be overthrown" (p. 309).

A fertile use of the coherence theory and its tenets was taken by Colonel Harry G. Summers, Jr. (1982) in his application of Carl Von Clausewitz's 150-year old theory about warfare, *On War,* to explain how America lost the war in Vietnam.

The United States Army was never defeated in Vietnam, yet the war was lost. How could that have happened? Summers explains that Von Clausewitz thought the role of theory was "to clarify concepts and ideas that have become . . . confused and entangled" (Howard and Paret, 1976, p. 133).

By using Von Clausewitz' theory, and the experience of the U.S. military in Vietnam to "correspond" to that theory's ability to explain, Summers derives the basic flaws in U.S. strategy. Von Clausewitz's theory is accepted as the best, most comprehensive, and complete of any theory available to provide such a strategic perspective, i.e., it coheres most appropriately to "the facts" as known (a kind of correspondence).

First, Colonel Summers follows Von Clausewitz's division of war into two categories: (1) preparation for war, and (2) the war proper. Summers avers that the United States confused these two categories in Clausewitzian theory, concentrating upon the development of the armed forces and their deployment. Applying those same forces to accomplish the political ends of the conflict was a failure, for Von Clausewitz indicated that the objective of war is peace which attains the nation's national policy objectives. Von Clausewitz counted a kind of "holy trinity" of war as the people, the government, and the army. These three elements must be balanced and woven together.

Summers (1982) notes that the North Vietnamese used and applied Von Clausewitz's theories to their own "people's army," and that Marxist–Leninist military thought was thoroughly permeated by them. Von Clausewitz saw an army as the expression of its people. When the people were committed, the army was committed. General Fred Weyand of the U.S. Army, the Commander of the U.S. withdrawal, said in 1976, "When the Army is committed the American people are committed, when the American people lose their commitment it is futile to try to keep the Army committed. In the final analysis, the American Army is not so much an arm of the Executive Branch as it is an arm of the American people" (Summers, 1982, p. 12).

President Lyndon Johnson never mobilized the American people. That would have endangered his Great Society program, so there never was a formal declaration of war in Vietnam. For a time, both civilian and military strategists believed that formal declarations of war were obsolete in the nuclear age. Summers disagrees based on Clausewitzian theory. "Pieces of paper do have value . . . it focuses attention, provides certain responsibilities and creates impediments to dissolution . . . we were under the delusion that we could disregard not only the *form* of a declaration of war but also its *substance*—the mobilization of the American people" (p. 17).

In this respect, America failed to take heed of Von Clausewitz's warning that the moral element must be considered along with physical force. By failing to mobilize the American people, the moral element was missing from American strategy. In contrast, the North Vietnamese were highly mobilized. The moral factor in their national will overcame their military backwardness when compared to that of the United States.

A second area where Clausewitzian theory dictates clarity is between waging war and the objectives of the war in the first place. Since war is a means of achieving political objectives, the objectives of a war must be stated in political terms. The Americans muddled the political objectives in Vietnam because of the American proclivity to confuse war with moral "crusades to punish evil" (Summers, 1982, p. 88). When the official justifications for actions taken in Vietnam were discussed and classified from 1949 through 1967, the North Vietnamese had one objective—the conquest of the South. During the same time period the United States had 22 (Summers, 1982, p. 90). A survey in 1974 of Army generals who commanded in Vietnam found that, "almost 70 percent . . . who managed the war were uncertain of its objectives" (p. 96).

Finally, Clausewitzian theory dictates that an army's offensive force be directed at the enemy's center of gravity. Such a place was defined as the hub of power and mobility. The American military misread where the enemy's center of gravity was in Vietnam. Throughout the war, the Americans viewed the Viet Cong as the center of gravity, when in fact it was North Vietnam itself. Summers' (1982) "evidence" to support his view was that in the 1968 Tet Offensive, the Viet Cong was all but destroyed, yet the war carried on in full force. Had the Viet Cong been the real center of gravity, the war would have been over (p. 117).

On the other hand, the North Vietnamese correctly read where America's center of gravity was located. It was not the U.S. Army, but rather, the relationship between the United States and South Vietnam. Driving a wedge between the nations with tactical attacks like TET led to the erosion of public support of U.S. troops at home, and ultimately, to the withdrawal of U.S. forces. When this happened, the North Vietnamese shifted their center of gravity to the Army of South Vietnam (ARVN) and accomplished their singular objective of unifying North and South under their rule (Summers, 1982, p. 119). Several American officers, notably Norman Schwarzkopf (1992), took the lessons from Clausewitzian theory regarding the enemy's center of gravity in Vietnam, and correctly used it in Operation Desert Storm to go after Irag's highly centralized system of command and control as their "center of gravity" (p. 319).

It is clear from Summers' book that Clausewitzian theory about war is more comprehensive, simple, consistent, and explanatory than any other as it pertains to waging war. The possibility that it is wrong does exist. The theory's *coherency* is a strong pull to apply it to the "lessons of Vietnam" however. The utilization of the theory does help explain what happened. It does assist in sorting out the confusion and "facts" about Vietnam. Despite these pluses, it could still be false, or other theories could have even greater power or coherency. It is important to note that more data would not be definitive in determining the superiority of a theory regarding war. So coherentist advocates are correct in arguing that "more" experiential information would not be helpful in deciding which theory of war to use. The decision does have to be made on a comparison from one theory to other theories on extra-empirical data. Popper (1979) uses a form of coherence in suggesting that better theories are those which have greater content, even before they are tested. Bolder theories are the result. Of course, the risk that the content is false is greater as well.

Redundancy Theories of Truth

Frank Ramsey (1931) took the position that the distinctions between *object language* and *metalanguage* were unnecessary; i.e., they were *redundant*. Alfred Tarski made such distinctions to avoid the problem of paradox.

Ramsey discerned that he could eliminate the words "true," or "false," from nearly all expressions. For example, the expression, "It is true that p," can be written as, "means the same as p" or, "For all p, then p" (Haack, 1988, pp. 127–128).

Ramsey therefore proposes a more simplified approach to language expression regarding truth or falsity. In his process, he is able to bypass the problem of "objects of belief." For example, in the statement, "It is true that p . . . is true," includes the idea that it is a predicate (the part of a sentence or clause that expresses what is said of the subject). It is an object of belief that truth is a property of something. However, by eliminating the word *truth,* it is no longer necessary to know what it is a property of, so the belief is redundant (Haack, 1988, p. 128). The solution to such semantic riddles and problems—even applying the logic of the redundancy theory to languages—has not eliminated the problem of paradox so far, which Tarski's theory was developed to do.

THE USE OF TRUTH IN SCIENCE

There are few absolutes in science. Popper (1965) has indicated that there are two points of view about the use of *truth* in scientific activities. The first use of truth is to prove things, i.e., that facts or propositions can be believed if they can be verified. In the process of verification they become worthy to be believed. Belief (Dewey's warranted assertibility) is the absence of doubt. To arrive at this state, one must produce positive evidence. Logical positivism or scientific empiricism lies behind this view of how truth is established. Popper's (1965) view is that such concepts have been discredited because positive reasons can never support the belief in a theory, whether buttressed by observation or probabilities in statistical manipulations (p. 228).

A second view is offered by the **falsificationists.** This perspective is that theories are never held to be true from empirical evidence. Rather, they are held in a state called **verisimilitude,** after rigorous testing has failed to dislodge them for the moment. Falsificationists, to which Popper belongs, are concerned only with testing theories in propositional form, and in continuing to test them ad infinitum. All theories are most likely to be shown false in time. So truth is simply what has not been shown to be false; at any given point it is a neverending quest. "We are not interested in establishing scientific theories as secure, or certain, or probable," says Popper (1965, p. 229).

Popper's perspective puts a different emphasis on theories of truth. If one is interested in "proving" something to be true, the various theories of truth are disconcerting. They show that there are few ways to conclusively do so. All of them are flawed to some extent, either logically, or in leading one into a morass of semantic traps and paradoxes that are difficult to resolve; some of the resolutions produce such minutia as to appear trivial in the real world.

On the other hand, if one is not trying to "prove" something, but is interested in testing it, the various theories of truth are illuminating. They suggest various ways to probe for weaknesses in arguments, lines of logical development, and inadequacies in presenting evidence or "correspondence." If one is not searching for certainty or even stability, but is in pursuit of a temporary state (verisimilitude), then the various theories of truth are quite useful in demonstrating what problems remain in that pursuit, what fallacies to avoid, and what remaining avenues are still open.

As researchers work with theories, they may produce evidence that does not "correspond" to predictions made by the theory. Contrary evidence never outright invalidates a theory. Rather, as Quine (1986) has shown, there is not a one-to-one relationship between data and propositions. Theories are comprised of bundles of hypotheses. Rarely is data ever able to identify which one may be false. Theories are usually underdetermined by data, "and not only by the observations we actually have made and will make, but even by all the unobserved events that are of an observable kind . . . our theory . . . is underdetermined by all 'possible' observations" (p. 6). So, even if some data does not correspond exactly to a theory, researchers will continue to use the theory until more and more of it is invalidated. This idea is called the **Duhem–Quine thesis** (Phillips, 1987, p. 13).

Sometimes discarded theories come back to life. The process may take centuries. For example, Feyerabend (1991) indicates that the theory of the motion of the earth existed in antiquity. It was criticized by Aristotle (384–322 B.C.) and was in disrepute until Copernicus revived it. A similar story can be told about atomic theory. Originally the creation of Leucippus in the fifth century B.C., it was refuted by Aristotle (342–322 B.C.) and was rejected into the nineteenth century. "It is good not to be guided by experience and experiment alone," comments Feyerabend (p. 8), despite its obvious shortcomings, correspondence, in its variety of forms, continues to be one of the major criterion in deciding whether a theory is worth criticizing.

PURSUING TRUTH IN EDUCATIONAL ADMINISTRATION

Early workers in the academic field of educational administration were influenced by classical Greek philosophy, notably Plato's concept of the ideal world which was fixed and impermanent. Culbertson (1988) notes that two of the discipline's earliest thinkers—William Torrey Harris and William Harold Payne—were devoted to making education a "new science . . . for a new management" (p. 4). They were trying to engage in a quest for a science that would envision schools as organizations that reflected a multidisciplinary perspective such as history, political science, sociology, and law. While Payne and Harris were searching for a compatible "new science," they soon found that one was emerging and were swept aside in the move toward logical positivism, as expressed in the ideas of August Comte and Herbert Spencer. The ideas of Comte and Spencer were cresting in the late nineteenth century. Spencer wrote in 1860 that, "Science is organized knowledge; and before knowledge can be organized, some of it must first be possessed. Every study, therefore, should have a purely experimental introduction; and only after an ample fund of observations has been accumulated, should reasoning begin" (p. 119).

The idea that science and the scientific method were quite superior to anything to be included in a school was captured by Spencer in this paragraph:

> By science, constant appeal is made to individual reason. Its truths are not accepted upon authority alone; but all are at liberty to test them—nay, in many cases, the pupil is required to think out his own conclusions. Every step in a scientific investigation is submitted to his judgment. He is not asked to admit it without seeing it to be true (p. 79).

Spencer's admonition about science bespeaks his view of it. Truth is established objectively in "seeing" it. This is verification by observation—the experimentalist position. Truth is established inductively, not by accepting a teacher's view or some deductive principle, but rather, by "testing" for it. Here, we have the correspondence theory in abundance.

As schools of education began growing, they added departments of educational administration that initiated the practice of surveying school systems to establish "the facts." Data gathered by these devices were supposed to be "representative" of the real world. It was from such information that scholars could create scientific laws and could establish a true management science for schools (see Tatsuoka and Silver, 1988, pp. 677–701).

Culbertson (1988) notes that between 1901 and 1925, educational administration was dominated by the desire of academics to find legitimacy in their new places in American higher education. The tool to accomplish this purpose was seen as gathering the data empirically. In the mid 1930s, a second generation of educational administration professors began looking to the social sciences as models of inquiry. The role of the survey was soon envisioned as too narrow, so experimental techniques were proposed as the appropriate tools to determine the truth.

Among the national leaders were Paul Mort, Arthur Moehlman, and Jesse Sears (Culbertson, 1988, pp. 12–13). It was Sears (1950) who advanced the thesis that schools should be seen as organizations that are parallel to government and business. Sears' ideas led the way to the present dominance of organizational theory as the contemporary theoretical umbrella for the study of educational administration.

An important interstitial movement was the rise of the Vienna Circle of philosophers and thinkers who advanced scientific empiricism, and logical empiricism, or the "unity of science movement" (Runes, 1984, p. 302, and Mises, 1956). This group blended the theories of many philosophers, among them Hume, Mill, Helmholtz, Duhem, Frege, Hegal, Whitehead, Russell, and Einstein (Runes, 1984,

p. 302). The unity of science was also indebted to linguistics and to the work of Ferdinand de Saussure (see Gadet, 1986).

The Vienna Circle was a bastion of empirical structuralism, a perspective that only by viewing a whole could any part make any sense or "mean" anything. One of the leading members was Herbert Feigl, whose ideas were incorporated in the birth of the "theory movement" in educational administration in the time period of 1960 to 1980 (see Evers and Lakomski, 1991, p. 3). As many of the Vienna Circle thinkers sought asylum in the United States prior to World War II, the impact on leading U.S. academics was accelerated and profound. The areas of psychology and sociology were deeply influenced by scientific empiricism. Because these are root disciplines to educational administration, it was not long before professors of educational administration such as Jacob Getzels, Dan Griffiths, Andrew Halpin, and Egon Guba were propelling the field toward "the theory movement" or "scientific empiricism" (see Lipham, 1988, pp. 171–184).

Despite the fact that the dominant view of educational administration has been criticized, perhaps beginning with T. B. Greenfield's (1975) attack on the organizational theory or structuralist metanarrative (as crippling the discipline's ability to deal with leadership), educational administration remains solidly anchored in scientific empiricism. As such, the professors and practitioners who make up the field overwhelmingly appear to support the objectivist view of truth. The majority appear to hold the view that truth can be considered apart from the context and culture in which it has been "discovered." Like Plato's ideals, truth represents fixed properties and relations between properties outside of life's temporal habitat.

The bulk of dissertation research in educational administration follows the form of scientific empiricism in which terms are to be defined, and boundaries are drawn between truth and nontruth, where certain topics or approaches are ruled out as applicable because they are not "scientific." These would include biographies, ethnographies, historiographies, and other forms of so-called "soft" research which are tainted by elements of "subjectivity."

All five theories of truth in this chapter are aimed at discerning a final version of truth which is "out there" and not "in there." "In-there" truth would be considered too "interiorized" to be called scientific research. While it is true that at some leading institutions in the United States, doctoral research has taken on new forms and incorporated different orientations, the field *as a field,* has been stabilized around what Lakoff and Johnson (1980) have called, "the building block theory" of meaning (p. 203). This theory of meaning centers on the Platonic notion that the real world is made up of things consisting of stable, bounded objects that can be captured by lingustic or mathematically expressed languages, piece by piece. Meaning is therefore *composed,* usually inductively.

A slight variation is made by some theorists such as W. V. Quine who acknowledged the peculiarities of specific languages in constructing ideas of truth. This shift, known as *ontological relativism* (Lakoff and Johnson, 1980, p. 203) concedes that languages are incommensurable, but insists that truth can be known objectively within them. Lakoff and Johnson (1980) criticize this stance as permitting the continuance of the doctrine of objectivism, "without any recourse to human understanding or cultural difference" (p. 203).

Educational administration, as a field, is neither lost nor drifting. Most of its research practitioners at the university level still see the world in binary objective–subjective terms, and therefore view truth in a way that, despite human linguistic and cultural differences, (which appear to be overwhelmingly abundant), is ultimately attainable by theoretical constructions, resulting in ontological stability. While the discipline has acknowledged the existence of qualitative (and softer) forms of inquiry as potentially valuable, it has yet to acknowledge that the objectivist account of truth is inherently flawed and unworkable in advancing the discipline further. It has yet to comprehend the view offered by Frederich Nietzsche in 1877:

> Let us beware of the tentacles of such contradictory notions as . . .'absolute knowledge' [or 'objective' knowledge—author's insert]. All these concepts presuppose an eye such as no living being can imagine, an eye required to have no direction to abrogate its active and interpretative powers—precisely those powers that alone make of seeing, seeing *something*. All seeing is essentially perspective, and so is all knowing. (Nietzsche, Golffing Translation, 1956, p. 255).

What the field of educational administration requires to advance is the creation of a **counter ontology.** Such a deliberately crafted view of reality would reject objectivism and any concept of truth as finality, for as Nietzsche eloquently observed, there can be no freedom until this notion of reality has been disposed of (Golffing, 1956, p. 287). To criticize the research in educational administration as unproductive, without changing its ontology, will be a futile endeavor. To successfully engage in counter ontology will require the rejection of a concept of truth, beginning with Socrates, and brilliantly extended by Plato's writings to the dawn of the twenty-first century. Thinking outside of the closed definitions of Greek logic poses a challenge to the field's most creative thinkers (see de Bono, 1992). It is unlikely that there will be any major breakthroughs until a new counter ontology is in place.

SUMMARY

The pursuit of knowledge, and in particular which knowledge may be considered true, is one of the oldest known activities of the human species. Since the era of the ancient Greeks, the idea of how to pursue knowledge has been embedded in a process called *logic.*

Scientific activity as we understand it today, arose in the seventeenth century and has taken on a number of traditions and methods over time. One of the legacies of scientific activity is the way in which the people pursuing science go about their business of developing knowledge, and discerning the true from the not-so-true or the false.

Scientific activity is directed by a number of often hidden assumptions, such as the concept of determinism, which rules out "free will," and posits that everything is caused by or connected to something else. These chains of causal events, means, and ends, are discoverable if one is persistent enough and knows enough.

Most recently, scientific activity is conceded to be indeterministic, governed by choice and chance as much as by anything else. Indeterminism cancels out the concept of progress as it has come to be understood in the West, because change is not always for the better, and because what is considered true today may not be considered so tomorrow.

Current concepts about truth are that it is embedded in language, culture, and temporal spatial relations which deny that it may be considered universal (Lakoff and Johnson, 1980, p. 227). Truth is contextually defined, and has either no meaning or a diminished meaning outside of the context in which it is located.

Verisimilitude is a concept by Karl Popper (1965) that is substituted for the concept of truth as a stable and enduring concept, fact, or idea. Verisimilitude represents the nearness to the truth rather than truth itself.

There are five major theories of truth: correspondence, semantic, pragmatist, coherence, and redundancy. Nearly all can be called versions of the correspondence theory in one way or another. The agenda of those proffering any of the five versions is to arrive at a final truth or statement about reality.

Researchers and scientists can roughly be divided into two camps: those who insist on some sort of positive evidence that something is true, and those who insist that something is false and determine ways to test statements derivative from theories in order to demonstrate their fallibility.

An emerging viewpoint is that there is a middle road between the binary term "objective–subjective" which is called *the experientialist* perspective. This concept revolves around the idea that truth only exists within various contextual systems, bounded by culture and context in any given period of time (see Lakoff and Johnson, 1980, p. 193). This version of an ontology is a kind of grand temporality, without resorting to subjectivism— the opposite of objectivity—in Greek logic. The breaking away from boxed definitions is the first step to constructing a new ontology for educational administration.

Perception Check and Applications

1. Comparing Language and Cultural Similarities

If no human language is ever really the same, no culture exactly like any other, and therefore no human experience like any other, how can humans communicate across languages, cultures, and time? In other words, how do humans communicate at all and share their experiences? One interesting work on this topic is W. V. Quine's (1974), *The Roots of Reference*. Other writings in the area of anthropology and history may provide clues to this question.

To provide an example, secure a copy of Martin Heidegger's (1984), "The Anaximander Fragment," as the oldest example of Western ontology. Indicate the ways that the dominant thought patterns in educational administration are examples of the concepts in Heidgger's essay.

2. The Concept of the Hermeneutical Circle

Dilthey's "hermeneutical circle" was based on the idea that unless one understood the larger context in which an event was being examined, it was nearly impossible to estimate its significance and attach meaning to it. Discuss the following events using the concept of the "hermeneutical circle":

1. The fall of the Berlin Wall and the reunification of Germany
2. The Matewan massacre in West Virginia in the 1920s
3. The Persian Gulf War
4. The kidnapping of Patty Hearst
5. The landing of men on the moon
6. The Los Angeles riots of 1992
7. The world AIDS epidemic
8. The resignation of Richard M. Nixon as U.S. President
9. The Iran–Contra Affair
10. The Scopes Trial in Tennessee in 1925

What information *as context* is necessary to understanding the fullest meaning of the event? What information is hardest to obtain? What information is most conjectural? What theory of truth were you using in determining the answers to the aforementioned questions?

3. Theories in Use in Education

Examine your experience in education as a classroom teacher or school administrator. Identify one or two theories that you have been using implicitly or explicitly in these roles. Have you been accepting all or parts of these theories? If parts, then identify the parts you've accepted and those you've rejected.

4. Indeterminism as a Metanarrative

Carefully consider which positions in education, classroom teaching, administration, learning, motivation theory, and the like are deterministic or indeterministic in their perspective. Inasmuch as the prevailing view of human activity is one of indeterminism (the metanarrative), explain the impact of what would or might be different in these activities if they were completely indeterministic.

5. Explaining Semantic Paradoxes

To find out if you really understand the nature of semantic paradox, explain how in either the Epimenides paradox or the liar's paradox, it arises and how it may be resolved with Tarski's semantic theory of truth or Ramsey's redundancy theory.

6. The Linguistic Inaccessibility of Language

Ludwig Wittgenstein has indicated in *Tractatus Logico-Philosophicus* that what is reflected in language, language cannot represent. Give several examples of

Wittgenstein's concept. Is there any way you could use language to reflect upon itself?

7. The Base of Scientific Activity

React to Karl Popper's (1968) statement that, "Science does not rest upon solid bedrock." Upon what does science rest? Describe a process where one could place the greatest amount of confidence in a scientific process or outcome. Describe the procedures you selected to ascertain "confidence."

8. Science as a Metalanguage

Using the difference described in the chapter between an object language and a metalanguage, establish a situation where science is a metalanguage for human experience. What problems did you or would you encounter in establishing science as a metalanguage? How do the problems relate to the idea of truth?

9. The Value of Theory

If true theories can generate false ones, and false theories generate truth, what is the value of theory in educational administration research?

Key Chapter Concepts and Terms

coherence theory of truth

The view that experience is not a definitive base upon which to select a superior theory. Rather, superior theories contain qualities in greater abundance than inferior ones. Superior theories are more complete, consistent, simple, comprehensive, and rich in content than inferior ones.

correspondence theory of truth

The idea that something may be considered to be "true," if it "fits" or "corresponds" to the facts, evidence, or other statements already believed to be true. More experienced data is usually believed to be definitive in arguments regarding the truth from this perspective.

counter ontology

Ontology is the study of reality, or of the question, "What is real?" A *counter* ontology is one that would reject the idea that reality is *either* objective or subjective. It would posit that reality may be something other than these binary terms suggest.

the critical method

A concept of Karl Popper's that he indicated was superior to the "scientific method." The critical method was a procedure to severely test theories, believing that none are most likely true in the long run. The critical method was an approach to falsification rather than to establishing truth with "proof."

disambiguated language

A language in which contradiction and paradox are removed, creating a truly logical language.

Duhem–Quine thesis

The notion that scientific theories are never totally proved or disproved, and that as data or evidence is encountered, adjustments are made in the overall theory to improve "correspondence."

falsificationists

Researchers or philosophers who believe that science is advanced not by positive assertion or evidence, but by subjecting statements or propositions to rigorous testing in order to demonstrate their falsity rather than their truthfulness.

the hermeneutical circle

A concept of the German philosopher Wilhelm Dilthey of expanding the idea of "text" from the printed page to the sociocultural aspects of a society and its ideas in order to gain greater understanding and hence, meaning.

modal logic

A logic based on the presumption of two languages being present, representing analytical truth (truth based on logic) and synthetic truth (truth based on experience and hence, correspondence). Analytical truth is carried in a meta-language and synthetic truth within an object language.

redundancy theory of truth

An approach to discerning truth by eliminating unnecessary repetitions in statements or propositions in which truth is being enunciated or tested.

right science

That "science" which is embraced by the government funding agencies or foundations as worthy of support. There is a certain type of politics involved in deciding what "right" science is.

the Sapir–Whorf hypothesis

The view that everyone is not persuaded by the same universe or evidence in it to see the same image or picture of it. This accounts for many of the language differences between various human language communication systems.

semantic theory of truth

The perspective that the use of natural language (object language) is fraught with a syntax that leads to antinomy and to paradox (contradiction). Therefore, a language to talk about language (a metalanguage) must be constructed to create rules (logic) that eliminates antinomy and paradox. Truth is a matter of engaging in statements that are free from paradox.

synechism (of reality)

The idea that reality is so overwhelming that no person or group could ever encompass all of it. For this reason, scientific theories are most likely going to be underdetermined.

truth

A statement, explanation, or theory that is believed to be substantiated by facts, evidence, coherence, or correspondence to what is believed to be "real," as opposed to not real (false), thus attaining a position of "objectivity"—i.e., beyond the personal or subjective fancies or beliefs of individuals within, but apart from, that reality.

verisimilitude

A concept of Karl Popper's that substitutes verisimilitude for truth. The former represents a "nearness" to truth rather than truth itself. Popper maintains that even if we should discern the truth, we may not recognize it. However, we are more apt to know what isn't true than what is. By this process, we advance closer to what is true without ever knowing if we perceive it directly or exactly.

References

Apple, M. (1991). "Regulating the Text: The Socio-Historical Roots of State Control," in Altbach, P. G., Kelly, G. P., Petrie, H. G., and Weis, L. (Eds.), *Textbooks in American Society.* Albany, New York: SUNY Press, pp. 7–26.

Appleton's American Higher Geography (1881). New York: D. Appleton and Company.

Asante, M. K. (1990). *Kemet, Afrocentricity and Knowledge.* Trenton, New Jersey: Africa World Press, Inc.

Associated Press (1992), "Tires Recalled so They Don't Tread on Allah," *Lexington Herald–Leader,* (July 25) p. A3.

Billington, R. A. (1973). *Frederick Jackson Turner*. New York: Oxford University Press.

Cherryholmes, C. (1988). *Power and Criticism*. New York: Teachers College Press.

Coe, M. D. (1992). *Breaking the Maya Code*. New York: Thames and Hudson.

Collison, M. (1992, February 26). "A Berkeley Scholar Clashes with Feminists Over Validity of Their Research on Date Rape," *The Chronicle of Higher Education*, 38:25, pp. A35–A37.

Coughlin, E. K. (1993, May 26). "New History of America Attempts to Make Good on the Claims of Multiculturalism," *The Chronicle of Higher Education*, pp. A9–10.

Crawford, J. T. (1992, September 30). *Hold Your Tongue: Bilingualism and the Politics of "English Only."* Excerpt in *The Chronicle of Higher Education*, 39:6, p. B5.

Culbertson, J. (1988). "A Century's Quest for a Knowledge Base," in Norman J. Boyan (Ed.), *Handbook of Research on Educational Administration*. New York: Longman, pp. 3–26.

Darwin, C. (1859). *On The Origin of Species by Natural Selection*. London, England: Murray.

Davidson, J. W., and Lytle, M. H. (1986). "Jackson's Frontier and Turner's," in *After the Fact*. New York: Alfred A. Knopf, pp. 85–114.

de Bono, E. (1992). *Serious Creativity*. New York: HarperCollins.

DeCamp, L. (1968). *The Great Monkey Trial*. New York: Doubleday and Company.

DeLoughry, T. J. (1991, December 4). "40 Scientists Call on Colleagues to Re-Evaluate AIDS Theory," *The Chronicle of Higher Education*, pp. A9–A15.

Denzin, N. K. (1978). *The Research Act*. New York: McGraw Hill.

Dewey, J. (1958). *Experience and Nature*. New York: Dover Publications.

Dewey, J. (1938). *Logic, the Theory of Inquiry*. New York: Henry Holt.

Duffy, J. (1979). *The Healers: A History of American Medicine*. Urbana, Illinois: University of Illinois Press.

Eco, U. (1990). *The Limits of Interpretation*. Bloomington, Indiana: Indiana University Press.

Eiselen, F. C., Lewis, E., and Downey, D. G. (1957). *The Abingdon Bible Commentary*. Garden City, New York: Doubleday & Company, Inc.

English, F. W., and Zirkel, P. A. (1989–1990). "The Great Monkey Trial: Scopes in Perspective," *National Forum of Applied Educational Research Journal*, 2:2, pp. 4–17.

Evers, C. W., and Lakomski, G. (1991). *Knowing Educational Administration*. Oxford, England: Pergamon Press.

Felperin, H. (1988). *Beyond Deconstruction*. Oxford, England: Clarendon Press.

Feyerabend, P. (1991). *Three Dialogues of Knowledge*. Oxford, England: Basil Blackwell, Inc.

Foucault, M. (1990a). *The History of Sexuality*. New York: Random House.

Foucault, M. (1990b). *The Use of Pleasure*. New York: Random House.

Gadamer, H. G. (1976). *Philosophical Hermeneutics*. Berkeley: University of California Press.

Gadet, F. (1986). *Saussure and Contemporary Culture*. London: Hutchinson Radius.

Golffing, F. (1956). *Friedrich Nietzsche: The Genealogy of Morals*. New York: Anchor Doubleday, pp. 147–299.

Haack, S. (1988). *Philosophy of Logics*. Cambridge, England: Cambridge University Press.

Hall, E. T. (1969). *The Hidden Dimension*. New York: Anchor Books.

Heidegger, M. (1984). "The Anaximander Fragment," in David F. Krell and Frank A. Capuzzi (Trans.), *Early Greek Thinking*. San Francisco: HarperCollins.

Herman, E. S., and Chomsky, N. (1988). *Manufacturing Consent*. New York: Pantheon Books.

Highwater, J. (1990). *Myth and Sexuality*. New York: New American Library.

Hintikka, M. B., and Hintikka, J. (1989). *Investigating Wittgenstein*. Oxford, England: Basil Blackwell Ltd.

House, E. R. (1991, August–September). "Realism in Research," *Educational Researcher,* 20:6, pp. 2–9, 25.

Howard, M., and Paret, P. (Eds. and Trans.) (1976). *On War* by C. V. Clausewitz. Princeton, New Jersey: Princeton University Press.

Howland, G. (1896). *Practical Hints for the Teachers of Public Schools.* New York: D. Appleton and Company.

James, W. (1991). *Pragmatism.* Buffalo, New York: Prometheus Books.

Jensen, H. (1969). *Sign, Symbol and Script.* New York: G. P. Putnam's Sons.

Kunhardt, P. B., Jr. (1983). *A New Birth of Freedom.* Boston, Massachusetts: Little, Brown and Company.

Lakoff, G., and Johnson, M. (1980). *Metaphors We Live* By. Chicago: University of Chicago Press.

Lipham, J. M. (1988). "Getzel's Models in Educational Administration," in N. J. Boyan (Ed.), *Handbook of Research on Educational Administration.* New York: Longman, pp. 171–184.

Matthews, G. H. (1965). *Hidatsa Syntax.* The Hague: Mouton.

McDonald, K. A. (1991, August 14). "Biologist Discovers That Survival of Common Orchid Challenges Darwin's Natural–Selection Theory," *The Chronicle of Higher Education,* pp. A6–A8.

Mises, R. V. (1956). *Positivism.* New York: George Braziller, Inc.

Ogden, E. H., and Germinario, V. (1988). *The At-Risk Student.* Lancaster, Pennsylvania: Technomic Publishing Co., Inc.

Outhwaite, W. (1991). "Hans-Georg Gadamer," in Q. Skinner (Ed.), *The Return of Grand Theory in the Human Sciences.* New York: Cambridge University Press, pp. 21–40.

Palmer, F. R. (1986). *Semantics.* Cambridge, England: Cambridge University Press.

Palmer, R. (1969). *Hermeneutics: Interpretation Theory in Schleiermacher, Dilthey, Heidegger, and Gadamer.* Evanston, Illinois: Northwestern University Press.

Peirce, C. S. (1934–1948). *Collected Papers* (4 vols.). Cambridge, Masssachusetts: Harvard University Press.

Peirce, C. S. (1955). *Philosophical Writings of Peirce.* J. Buchler (Ed.), New York: Dover Publications, Inc.

Phillips, D. C. (1987). *Philosophy, Science, and Social Inquiry.* Oxford: Pergamon Press.

Popper, K. R. (1965). *Conjectures and Refutations: The Growth of Scientific Knowledge.* New York: Harper and Row.

Popper, K. R. (1968). *The Logic of Scientific Discovery.* New York: Harper and Row.

Popper, K. R. (1979). *Objective Knowledge.* Oxford, England: Clarendon Press.

Popper, K. R. (1988). *The Open Universe.* London, England: Routledge.

Quine, W. V. (1974). *The Roots of Reference.* La Salle, Illinois: Open Court.

Quine, W. V. (1980). *From a Logical Point of View.* Cambridge, Massachusetts: Harvard University Press.

Quine, W. V. (1986). *Philosophy of Logic.* Cambridge, Massachusetts: Harvard University Press.

Ramsey, F. P. (1931). *The Foundations of Mathematics.* London: Routledge and Kegan Paul.

Rickman, H. P. (1976). *Dilthey.* Cambridge, England: Cambridge University Press.

Ridpath, J. C. (1874). *History of the United States, Prepared Especially for Schools.* Cincinnati, Ohio: Jones Brothers & Co.

Runes, D. D. (1984). *Dictionary of Philosophy*. Totowa, New Jersey: Rowman & Allanheld.

Ruse, M. (1979). *The Darwinian Revolution*. Chicago: University of Chicago Press.

Sapir, E. (1949). *Selected Writings of Edward Sapir in Language, Culture and Personality*.
G. Mandelbaum (Ed.), Berkeley, California: University of California Press.

Schrag, F. (1992, June–July). "In Defense of Positivist Research Paradigms," *Educational Researcher*, 21:5, pp. 5–7.

Schwarzkopf, N., and Petre, P. (1992). *It Doesn't Take a Hero*. New York: Linda Grey, Bantam Books.

Sears, J. (1950). *The Nature of the Administrative Process*. New York: McGraw–Hill.

Sears, S. S. (1983). *Landscape Turned Red*. New Haven: Ticknor & Fields.

Spencer, H. (1860). *Education*. New York: D. Appleton and Company.

Summers, H. G., Jr. (1982). *On Strategy: A Critical Analysis of the Vietnam War*. Novato, California: Presidio Press.

Tannahill, R. (1982). *Sex In History*. New York: Stein and Day.

Tarski, A. (1956). *Logic, Semantics, and Metamathematics*. Oxford, England: Oxford University Press.

Tatsuoka, M., and Silver, P. (1988). "Quantitative Research Methods in Educational Administration," in N. J. Boyan (Ed.), *Handbook of Research on Educational Administration*. New York: Longman, pp. 677–702.

Tschanz, D. W. (1992, January–February). "The Fate of the Wounded in the American Civil War," *Command*, 14, pp. 34–37.

Whorf, B. L. (1956). *Language, Thought and Reality: Selected Writings of Benjamin Lee Whorf*.
J. B. Carroll (Ed.), Cambridge, Massachusetts: MIT Press.

Winkler, K. J. (1992, July 8). "A Scholar's Provocative Query: Was Huckleberry Finn Black?" *The Chronicle of Higher Education*, 37:44, pp. A6–A8.

Wittgenstein, L. (1921, 1961). *Tractatus Logico-Philosophicus*. London, England: Routledge & Kegan Paul.

A Typology of Metanarratives in Educational Administration

A **typology** is a study or classification of types. A type is a model or impression. What this chapter will present is a typology of metanarratives, or "grand theories" as they are sometimes called (Skinner, 1991). Since there is no way to make sense of so-called "facts," apart from the theories in which they may be imbedded, and since theories cannot be compared on a common scale, a rough kind of typology is all that is most likely possible to create in order to understand different theories (English, 1993).

Metanarratives assume privileged positions as scientific theories, i.e., the theories themselves are incommensurable (Skinner, 1992, p. 10) because they rest on assumptions that are not open to refutation. In this sense, Nietzsche (1956) was correct in stating that faith in science is essentially metaphysical (p. 88).

The diversity of the metanarratives—their differences—may not always be stated boldly by their proponents or even their critics. Sometimes they are buried in the explication, rationale, or even the narrative itself. Each metanarrative can be considered a text in the hermeneutical sense of the word. The purpose is to give the reader a general overview—mostly, though not exclusively—in very rough chronological order of the development of texts in the discipline. The sequences often overlap because there are no clear boundaries when one is tracing the development of ideas. As a discourse, the history of ideas pays little attention to the rules of sequence or succession (see Foucault, 1972, p. 169). Sometimes ideas lay dormant for a considerable time and later re-emerge transformed. This has certainly been the case with scientific management.

The distinctions between the types may be considered less as categories, and more as a set of interpositivities which will illustrate the various transformations of ideas and concepts in educational administration. While these interpositivities illustrate the transformations over time, they cannot be considered inclusive, nor represent the totality of the field. In this sense, the metanarratives are illustrative of Foucault's (1972) concept of the archaeology of knowledge of a discipline presented as a kind of rough historical enunciative discourse (p. 164).

In the process of interpretation, we should remember that Hans-Georg Gadamer noted that the social sciences were plagued by a *double hermeneutic*. This means that the researcher in the social sciences approaches the world through theoretical lenses and must remember that data produced with these a priori configurations is what the analysis is all about. Understanding that theory preshapes the data to be analyzed is the problem of the double hermeneutic (Outhwaite, 1991, p. 34).

THE DEVELOPMENT OF EDUCATIONAL ADMINISTRATION

Educational administration, as commonly conceived in the United States, was the progeny of the growth of schools in the population expansion and migration to the cities during the time period of 1820 to 1860 (see Tyack, 1974, pp. 30–31). Prior to this population explosion in the cities, the first state superintendency was created in New York in 1812, the County superintendency in Delaware in 1829, and the local superintendency in Buffalo, New York, in 1837 (English, 1987, p. 33).

The development of the superintendency capped a long road beginning with the creation of the "principal–teacher," or principalship during the same time period (see Otto, 1954, p. 652). The emergence of school administrators directly paralleled the development of bureaucracy in American schools. Bureaucracy develops when there are offices arranged in hierarchical order within an organization resembling the arrangement of classical Roman military organization. Bureaucracies were more independent politically than prebureaucratic agencies had been. Officers were advanced on merit and not on their political connections.

Efficiency was the watchword of bureaucracies. The development of bureaucracy involved the centralization of its authority structure into functional offices or bureaus. The creation of bureaucracies based on merit and expertise was part of the reform movement in American public life that re-shaped its cities following scandals such as the exposé of Tammany Hall's plundering of the city and its schools in 1864 (see Ravitch, 1974, p. 99).

City and school reformers promoted the advancement of scientific management in the form of bureaucracy as the antidote to the "ward politics" of the day. Kaestle (1983) cites three dominant metanarratives which resulted in the development of a plank for school reformers during this time period. They were *Protestantism, republicanism,* and *capitalism.* The major focal points for these three positions were encapsulated into these ideologies: (1) ideas about the sanctity and fragility of republicanism which included beliefs regarding individualism, liberty, and virtue; (2) the primary role of character in shaping social morality; (3) the necessity of the work ethic in shaping individual moral integrity; (4) the definition of a role for women which included respect but limited social standing and mobility outside the home; (5) the importance of character building; (6) the inviolability and virtue of property; (7) the open opportunity for economic advancement in the United States; (8) the superiority of American Protestant values; (9) the larger manifestation of American destiny in the world; and (10) the prerequisite for change to assure that the nation's immigrants were "assimilated" or aligned to these ideologies. The schools were seen as the social agents to insure the continued domination of the immigrants (pp. 76–77).

The development of school administration in America was part and parcel of a definite "power–knowledge" continuum. The school reformers were moved to fight against municipal corruption, which meant taking away local control from the wards in which large numbers of immigrants were housed. It meant removing local board members who represented these classes. Since the reformers were outnumbered by the popular vote within the wards, their strategy was to remove the political power of the ward boards by declaring them political non-entities through the state legislatures. This was accomplished by moving to "at large" elections and reducing the size of the remaining boards. In a deft "re-structuring" move, the New York City board was reduced over a 20-year time frame, from 46 people to seven. The instigators of reform and school centralization were "business and professional men, advocates of efficiency in schools as well as in city governments, and also old-fashioned Protestant moral reactionaries" (Button and Provenzo, 1989, p. 212). With fewer board members, the elites who controlled the banks, newspapers, legal, and other professional services came into control of the schools. Nasaw

(1979) explains that during the time period of 1882 to 1905 in Philadelphia, the major agencies for reform of the schools were comprised nearly exclusively of wealthy businessmen. "One hundred percent of the Civic Club and 75 percent of the P.E.A. [Public Education Association] officers were listed in either the *Blue Book* or the *Social Register*" (p. 108).

The rapid centralization of city school districts created the need for trained educational "experts." It is not an accident, therefore, that school administration was the beneficiary of bureaucratic centralization based on notions of efficiency that were firmly grounded in fundamental Protestant–capitalistic, socioeconomic ideologies of the reform of the cities and the domination of them by business–professional elites.

Administrators who claim that they are "nonpolitical" are incredibly naive about how their roles came to exist in the first place. Their ignorance regarding the nature of politics and its relationship to socioeconomic relationships is a case of self-delusion. School administration as we know it today in America was the outcome of a long struggle to change the political landscape of the nation, to wrest political power away from one group and transfer it to another, and to reinforce a set of socioeconomic–political ideologies that appeared to be threatened at the time under the banner of "better management" (Nasaw, 1979, p. 109). The preoccupation with management has been school administration's legacy to its own *raison d'etre*. Under no circumstance could it be considered *apolitical* or *neutral*. School administration was the child of "efficiency." To a very large extent, it remains in this ideological rubric to present times.

THE KNOWLEDGE BASE OF SCHOOL ADMINISTRATION

Culbertson (1988) claims that the first book on school administration was written by William Harold Payne in 1875 (p. 3). Actually, there are exemplars of such texts at least three decades prior to Payne's book. Potter and Emerson's (1842) book, *The School and the School Master,* and Randall's (1844) *A Digest of the Common School System of the State of New York* could be considered "texts" in school administration. They both contain examinations of the problems facing school persons, together with prescriptions regarding rules, pupils, curriculum, teaching, and other administrative problems facing schools of their times.

The Potter and Emerson (1842) text contains prescriptions on the mental and moral qualities that are important in a teacher, the division of curricular studies, the duties of teachers, the organization of the school, and a discussion of the mental and physical attributes of a schoolhouse that were conducive for learning.

Beginning with the notion of organization, Potter and Emerson note:

The teacher is to establish a system or organization, the object of which is to prevent irregularities, and to save time; to enable him to do as much for each, and for all, as possible; and to exercise each pupil according to his capacity and advancement, not over-tasking him, nor leaving him unoccupied. This system should be comprehensive enough to embrace all the operations of the school, and so simple that all the children may be able to understand it; so that, when once established, it shall almost keep itself in operation, leaving the teacher his whole time for other duties (p. 394).

The text explains that there are five matters which will require the attention of the teacher. They are: (1) general exercises, (2) the time, order, and length of the exercises of the several classes, (3) interruptions, (4) recesses, and (5) the punishment of offenses.

Under the recommendation regarding general exercises, the authors suggested two types. The first concerned general classroom instruction for all students on *duties,* and the other regarded useful practical knowledge. All remaining instruction consisted of small groups or of individuals being taught.

On the matter of interruptions, Potter and Emerson (1842) take note of five types: (1) mending pens, (2) giving leave to whisper or leave seats, (3) explaining sums and answering questions in regard to studies, (4) tardiness and hearing excuses for tardiness, and (5) punishing offenses as they occur. They note that if the teacher fails to regulate these aspects of classroom life, "they will be continually occurring to harass the teacher, distract his attention from the proper exercises of the school, to overwhelm his faculties, and wear out his spirits" (p. 397).

On administrative matters directly, Potter and Emerson (1842) note that, "The art of governing a school naturally divides itself into, 1. The preservation of order; 2. The prevention of wrong; 3. Incitement to study" (p. 487).

In speaking on how to attain these aims, the authors indicate, "Towards the accomplishment of all these the first requisite is *to render your school pleasant* [original text italicized]. A pleasant school is one that is properly cared for, ventilated, [and] airy, with proper seats and the like." Finally, "order is not unpleasant . . . study is not unpleasant. When the thing studied is understood, nothing is more pleasant. . . . An exercise should cease before any one has become weary" (p. 488). These most practical matters in school organization, management, and operations are most certainly topics in school administration today.

The Randall text (1844) is a published list of duties of town and county superintendents, town clerks, teachers, and librarians. It specifies the purchase, custody, and sale of schools, the employment and payment of teachers including teacher contracts, annual reports, accounts, and how to handle various types of lawsuits. The book includes subject matter in the following courses now offered in school administration: law, finance, personnel, organization, facilities, curriculum, board and community relations, and educational history.

These texts indicate that the field of educational administration emerged around 1800 in response to legislation introduced in the late eighteenth century. Larry Cuban (1988) found the title of superintendency in a Congressional document in 1804 granting certain powers to the District of Columbia's City Council. Cuban also noted that the title of **school superintendent** was used by the Methodist, John Wesley, beginning in the 1780s in the United States when bestowing bishoprics in that religion (p. 111). Factory managers were also called superintendents. Taking 1800 as a convenient year, school administration as a field is over 190 years old. Considering how long medicine, law, ministering, engineering, and accounting have been around, it is a very young field.

ADMINISTRATIO VS. PRINCIPALIS: A COMMANDER OR A COUNSELOR?

It should be clear that educational leadership, or simply leadership, is as old as humanity. School administration is the product of the bureaucratization of schools and districts, the genesis of which was the industrial revolution in America and subsequent demographic shifts which brought large numbers of persons from rural areas to the cities, including successive waves of immigration from Europe.

Administrator is derived from the Latin word *administratio,* which means, "He who is at one's hand, i.e., aids, assists, in the care of a thing" (Freund and Andrews, 1854, p. 35). A derivation of the word is the French *administrare,* which means "to serve," as in *minister* (Webster, 1972, p. 12). *Minister* is also a Latin word which stands for attendant, waiter, or servant. The Latin view was that a minister was an "under official," or an "inferior officer" (Freund and Andrews, 1854, p. 951). Clearly, the heritage of the word *administrator* was not the idea of a visionary or missionary leader of an organization that has come to epitomize discussions regarding the topic of administration today.

"School" is from the old English word *scol* and the Latin *schola,* which meant "leisure given to learning or a learned conversation or debate" (Freund and Andrews, 1854, p. 1367). Thus, one translation of school administrator from antiquity is a "minor official who supports and tends to learned conversation or dialogue." *Administrator* with a bit more emphasis from the French emphasis would point to a person who *serves* a learned conversation or dialogue. It is clear from the Latin that in no case would this person direct or *control* a learned conversation or dialogue. Nor is there a hint that *administratio* means "to define" or "to limit" that which is at hand or must be served.

The connotation of *school administrator* from the Latin is a soft type of phrase to cover the work of minor officiating of a relaxed, or leisurely, activity—a kind of counseling which is a far cry from the hard and controlling vocabulary replete in texts dealing with school administration in post-industrial revolution societies.

Consider, for example, Chicago school superintendent George Howland's (1896) description of the school principal's duties:

> His is the life, the impulse of the school, its controlling and directing power, its inspiration and its hope; adjusting and harmonizing its various parts, encouraging here and checking there, making his presence felt for good by teacher and pupil at once, omnipresent in his influence, never obtrusive, but alive to the working of all the mental and material machinery intrusted to his care (p. 152).

The passage clearly shows the factory model at work in the words "adjusting and harmonizing" and in the phrase "mental and material machinery." However, Howland elaborates and leaves no doubt as to his view of the matter:

> The plan of the school should be as clearly defined in his thought as that of a coming battle in the mind of the commander. . . . With wise and calm decision and prompt action should he put his plans into operation, unruffled by the countless questions and suggestions of pupils and parents; every teacher in her place, every pupil promptly to his

seat, ready for the work, so that almost with the morning bell the whole school may start off, like the machinery of a vast factory at the touch of the lever that puts it all in motion, with no jarring, no friction, no undue tension, but quietly, smoothly, strongly, all in perfect accord for the working out of earnest, industrious, well-informed, self-controlled, intelligent and worth characters (p. 153).

Howland's picture, his metaphors, make it plain that the principal decides *alone and without consultation* how this factory will work. He puts it into effect *despite* questions or suggestions from pupils or parents because he is the equivalent of a military *commander.*

Howland's paternalism and advice make it singularly clear that the principal is no minor official "supporting" a learned dialogue in a later passage:

Yes, my fellow-teachers, though yours is the work, as has been my continual theme, and stronger and strong my belief, as the years go by, the principal is the school; the school is what he makes it. The organization, the plan of the work is his, and his the spirit that shall animate, the methods that shall execute, and the character that shall control (p. 155).

In these pursuits, the person in the school ceases to minister or support. The principal, from the Latin *principalis*, means "first in ranking," or "of or pertaining to a prince or ruler." The Latin *principes* refers to the second line in the order of battle (Freund and Andrews, 1854, p. 1201).

So while *administratio* is passive, supporting, and indirect, the *principalis* is controlling, contentious, and commanding. These two views are inherent in the traditions of school administration today. One view is the *administratio*, the supporting, the passive, the protecting of the learned dialogue—the kind of leadership that Burns (1978) named "transformational." The second is the *principalis*—the authoritarian, directing, controlling, and continually subordinating others to command— the "transactional." These tensions and opposites have been encapsulated in the history of the discipline. They present the superintendency with the same kind of ambiguity. In Latin, the word *super* means "above" or "over in number or quality." A *superintentor* is an "overseer" (Freund and Andrews, 1854, p. 1495). It comes from the verb *superintendo*, which means "to have the oversight of." An overseer is not a commander in the same vein as the *principalis*.

THE FIRST SUPERINTENDENCY: WHAT MANNER OF JOB?

The very first American school superintendent was most likely Mr. Gideon Hawley, Esquire, of Saratoga, New York. He was selected by the Council of Appointment, for the State of New York, as a consequence of the passing of the law in 1812 that created a state system of common schools. (Randall, 1844, p. 19).

Assuming his duties in January of 1813, Mr. Hawley had the task of overseeing the creation, development, and extension of public education throughout the Empire State. The law created no specific duties for the first superintendent. It simply stated that, "the whole system be placed under the superintendence of an officer appointed by the Council of Appointment" (Randall, 1844, p. 16).

Lawyer Hawley served for eight years as state superintendent until he retired and his job was abolished. His duties were assumed by the secretary of state. Exactly what did he do? We are provided some clues in the statement summing up his accomplishments after his eighth term by Randall (1844):

> At a period when everything depended upon organization; upon supervision; upon practical acquaintance with the most minute details; and upon a patient, perservering, laborious process of exposition, Mr. Hawley united in himself all the requisites for the efficient discharge of the high functions devoted upon him by the legislature. From a state of anarchy and confusion, and complete disorganization, within a period of less than eight years, arose a beautiful and stately fabric, based upon the most impregnable foundations, sustained by an enlightened public sentiment, fortified by the best and most enduring affections of the people, and cherished as the safeguard of the state—the true palladium of its greatness and prosperity (p. 29).

Such flowery words are rarely seen in state reports in modern times. In concrete terms, Gideon Hawley oversaw the development of a system of common schools in New York that doubled the number of school districts and increased the percentage of elementary school children in school from four-fifths to twenty-four, twenty-fifths. Years for which data is available show the funds alloted to school districts from the state rose from $55,720.98 for 2,755 school districts educating approximately 176,449 children age five through sixteen in 1815 (the year of the first statistical report) to $157,195.04 for 6,659 school districts educating approximately 332,979 children in the same age ranges in 1821, the last year of Gideon Hawley's tenure (Randall, 1844, p. 83). In 1841, the New York legislature adopted into law a system of county superintendents of common schools. By that time, there were 10,886 school districts educating 583,347 children with the state dispersing $658,954.70 to the same districts (Randall, 1844, p. 83).

The duties of the County Superintendent are specified in the act of 1841 in New York as follows (Randall, 1844):

1. To visit and examine all the schools and school districts committed to his charge as often in each year as may be practicable . . . to inquire into all matters relating to the government, course of instruction, books, studies, discipline and conduct of such schools, and the condition of the school houses, and of the districts generally; and to advise and counsel the trustees and other officers of school districts in relation to their duties, particularly in relation to the erection of school houses, and to recommend to such trustees, and the teachers employed by them, the proper studies, discipline and conduct of the schools, the course of instruction to be pursued, and the books of elementary instruction to be used therein.
2. To examine persons offering themselves as candidates for teachers in common schools, and to grant them certifications of qualification;
3. By and with the consent of the Town Superintendent of any town to annul any certificate granted to any teacher in said town, whenever such teacher shall be found deficient.

4. And generally, by all the means in his power, to promote sound education, elevate the character and qualifications of teachers, improve the means of instruction, and advance the interests of the schools committed to his charge (pp. 265–266).

The expansion of the role of superintendent, originally an overseer, now shifts to include inspection and supervision. *Inspectatio* in Latin means "a looking into," while an *inspectator* is an overseer (Freund and Andrews, 1854, p. 814). Supervision includes the idea of "over" or "above" with *visio* meaning "the act or sense of seeing" (p. 1638).

The necessity of inspection and supervision to early educators, legislators, and common school advocates was a necessity to "execute" the law. In New York, as early as 1826, distinguished statesmen were advocating to the legislature the advantages of inspection on the county level to force school boards to hire more competent (instead of the cheapest) teachers. (Randall, 1844, p. 38). One of the remedies to the problem of incompetent teachers was to develop "teacher seminaries" and the so-called "Prussian plan" of education. Put forth in 1840 as a model to emulate, the then-Superintendent of Common Schools in New York indicated that "The Prussian system not only prepares the teachers, but compels the school districts to employ them. Our whole system proceeds upon the principle of accomplishing by persuasion what the Prussian effects by force" (Randall, 1844, p. 69).

In that same 1840 report, the superintendent mustered as much force as he could by imploring, "All writers on public education concur in the unanimous and decided opinion, that effectual inspection and supervision are more essential to the proper management of schools, and more indispensable to their improvement than any other agency or all other agencies combined" (Randall, 1844, p. 70).

Twenty years later in the Superintendent of Common Schools Report in Pennsylvania (Burrowes, 1860), Charles W. Quick, Allegheny County Superintendent of Schools, reported that:

Between October 2, 1859, and June 1, 1860, thirty townships, eleven boroughs, and thirteen ward districts were visited. . . . The Superintendent traveled one thousand six hundred and sixty-eight (1,668) miles, and that of that distance seven hundred and sixty-seven miles were traveled on foot (p. 19).

Another Pennsylvania county superintendent, David Evans, confided in his report the nature of his visitations as follows:

Four schools were visited in a day. From one and a half to two hours were generally spent in each . . . A common opinion prevails that this time is too short, to arrive at any accurate estimate of the state of a school. But this error arises from a wrong impression which many persons have of the object of a superintendent's visit. But so far as he has to do with the teacher, as soon as he is satisfied with the nature of his discipline, and of his attention to his pupils, his object is satisfied. Yet when anything wrong was seen, it was always pointed out, and ways of correction suggested. Questions were also given to classes, especially when there was suspicion that preparation of particular lessons was made for my visit (p. 59).

The 1860 *Report* is filled with reflections by county superintendents regarding how their own role was being accepted by the general populace. Most conceded that it was accepted. Perhaps the most candid reaction was filed by Henry Houck, Lebanon County Superintendent, who wrote in his annual report:

> *County Superintendency*—This office is slowly gaining in popularity in this county, as in others, where its nature is being more properly understood, and its duties rightly exercised. It has its *warm* friends and its *warm* enemies, and five years ago the name of the latter was 'legion.' The opposition comes from three distinct classes of individuals. The first,— comparatively small—those who contend that in educating our children we are only giving them the requisite qualifications to commit crime, and who are opposed to all innovations. The second class is composed of persons who are, as a general thing, intelligent, but have paid very little attention to our common schools. This fact accounts for the position they hold; and as they become more acquainted with school matters they become friends of the office. The other class,—by far the smallest, and the most difficult to contend with—is made up of such as would support the County Superintendency to a man, because they are convinced of its utility, were it not for the *salary appendage* (p. 62).

In 1878, J. P. Wickersham, Superintendent of Public Instruction in Pennsylvania, summarized the history of the county school superintendent in his annual report:

> The act establishing the county superintendency was passed in 1854, and has consequently been in operation twenty-four years. The office was at first very unpopular, but its usefulness is now universally acknowledged except where men fill it who are incompetent in the first place. Those acquainted with the history of common schools in Pennsylvania for the last quarter of a century, must accord to it the higher honor of being the principal agency in the movement that has revolutionized our system of public instruction, making it one of the most efficient in the Union (p. vii).

In the same report, Wickersham presented a case to the legislature for more fully developing the local superintendency. First, he cited a need for greater supervision: "Close and intelligent supervision is the life of a system of schools. Nowhere in the whole world has there ever been a system that reached a degree of efficiency without it." Then he switched to Pennsylvania, saying it had accomplished much but that, "in many of the county districts it operates at too great a distance from the schools and covers too much ground to be effective" (p. xvi). The solution, he insisted, was not a radical new law, but rather, the modification of an old one. Reminding the legislature that local school boards could appoint their secretary as district superintendent, he argued for such an appointment from the ranks of teachers instead of the board on the grounds that, "the inspector of schools should always be a practical teacher, of acknowledged skill." He envisioned that such a person "would in a short time double the efficiency of the schools" (p. xvii).

Cities had hired school superintendents beginning with Buffalo, New York, and Louisville, Kentucky, in 1837 (see Reller and Gilland, 1935). By 1890, nearly every major American municipality had hired a local superintendent of schools, including Nashville, Tennessee; Milwaukee, Wisconsin; Savannah, Georgia; Richmond, Virginia; and Salt Lake City, Utah (AASA, 1952, p. 55).

When Payne (1875) wrote his textbook regarding school administration, he listed the work of the superintendent as follows:

1. To classify pupils according to their attainments;
2. To advise the Board of the qualifications of the teachers employed, and to anticipate the vacancies which are likely to occur;
3. To enforce an observance of the course of study and the use of prescribed textbooks;
4. In cases of difficulty, to assist teachers in the discipline of pupils, and to secure an observance of the rules and regulations of the Board;
5. To prescribe rules for the conduct of pupils in the school buildings and on the school grounds;
6. To direct teachers in their methods of instruction and discipline (pp. 28–29).

By the time George Howland, the Superintendent of Chicago, wrote his book on administration nearly 30 years later (first copyrighted in 1889), he noted that, "The superintendent has become an important factor in our American schools" (p. 176). Howland carried the major duties of the county superintendent, i.e., visitation and inspection, into his descriptions of the duties of the position.

> The grandest work of the superintendent is to carry the best, the wisest, and the worthiest of each and every school into all the schools. . . . It is this intercommunication between teachers and schools, under the direction of the superintendent, which alone can insure to them all a wholesome life and fruitful progress (p. 186).

In Howland's description of duties, there is no mention of the words "chief executive officer," no strategic planning dictates, no sense of military commanding, and no allusions to corporate presidents. The description of the superintendent is far less militant than words he reserved for the principal.

All of this swiftly changed after the turn of the century. When Leonard Ayers (1916) performed his analysis of the problems in the Cleveland, Ohio, public schools, he found that mismanagement was rampant at the upper levels of the school district. Part of the problem was that the superintendent of schools was competing with the business manager for control of the system. Since the Cleveland Board of Education spent more time in its meetings on business, the business manager had more authority than the superintendent.

Ayers solved the problem by recommending the supremacy of the superintendent:

> The proper form of administration and the one recommended in every recent responsible book on the subject is one which places the superintendent as the executive head of the entire school system and gives him co-ordinating power over all departments. . . . The superintendent should be the real head of the school system as well as its titular head (pp. 78–79).

This recommendation shows the shift from school visitation and "intercommunication" being the major duty of the superintendent, over to the executive officer. *Execution* stems from the Latin *exsecutio,* meaning "an accomplishing, performance, or execution," with *exsecutor* being "a performer or executer" (Freund and

Andrews, 1854, p. 579). Officer is from the Latin *officium* meaning "the rendering of a service," whether voluntarily or involuntarily. Executive officer is more directive and controling than superintendent—a mere overseer. A superintendent as an overseer of an enterprise is different from a performer of a service. The shift is subtle, but it moves from watching something (without interfering and changing it, except as in inspection) to being the focus of an act as *the performer of the act itself* (the object itself). The shift to executive officer clearly centers the superintendent as *the person* himself or herself. By the time Elwood P. Cubberley (1929) writes about the superintendent of schools, this role has become the "chief executive officer of the school system" (p. 241). The derivation in Latin is *caput* or "head"—that which is pre-imminent (Freund and Andrews, 1854, p. 241).

But Cubberley (1916) uses another synonym to describe this educator; he refers to the superintendent as "the supervisor of the instruction in the schools, and also the leader, adviser, inspirer, and friend of teachers" (p. 132).

By 1929, Cubberley goes beyond mere supervision being the role of the superintendent as chief executive officer. The superintendent is "the educational leader of a city" (p. 227) and is also "a community leader . . . one of the most important of all city officials" (p. 250). In this shifting meaning of superintendent, various writers redefined and re-centered just who the superintendent was in public education. Thus, we have seen a constant attempt to upgrade, enhance, and embellish the authority of the superintendent—from an overseer to the person who is pre-imminent, from an inferior officer, to the supervisor, to the *leader*.

The word *leader*, from *lead*, traces its roots to the old English, *lithan*, "to go" or German *leiten*, "to lead." The Latin *duco* and such forms as *abducere*, and *deducere*, mean "to lead, conduct, draw, or bring forward" in any direction as it pertains to his will or opinions (Freund and Andrews, 1854, pp. 505–506).

Applying the idea of leadership to educational administration is a semantic shift largely of the twentieth century. It occurred late in the development of educational administration. For example, in Howland's (1896) text, the word *leader* is never used to describe the role or duties of a principal or superintendent. In Samuel Dutton's (1903) *School Management,* the word *leader* or *leadership* is never applied to describe the real or ideal role of the school principal or superintendent. In a passage where one would find the topic of leadership in most contemporary texts, Dutton never even applies the word "leadership":

> Nothing is so good for a school system, or is regarded with more favor by the public, than a superintendent who has ideas for which he is willing to stand or fall; things in which he believes and which seem to him especially pertinent to the situation. Every community has its own local needs and peculiarities. A superintendent should be quick to recognize these. He should not be too stubborn nor too hasty in announcing his policy (pp. 235–236).

Campbell, Fleming, Newell, and Bennion (1987), in *A History of Thought and Practice in Educational Administration,* list only three works in school administration published prior to 1900, and none were cited in any section concerning leadership. Rost (1991) found no definitions of leadership in books before 1900 (p. 47). Immigart (1988) cited no work on leadership or leadership behavior prior to 1948 in *The Handbook of Research on Educational Administration* (pp. 259–278). In Smith,

Mazzarella, and Piele's (1981) book *School Leadership,* the oldest citation regarding the topic was 1940. Stodgill's (1974) *Handbook of Leadership* contained a massive 150-page bibliography of references from books and over 61 journals worldwide. Stodgill cited only four sources published before 1900, and none of these were mentioned in establishing a definition or theory of leadership.

Elwood P. Cubberley (1914) used the term "leadership" generically in his book, *Rural Life and Education,* when he said, "Unless there is an effective leader of leaders to stimulate and to direct, rural educational progress is almost certain to prove sporadic and ineffective" (p. 306). Later in his *Public School Administration,* published in 1916, 1922, and 1929, he applied the idea of *leadership* to the school superintendent.

The scholar is aided in this search for the use of the concept of leadership of school offices because Cubberley annotated his bibliographic references. The oldest reference to Cubberley's chapters on the superintendent was to J. H. Beveridge from the *Proceedings, Department of Superintendence, National Education Association* in 1898 in which Cubberley indicated that this address contained the "needed scholarship, background, knowing the job, courage, self-control, resistance, and personal qualities" (p. 231).

Two references from Cubberley use the term "educational statesman" to describe the superintendent—one published in 1904 and the other in 1906. Another source was listed in Samuel Dutton and David Snedden's book, *The Administration of Public Education in the United States* (1908). They referred to the superintendent of schools as "the peer of the ablest man in other professions. He must possess those qualities of leadership and statesmanship which shall render him well-nigh invincible" (p. 231). Dutton and Snedden both taught at Columbia University's Teachers College in New York where Cubberley received his doctorate in 1905. A specific citation in which leadership was applied to the superintendency was from Jesse Newlon (1925) and was entitled, "Why is Superintendence," in which Cubberley annotated, "Direction and management necessary. Importance of leadership. Chief function of the superintendent" (p. 302).

By the mid-1920s, professional textbook writers (Gist, 1928) in educational administration were saying such things as, "The efficient principal possesses leadership of a highly professional type. . . . He must have a broad outlook upon life's problems and keen vision to realize the educational opportunities to the fullest extent" (p. 287).

Cubberley's lifting up of the superintendency from *administratio*—an inferior official, an underling—to the head, the executive of the system, was no mere feat. He succeeded in rescuing the administrator and reincarnating the idea into something beyond that which was certainly originally anticipated. The creators of administrative offices established and abolished them because they were not considered major offices. When Gideon Hawley retired, his position was merged with another—the secretary of state—and the role remained bifurcated for 32 years. Clearly, this was possible only if the superintendent was an administratio, and not an exsecutor. The superintendencies of Philadelphia, Cleveland, Baltimore, and Detroit were all abolished and later reestablished (AASA, 1952, p. 52). We have therefore traced the rise of the idea that an educational administrator is more than an under-officer; he or she is a *leader.*

It should be recognized that this shift in emphasis from a minor educational official to a major educational leader is less than 100 years old. The beneficiaries of the redefinition are clearly those who occupy administrative positions, and those whose interests rely on the judgments of administrators. The rise of school administration was fueled by a re-distribution of political power in the cities. That re-centering process took many decades to unfold, and it was fraught with conflict and chaos (Ravitch, 1974). But the transformation firmly established the rise of school administrators from minor officials to the captains of education (see Callahan and Button, 1964, p. 85).

THE LONG VIEW OF LEADERSHIP

Once school administrators were proclaimed "leaders," and authors describing their functions switched their allegiance from short-term measures of efficiency to more longer lasting perspectives, educational administration came face to face with the inadequacies of its own traditions—notably its emphasis upon scientism, behaviorism, and structuralism. These metanarratives were not inclusive enough for the view of leadership that has the longest tenure in human affairs. This exists in the arts and the humanities.

Part of the frustration and flux within educational administration today is understanding the shortcomings of the challenge to leadership, and at the same time recognizing the shallowness of the field's narratives and investigative traditions. Behaviorism is simply not adequate to define leadership. Scientism in the form of scientific management and some of its modern-day offspring (such as total quality management, as a largely statistical driven effort) are not adequate either. Finally, structuralism promised answers of permanency and unity which it was totally unable to deliver upon.

To connect the traditions of the humanities and arts to the relatively short history of educational administration, the connective strand of leadership as the larger phenomenon is required. The typology presented in this chapter deals with metanarratives and not paradigms. Pohland (1992) has presented a convincing case that educational administration is not a mature enough field to have developed its own paradigms. The typology therefore utilizes the idea of metanarratives as being privileged positions in conducting inquiry within this evolving field.

Each level is described briefly with representative texts that can be grouped at that level. The levels and the texts will be described in greater detail in subsequent chapters.

TYPOLOGICAL LEVEL 1: PRE-SCIENTIFIC IDEAS OF LEADERSHIP

Ideas about leadership and leaders are certainly found in antiquity. The heroes and heroines of mythology that are nearly universal in all human cultures are the earliest examples of the phenomenon of leadership, certainly as human desire, perhaps even projection, of the human spirit into the unknown. Joseph Campbell (1973) has called myths "the secret opening through which the inexhaustible energies of the cosmos pour into human cultural manifestations" (p. 3).

Myths are traceable to documents and displays that are over 4000 years old. The word *myth* is a derivative of the Greek word *muthos,* which means "word," "speech," "the thing spoken," or "the tale told" (Larue, 1975, p. 5). Myths served the need for all peoples to attain "psychic survival," because they provided answers where there were none. Myths filled the void, and helped to provide sustenance in a universe which seemed totally barren and hostile to human habitation (Larue, 1975, p. 8).

Campbell (1973) sees the primary function of myth as defying death by the process of renewal, both spiritual and physical. "Within the soul, within the body social, there must be—if we are to experience long survival—a continuous 'recurrence of birth'" (p. 16). The mythic hero, the leader, performed a function necessary to human survival and stability—triumph over the one unalterable fact that humanity can neither avoid, nor conquer in any single lifetime, its own expungement in death.

Campbell has therefore analyzed myths from the perspective of this function, and found forms for the **nuclear unit of the monomyth** in which the hero must traverse a certain rite of passage in separation—initiation—and return (p. 30). This same tale is told from the Great Struggle of Buddha to the crucified Jesus Christ who rose from the dead and promised to come again to Earth. "Mythology, in other words," notes Campbell (1973), "is psychology misread as biography, history, and cosmology. [It is] a powerful picture language for the communication of traditional wisdom" (p. 256).

Clarissa Pinkola Estes examined the nature of mythology from a feminine perspective in her best-selling book, *Women Who Run with the Wolves* (1992). Her work involves not only classic stories from the old world and the new, but interpretations drawn from Jungian psychology as well. She writes movingly about the return to a woman's "soul home," or her "wild home." Fairy tales or folk stories carry what Estes calls "dense instruction" for women from one generation to the next. These stories serve to reconnect women with their "deep templates" of a common psychological ground carrying far back into antiquity (pp. 264–265). In the next chapter, we will examine ideas about leadership from these sources more closely.

TYPOLOGICAL LEVEL 2: PROTOSCIENTIFIC VIEWS OF LEADERSHIP

A source of leadership that spans the body of knowledge of myths and history would be that of Homer—a poet–musician of the ninth or eighth century B.C. who described the Trojan War and the wanderings of Odysseus (Ulysses) in the two classics, *The Illiad* and *The Odyssey.* The Trojan War is believed to have occurred between 1200 and 1100 B.C. (Wood, 1985, p. 16). Both of these timeless tales interweave mythological figures and human ones. Who could ever forget the picture of Helen, whose beautiful face launched a thousand ships, or the brooding Achilles, who took revenge upon the Trojans for killing Patroclus dressed in his armor by slaying the great Hector before the walls of Troy, announcing, "Lie dead there; I am ready for my own death whenever Zeus and the other immortals send it" (Richards, 1950, p. 181).

Protoscientific works are those which combine elements of narrative or tradition that embody history and biography, or statescraft that provide pictures of leadership and leaders, or indicate important thinking about them. The work of Xenophon in the time period between 400 and 300 B.C. provided American schoolchildren with a source for reading in Greek for many years in his *Anabasis* (Owen, 1851; White, 1883). The *Anabasis* was the story of the war of Cyrus the Younger against his brother Artaxerxes II. Xenophon served in the army of Cyrus and recorded his life and adventures in it. He later assumed command of the Greeks when Cyrus was killed.

Other protoscientific writers were Thucydides, 400 B.C., who wrote *History of the Peloponnesian War* and was considered the greatest historian of antiquity, and Herodotus, who has been called "The Father of History" (Webster, 1983, p. 469). Thucydides provided glimpses of leaders and their actions. Consider his description of Alcibiades, the Athenian general and politician who argued for an alliance against Sparta in the Peloponnesian War:

> The position he [Alcibiades] held among the citizens led him to indulge his tastes beyond his real means, both in keeping horses and in the rest of his expenditure; and this later on had not a little to do with the ruin of the Athenian state. Alarmed at the greatness of his license in his own life and habits, and of the ambition which he showed in all things he undertook, the mass of the people set him down as a pretender to absolute power, and became his enemies . . . individually his habits gave offence to everyone, and caused them to commit affairs to other hands, and thus before long to ruin the city (Livingstone, 1949, pp. 279–280).

Another writer and speaker of antiquity who spoke to issues involving leadership and statesmanship was Demosthenes (384–322 B.C.), whose famous speech, "On the Crown," has been studied in schools throughout the world as an example of logic, oratory, and leadership, and was imitated by such writers as Milton (Kennedy, 1897, p. 136). In a stunning passage, Demosthenes contrasts his life with that of his rival, Aeschines, as follows:

> Contrast now the circumstances of your life and mine . . . Aeschines; and then ask these people whose fortune they would each of them prefer. You taught reading, I went to school: you performed initiations, I received them: you danced in the chorus, I furnished it: you were an assembly-clerk, I was a speaker: you acted third parts, I heard you: you broke down, and I hissed: you have worked as a statesman for the enemy, I for my country. I pass by the rest; but this very day I am on my probation for a crown, and am acknowledged to be innocent of all offense; while you are already judged to be a pettifogger (Kennedy, 1897, p. 136).

Of course, Plato also had much to say about leadership in his work *The Republic*. In proffering the "philosopher–king" as the model for leadership since philosophy is the pursuit of the ideal of "good" (the true end of being), Plato notes:

The man who really applies his intellect to reflect on true being, probably has no leisure to look down on the little affairs of mankind, and by fighting with them, become filled with envy and ill-nature; but on the other hand, beholding and contemplating objects that are orderly, always self-consistent and stable, such as neither injure nor are injured by each other, but are in all respects beautiful and consonant with reason, these he imitates and resembles as far as possible (Davis, no date, p. 188).

The Romans were blessed with *Plutarch's Lives,* or more accurately, *Parallel Lives.* Plutarch was a Greek (46 A.D. to 119 A.D.) who taught in Rome and wrote a work that dealt with famous Greeks and Romans in pairs. For example, he compared the Greek orator Demosthenes to the Roman orator Cicero. As Lindeman (1953) has pointed out, Plutarch was not a biographer. He was a moral philosopher and an eclectic one at that. He wrote portraits of 65 famous persons, of which 50 have survived into contemporary times. Plutarch was attempting to measure the moral qualities of his subjects, along with their traits and influence within their own times.

Alcibiades comes off poorly in Plutarch's descriptions, as he did with Thucydides. Says Plutarch:

But all his great abilities in politics, his eloquence, the reach of his genius and keenness of perception were tarnished by his luxurious living, his drinking and debauches, his effeminacy of dress and his insolent profusion . . . in the wars he bore a shield of gold which had none of the usual ensigns of his country but instead a Cupid bearing a thunderbolt (Lindeman, 1953, p. 104).

Alcibiades' ability as a charmer and seducer of women was established in his affair with the Queen of Sparta, who bore him a child which she bragged about to servants in the palace. The Spartan King, Agis, had the child declared ineligible to inherent the crown (p. 112). Plutarch declares Alcibiades a kind of hydra, a person who with one head was both a charmer and brilliant general and with the other was a traitor, a raconteur, and a debaucher. In the end, this imbalance caused the downfall of Athens and the end to Alcibiades, who was killed by a set of jealous brothers whose sister had been violated by the man who wore a Cupid with the thunderbolt (Lindeman, 1953, p. 126).

One of the most notable of the medieval treatises on leadership (which is still widely read today) is Nicolo Machiavelli's *The Prince.* Nicolo Machiavelli (1469–1527) was an Italian philosopher and diplomat. He served the city of Florence for a time, but was driven from office when the Medici came to power. It was Machiavelli who developed the concept of the *esecuzioni,* or the **executive,** that we have come to accept as "natural" in modern times (Mansfield, 1989, p. 122). Machiavelli embraced the idea of *force* as an instrument of law in order to compel compliance to the law. Part of an executive's effectiveness was his or her ability to act "by surprise" and to exceed the law in situations where language ambiguity did not include specific instances where the executive was "to execute." The fact that today Machiavelli is regarded as a philosopher with much to say about contemporary leadership is indicative of his increasing stature based on his writings. While his work would not be called "scientific" by some, it nonetheless would be considered so originally insightful as to be worth reading to gain greater understanding and meaning about leadership. As our concept of science undergoes changes to include areas where scientism, behaviorism, and structuralism have tended to emasculate humans and discard their motives and feelings, Machiavelli restores them in spades. His work provides the basis to re-examine the inadequacies of contemporary research on leadership.

Great works of literature also provide portraits of leadership, and drama has offered insights into human leadership as well—from the inception of the Greek tragedy such as Sophocles' *Oedipus the King,* through Shakespeare's *Hamlet, Othello, King Lear,* and *Julius Caesar.* English poetry is filled with pictures of heroes in *Sir Gawain and the Green Knight* and Chaucer's *Troilus and Criseyde.*

In France, the plays of Jean-Baptiste Poquelin (Molière) satirized the evils of the day, including his most famous *The Misanthrope,* which has been called "the French *Hamlet"* (Grebanier, Middlebrook, Thompson, and Watt, 1957, p. 1130). And who can ever forget the portrait of the hero, leader, poet, and cavalier— *Cyrano de Bergerac*—of Edmond Rostand? It was Cyrano who dispatched his opponents with these lines:

> Prince! Pray God, that is Lord of all,
> Pardon your soul, for your time has come!
> Beat—pass—fling you aslant, asprawl—
> Then, as I end the refrain—Thrust home!
> (Rostand, 1923, p. 57).

The respository of the arts has been a rich source of testimony to all sorts of leaders throughout history. The fact that many of these plays are still performed and enjoyed by audiences today indicates that the themes the playwrights and authors pursued are still considered "fresh" and relevant. That is why they are called "classics."

TYPOLOGICAL LEVEL 3: PSEUDOSCIENTIFIC VIEWS OF LEADERSHIP

Pseudoscientific views about leadership were once considered scientific. Beginning with the work of Frederick Taylor and the rise of scientific management, others such as Henry Gantt, Frank and Lillian Gilbreth, Horace Hathaway, Sanford Thompson, and Harrington Emerson were quick to capitalize upon the new doctrine of efficiency (Gross, 1964, p. 38). The scientific management approach pioneered by Frederick Taylor in the Midvale Steel Company in 1881 was an unabashed approach for improving efficiency in industry. Taylor employed a stopwatch in analyzing work methods that he originally called "task management," or "the task system" (Gross, 1964, p. 38).

The idea was to raise worker output by determining which worker movements were "on task," and which ones were "off task." Then, by means of a stopwatch, the manager was to select the "on task" movements that accomplished the job the fastest (Barnes, 1940, p. 7). Taylor's methods led to standardization of tools and to establishing a rate of pay which was based on output per worker. Thus, pay and output were the products of Taylor's "system."

There was little that was "scientific" about Taylor's studies. An investigative report by Professor Robert Hoxie in 1915 concluded that Taylor failed to include the human aspects of work in his calculations, and that his results were not established by science, but rather, by arbitrary selections of motions he analyzed (Gross, 1964, p. 38).

Taylor was an enthusiastic positivist. He insisted that there was always one "best way" to do any job, and that the worker and the work could be separated, just as the positivist insists that reality can be separated from the perceiver of reality. When this occurs, the "truth" is discerned and is "context-free," i.e., generalizable from one setting to another without problems of transference (English, 1992, p. 37).

The second part of "scientific management" was developed by Frank and Lillian Gilbreth and was called "motion study." Motion study began when the young Frank Gilbreth studied brick layers to find the one "best way" to lay brick. He used photography to study methods, and rather than use a stop watch as Taylor did, he searched for methods that were less complicated and produced less fatigue in workers. Gilbreth developed the chronocyclegraph in which a motion picture camera is employed to record the motions of a machine operator with a light attached to a finger, hand, or other part of the body. By watching only the path of the light, Gilbreth selected the most appropriate body motions for any given piece of work (Barnes, 1940, p. 15). Gilbreth and his wife—Lillian, a psychologist—developed a list of 18 basic work motions common to any type of motion. He dubbed these "therbligs," which was Gilbreth spelled backwards (Barnes, 1940, p. 62).

Educational leadership, using the bias of "scientific management," involved a search for the one best way, method, process, or system. The motivation for the search was economic; it was simply cheaper. Educational administration has been dominated by the search for this one best method since Taylor and the Gilbreths created the time motion study. Behaviorism strongly reinforced the search for measurable units in educational administration, perhaps best exemplified in the work of Daniel Griffiths' search for OTUs (organizational taxonomic units) which could be classified and compared.

Griffiths' work utilized the same process as Taylor and Gilbreth; i.e., he created a rationale to separate administrative behavior into purposeful and nonpurposeful activities, and then moved into separating them out into Y factors (energy expended in administration) versus X factors (actual decision making) (Griffiths, 1969, p. 67).

While such studies use systematic approaches to examining human work or human decisions, the word *scientific* is misapplied to them. Being systematic and using statistical tools does not automatically qualify work to be called "scientific" (see Gribbins and Hunt, 1981). Science is a pursuit of knowledge that is reflectively critical. A belief that systematic or statistical work is "scientific" on its face is "scientism"—a mimic of science that is "sciencelike," but not science itself. It is *pseudoscience.*

Educational administration has a long strain of theorists and practitioners who have devoted years to systematizing the field with methods and data, and to constructing a knowledge base rooted on such concepts. They have not, however, created a "science" for the field. The so-called "knowledge base" is simply the residue of their efforts rather than one on which a science could be constructed.

Scientific management and its offshoots are not based on a theoretical framework that courts refutation since there is no theory that is really being tested in its application. It is, rather, an *ideology* encapsulated as a *method*. The same criticism can be applied to W. Edwards Deming's total quality managemennt, which is being touted as "the" management posture of current times (see Gabor, 1990).

While Taylor's work led to a piecemeal rate structure based on task analysis, Deming's method rejects individual pay tinkering, but ends up embracing hierarchical management authority to alter the work environment and enhance individual worker productivity. Both are *methods* which fit into and reinforce the socioeconomic–political status quo. Neither method, for example, ever questioned the **androcentrism** of the work world, nor ever proposed altering the power–knowledge structure found there (see Capper, 1992).

TYPOLOGICAL LEVEL 4: EARLY SCIENTIFIC CONCEPTS OF ADMINISTRATION AND LEADERSHIP

Emergent concepts of administration began with the work of Henri Fayol (1842–1925), a Frenchman who is credited with creating the first "general approach" to administration as it is understood in human organizations. He has been called the Father of Modern Management Theory (Hodgetts and Kuratko, 1988, p. 37).

Fayol became president of a mining company that was floundering. In exercising management of the company he developed an approach to viewing administration and its functions. He believed that there were five primary functions of administration: *planning, organizing, commanding, coordinating,* and *controlling.* In commanding, leadership was exercised.

From these essential functions, Fayol extrapolated 14 principles that dealt with the division of labor, authority and responsibility, discipine, unity of command, unity of management, subordination of individual interests, remuneration, centralization, the hierarchy, order, equity, stability, initiative, and esprit de corps or morale.

In this early category of truly scientific work in administration and leadership, we must also consider the work of Mary Parker Follett, Elton Mayo, Chester Barnard, Luther Gulick, and Lyndall Urwick. These pioneers were trained in political science, psychology, and philosophy, and were not merely engineers in the vein of Taylor and the Gilbreths. They brought experience from many disciplines to their ideas and had insight into practical applications in business, government, and industry. Their thoughts roamed far beyond *efficiency,* and confronted the full range of issues facing the leaders in organizations.

Mary Parker Follett (1868–1933) developed ideas in management far ahead of her time. In fact, they are just beginning to be appreciated for their depth and complexity today (Massie, 1965, p. 395). One concept she developed was called **the law of the situation.** Follett saw that authority was not solely determined by the administrative hierarchy, but by the situation itself, and by the person who could exercise competence and leadership in that situation. This insight was developed around an assumption that people were not simply motivated by personal gain, but by what was "good" for the group as well (Hodsgetts and Kuratiko, 1988, p. 38). Her belief was later validated in the famous Hawthorne studies conducted at the Western Electric Company plant in Chicago.

Follett believed that there were four primary principles of organization. All of them revolved around the idea of *coordination* because management was a social process. She developed the idea of conflict management because she recognized that conflict was inherent in all of management's work. She advised three methods for dealing with conflict: (1) domination, (2) compromise, or (3) integration. Follett argued for integration as the preferred method of resolving organizational disputes by bringing the differences between parties into the open (Massie, 1965, p. 395). In this respect Mary Parker Follett laid the groundwork for much of what today is called *organization development* (French and Bell, 1973).

The thoughts and writings of these early authors in administration and leadership are called "classical" today because they laid the foundation for the study of organizations. Their work also made management a respectable field of studies in collegiate business schools, public administration, and educational administration.

TYPOLOGICAL LEVEL 5: THE METANARRATIVE OF BEHAVIORISM

The breakpoint in the typological categories between classical and modern occurs in the work of Herbert Simon, whose book *Administrative Behavior* (1945) is the first great work centered on behaviorism/logical positivism in administration. Simon's focus on decision making in organizations was on *rational man* driven by economic motives which he/she found *satisficing.* Simon focused on the "operative employee" as his unit of analysis, noting that "insight into the structure and function of an organization can best be gained by analyzing the manner in which the decisions and behavior of such employees are influenced within and by the organization" (1957, p. 3).

The concept of **rationality** within an organization was simply where one was "concerned with the selection of preferred behavior alternatives in terms of some system of values whereby the consequences of behavior can be evaluated" (p. 75). Simon's work was expanded by those who analyzed the behavior of the person *within* a human organization, motivating employees to work, and participating in the work of the organization (March and Simon, 1958; Herzberg, Mausner, and Snyderman, 1959). Renewing organizations through individuals became a focus of those engaged in organization development (Lippitt, 1969).

Much of **contingency theory,** as exemplified in school climate studies (which are really individual/group interactive behavioral patterns—such as Halpin's [1966] work on bomber pilots and later school principals), is distinctively behavioral in focus. Halpin's work was preceeded by the best-selling book *The Human Side of Enterprise* by Douglas McGregor (1960), who examined management's influence and control through two views which he labeled "Theory *X*" and "Theory *Y.*" The pursuit of these different paths in management created a psychological **climate.** Says McGregor:

> The climate is more significant than the type of leadership or the personal "style" of the superior. The boss can be autocratic or democratic, warm and outgoing or remote and introverted, easy or tough, but these personal characteristics are of less significance than the deeper attitudes to which his subordinates respond (p. 134).

Fiedler's (1967) concept of *style,* based on an interaction between a leader's disposition to emphasize people or work tasks leading to an interpersonal setting that could be identified, is Simonian in nature as well. A leader's "position power" was the result of the interaction of a leader's style with the group.

Any study of organizations in which individuals and their behaviors are the focus of the work is usually an example of the behavioral metanarrative in operation. Behaviorism abhors the "subjective," the feelings, emotions, cultural leanings, and predispositions of humans. These are neither objective nor directly observable. Behaviorism is steeped in logical positivism and the concept of verification by observation. If at all possible, the necessary behaviors are reduced to numerical equivalents so as to display their "objectivity" (see Cyert and March, 1963).

Another example of the behavioral metanarrative in action is the **intervention method** of Chris Argyris (1970). The intervention method described by Argyris is not used with individuals, but with organizations. Individuals in the organization are referred to as "clients" (an impersonal term), and the organization as the "client system." Argyris also employs the concept of "open" and "closed" systems as composite categories within an organization. Closed systems are seen as those in which, at lower hierarchical levels, client systems are characterized by "fighting, withdrawal, apathy, indifference, goldbricking, distorting information sent upwards, and developing internal defensive establishments" (p. 136). Open systems are those where the strategy is "reaching out, learning, and becoming competent in controlling the external and internal environment so that its objectives are achieved and its members continue to learn" (p. 136).

The most modern adaption of behaviorism using Argyris' notion of an open system is exemplified in Peter Senge's (1990) book, *The Fifth Discipline.* Senge characterizes an effective organization of the future as a "learning organization" which is the result (like climate) of an interaction between patterns of behavior and systemic structure (p. 52).

As a metanarrative, behaviorism has left a long and lasting imprint on educational administration and several generations of students and researchers. As Senge's book testifies, it is far from being a defunct metanarrative. Behaviorism is still alive and well in the work of the National Policy Board of Educational Administration (NPBEA) (Thomson, 1992), which is attempting to validate and codify the knowledge base in the field (see Capper, 1992).

TYPOLOGICAL LEVEL 6: TRANSITION WORKS COMBINING BEHAVIORISM AND STRUCTURALISM

Once the unit of analysis begins to shift from the behaviors of people within an organization to the organization itself, the metanarrative re-centers itself on an emphasis to the context or organizational structure in which a person must work. Structuralism is based on the premise that a study of whole units or structures represents the key to understanding individual phenomena (behaviors). It is like turning a sock inside-out. Instead of using behaviors to predict impact on the organization or structure, one begins with the structure and assumes it impacts behaviors. Thus, behaviorism fits neatly within a structural metanarrative and is mutually reinforcing and supporting of it.

One of the important transition works between behaviorism and structuralism is Katz and Kahn's (1966) book, *The Social Psychology of Organizations*. This important work combined the view of psychologists and that of sociologists (the latter influenced by Marxian concepts of social class), attempts to build superorganic sociological models as exemplified in the works of Emile Durkheim (1858–1917) and his idea of the "group mind," and Talcott Parsons (1902–1979) who worked to integrate findings from economics, anthropology, and sociology into one systematic approach. Another prolific writer–researcher in the structuralist tradition is Rensis Likert (1961), who studied at the Institute for Social Research at the University of Michigan.

Perhaps the most influential of disciplines in educational administration as it pertains to structuralism is **general systems theory.** General systems theory is derived from biology, and the writings of Ludwig von Bertalanffy (1968). A system has been defined as "a set of interacting units with relationships among them" (p. 3) by Bertalanffy. A system can only be understood as the sum of its parts. This emphasis on wholes emanates from a study of human languages, specifically the work of Ferdinand de Saussure (1857–1913) (see Gadet, 1986).

A controversial work which combines the behavioral view of humans within organizations as *situations* would be that of Cohen and March (1974). These two authors examined the college presidency and found that a president works within an **organized anarchy.** The latter situation exists when there are *problematic goals, unclear technology,* and *fluid participation* (p. 3). Cohen and March called the role of the college president an example of "garbage can leadership," in which the major job of the president was to sort problems into the right "garbage cans" (p. 211). The purely behavioral view of leadership has receded from the limelight, except perhaps in discussions regarding national licensing of educational administrators. Some training models are still deeply anchored in behaviorism.

TYPOLOGICAL LEVEL 7: BROAD FIELDS VIEW OF LEADERSHIP AS SITUATIONAL

This typological level moves beyond the classical behavioristic framework for examining what leaders do. Such metanarratives are often centered on very broad disciplines, usually involving psychology, history, anthropology, and sociology. A far reaching work that won a Pulitzer Prize and the National Book Award was James MacGregor Burns' (1978) book, *Leadership*. Burns uses very broad strokes in painting pictures of two types of leaders: transactional and transformational. Transactional leaders function in an exchange relationship with subordinates, while transformational leaders are after subordinate empowerment. Burns works back and forth between very broad disciplines and the actions of leaders. His work is beyond simple behaviorism, but is nonetheless an example of dynamic, situational, or contingency leadership concepts in which psychology and the individual's growth and development are critical parts of the leader's emergence. Burns' idea of the transformational leader as one who empowers others rather than subordinating others is very contemporary in the discussions regarding empowerment as one of the major functions of administration (see Kreisberg, 1992). Other works in the Burns tradition of broad fields human developmental perspectives dealing with leadership are Sarah Lawrence Lightfoot's (1983) *The Good High School,* James David Barber's (1985) *The Presidential Character,* and John Keegan's (1987) *The Mask of Command.*

Keegan's views on leadership center on generalship, since Keegan is a historian who teaches at the Royal Military Academy at Sandhurst (England). Keegan rejects trait theory and behaviorism in examining military leaders. They are the methods of social scientists, asserts Keegan, "and, as with all social science, condemn those who practice them to the agony of making universal and general what is stubbornly local and particular" (p. 1).

Keegan concedes that military leaders must have individual traits and behaviors that are exceptional. That is taken for granted. What he believes is critical is how any society defines the manner in which such qualities are to be presented.

> Any leadership—is, like priesthood, statesmanship, even genius, a matter of externals almost as much as internalities. The exceptional are both shown to and hidden from the mass of humankind, revealed by artifice, presented by theatre (p. 11).

The context of societal expectations upon its leaders requires them to put on a **mask.** To understand **leadership,** whether military, artistic, religious, pedagogical, athletic, or political, involves an effort in penetrating the expected social mask that leaders must present in the theatre of their times. This effort clearly involves history, literature, drama, art, and music. It eclipses social science in the longer and wider traditions of learning and knowledge involving humanity.

Keegan concludes his work analyzing the masks of command presented by Alexander the Great, the Duke of Wellington, Ulysses S. Grant, and Adolf Hitler with a surprising twist: a plea for a nonheroic leader who, by historical standards, would be no leader at all. The nuclear age requires no one to pull the trigger, and no parades through Persepolis; "today the best must find conviction to play the hero no more" (p. 351).

In offering an illustration to demonstrate the **anti-heroic** leadership portrait of the modern occasion for decision making, Keegan cites the 1962 Cuban missile crisis in which a leaderless group with no chairperson, no hierarchy of command, and only one military personage present came to a decision to blockade Cuba which the Soviet Union accepted. Everyone on the Executive Committee spoke as equals in the crisis. There were no privileges of command and no rank. This "leaderless" group came to a decision which saved the world from a nuclear war. In their deliberations, the ExComm utilized the benefit of history unusual analysis of situational assumptions, and began to think about the Soviet leader, Khruschev, "as a person, with a history of his own" (Neustadt and May, 1986, p. 12). The resolution of the crisis depended upon more than trait theory, behaviorism, or even simple situational stimulus–response models of climate. *The real world is broad fields and multidisciplinary.*

TYPOLOGICAL LEVEL 8: THE METANARRATIVE OF STRUCTURALISM IN EDUCATIONAL ADMINISTRATION

Purely structural works in administration today are represented in these writings Blau and Scott's (1962) *Formal Organizations,* James Thompson's (1967) *Organizations in Action,* John Galbraith's (1973) *Designing Complex Organizations,* Henry Mintzberg's (1983) *Structure in Fives,* Deal and Kennedy's (1982) *Corporate Cultures,* and Bolman and Deal's (1991) *Reframing Organizations.* Structuralistic viewpoints center their metanarrative on the importance of structural functions within organizations in understanding what people do in them, and how they might be put together differently. The works in this area can be grouped under the title **organizational theory.**

The Bolman and Deal book centers on the idea not of finding the one right organizational pattern, but of knowing how to select the right perspective or "frame" to view problems. This is **frame theory.** Bolman and Deal offer four basic organizational "frames" from which to select: the structural frame, the human resource frame, the political frame, and the symbolic frame (p. 15). The job of the leader is to select the right frame and to ride the waves of change like surfers (p. 450).

Bolman and Deal do not break out of the frames of structuralism as a metanarrative because they see organizations as "organic forms in which needs, roles, power, and symbols must be combined to provide direction and shape behavior" (p. 450). Such wholes are structures or complete systems. It is assumed that they possess a unity that subsumes their respective parts. Thus, even while the Bolman and Deal frame theory model appears to be selective, it is in reality a rationale for knowing what behavioral/structural "frame" will yield what when imposing it upon an organization. The choices are limited to purely structural alternatives. Bolman and Deal never postulate the essential immutability of the wholes governing and directing the parts—an idea in language called logocentrism (Lefkovitz, 1989, p. 63). Frame theory's logocentrism itself is never disputed or questioned. It is upon this line that the post-structural metanarratives cross.

TYPOLOGICAL LEVEL 9: DRAWING THE LINE ON PREVIOUS METANARRATIVES—THE EMERGENCE OF FEMINIST AND CRITICAL THEORY

Feminist theory has pointed out that educational administration has been androcentric (male centered) since its inception (see Shakeshaft, 1989). As a discipline, educational administration rests on the binary field of male/female gender polarization, which not only continued the gender cultural typecasting of female subservience, but also eliminated any kind of psychosocial orientation except "real male" or "real female" culturally approved opposites.

One result of the dominant gender schema being perpetuated without question has been the priviliging of heterosexuality as the "proper" sexual orientation (see Bem, 1993, pp. 146–147). Thus, homosexuals were not allowed to be leaders or school administrators by excluding them as neither "real males" or "real females."

Critical theory is not behavioral, but it may be argued that it borders on structuralism. Much of it represents a kind of dialectical analysis of the literature and ideas in educational administration. The best known North American works in this metanarrative are those of William Foster (1986)—*Paradigms and Promises;* Henry Giroux (1988)—*Schooling and the Struggle for Public Life;* and Spencer Maxcy (1991)—*Educational Leadership: A Critical Pragmatic Perspective.*

Critical theory looks outside school or organizational structures and examines the linkages between them and the larger sociopolitical network and forms of power. William Foster (1983) criticizes both frame theory and other forms of organizational theory: "Traditional studies have focused on the organization as if it existed in a time warp. A processual analysis would attempt to look at the organization over time, and to analyze the processes of change and innovation to see how they occur in relation to other changes in the social system" (p. 146).

The emphasis on the social system and values within that system have led to the development of a discussion regarding the place of values, morals, and ethics in educational administration.

Spencer Maxcy (1991) comments:

> Leadership is characterized as a superordinate class of philosophic or intellectual insights, while on the other hand, leadership is taken to be synonymous with administration and tends to be reduced to the tasks of managing the school. These tasks are specifiable and lend themselves to repeat performance. Leadership given this latter view is nothing but the routine tasks of management (pp. 56–57).

Maxcy argues for moving away from situational models of leadership, or observed behaviors or traits, to "a shared value intimately tied to the democratic context" (p. 48). He observes that leaders must once again be seen as "artists" and "philosophers" and "must involve teaching and learning" (p. 50).

Critical theory involves "the turning back upon itself" of thought about educational administration. Critical theory is forcing educational administrators to see themselves not as isolated figures in a specialized world, but as connective leaders within a much larger socioeconomic–political milieux. As such, educational administration is forced to rethink its boundaries as a discipline, the manner in which it has conceptualized problems, the lines along which it conducts formal inquiry, and the proper content of its knowledge base. Despite its penchant for reflective inquiry, even critical theory does not question its linguistic heritage and the logocentrism of language in conveying thoughts and concepts. Were it to do so, it would have crossed the line into post-structuralism, or post-modernism, in an important way.

Because critical theory often "shadows" rather closely the traditional texts it critiques, indirectly it can be a kind of covert structuralism without a label. This predicament is the same one which presents itself to those directly criticizing structuralism. Marxist-based critical theory would definitely be a kind of structuralism. Saussaurian structuralism looks inward to the *text*. Marxian critical theory looks outward to *context*.

TYPOLOGICAL LEVEL 10: POST-MODERNISM IN EDUCATIONAL ADMINISTRATION

Post-modernism in science and education moves far beyond critical theory. Post-modernism is centered on hermeneutics and the ideas of deconstruction as fashioned by Jacques Derrida (1976), an Algerian-born Jew of Sherpardic parents, who teaches at the École Normale Supérieure in Paris. Derrida is the intellectual father of deconstruction as a popular critical method in literary studies, though its precedent can be traced to Martin Heidegger's concept of the destruction of ontology in his philosophical writings (Rapaport, 1989, p. 9).

Deconstruction is a powerful hermeneutical tool to analyze texts, searching for hidden meanings and concepts. "Any text, any system of signs, can be shown to compromise itself from within," writes David Lehman (1991) in his critical analysis of deconstruction. "To deconstruct is to debunk, systematically, rigorously, ruthlessly" (pp. 67–68).

The meaning of a word is found in its difference from other words. The problem of definition was broached in the concept of infinite regress from Popper (1968, p. 29). Deconstruction likewise understands that meaning is always moving between words. Meaning is shifted endlessly, deferring any final determination. Meaning can never become concrete or fixed in the present. It is too fluid and indeterminate.

The hermeneutical tradition of deconstruction is to abandon the search for certainty, and to accept the premise that uncertainty and indeterminancy are "givens." "In the absence of a center or origin, everything became discourse. There are no facts, only interpretations, and no truths, only expedient fictions" (Lehman, 1991, p. 98).

To speak of leadership in a deconstructed world—a world of primary indeterminancy—a world where causality is a victim itself, where recognition that no one thing is ever singularly responsible for any other thing, one to one, is to recast and re-center our concept of leadership. The re-centering moves from a single person acting independently and conclusively (heroically) to multiple interactions between people. In this shift, internality (as opposed to externality) is the center of the exchange and influence between leaders and the led. The changes preclude either one or the other dominating by observed or measured behaviors. Deconstructed leadership is counterhegemonic. It is neither behavioral nor structural, exclusively one or the other, or dualistically interwoven as a single unified text.

The study of leadership must be recontextualized, reconsidered, and recast as a kind of intertextual theatre. In this enterprise, the audience is the actor, the player, and the voice of the led, and the play itself is the concept of leadership unfolding dialectically between the two. The intertexts are both the academic disciplines involved in describing leadership which are dynamic and nonstatic definition that have no final meaning or certainty. In this situation, morality is not only an interrelationship, but also an encompassing process and presence. Morality is more than behaviors between the leader and the led. Morality is the ontology of humane decisions, interactions, and consequences within a temporal human conscience—fallable and finite. Morality is to the human world as oxygen is to the ocean—every living thing in it breathes to keep living. Without morality in the human sea, leadership is rudderless.

Sergiovanni (1992) points out that an expanded view of leadership which includes **the moral dimension of leadership** "may require us to reinvent the concept of leadership itself" (p. xiii) and provides as an example the dictum "it seems obvious that leadership breeds followership. Less obvious is the idea that the practice of followership provides the basis of leadership" (p. xiii). Sergiovanni's turning the leadership–followership dyad inside-out is an example of deconstruction. Postmodernism challenges many notions of leadership, from those contained in antiquity within the immortal lines of *The Illiad* of Homer, to social science portraits contained in Halpin's school climate narrative or Argyris' open system contextual sketch. These and other possibilities will be explored in greater detail in subsequent chapters.

SUMMARY

This chapter presented a typology of metanarratives in leadership. A typology is simply a categorization of types. The types used in this typology were interpositivities, called metanarratives, regarding the nature of leadership and classified by their assumptions—overt and covert—and their methodologies and procedures of inquiry and investigation. Important or illustrative works have been assigned to the groupings within the typology, but they were not exhaustive.

Educational administration, as a field in America, is barely 190 years old. Originally, administrative roles were conceived as minor officials presiding over an enterprise largely run by teachers and board members. Since the first principal–teachers evolved, there has been a constant reshifting of the idea of administration as reflected in the development of the *principalship* and, later, the *superintendency*. The actual re-centering of a forceful and authoritative militarylike figure occurred in the description of the American superintendent as a "leader"—a kind of "captain of the ship" metaphor. This occurred after the turn of the century and was reflected in the texts for school administrators written by Elwood P. Cubberley. When one considers an educational administrator as a *leader,* then a much longer body of literature and knowledge is connected to discussions regarding school administration.

The larger body of literature regarding leadership has been reviewed and grouped into ten typological interpositivities, beginning with pre-scientific ideas about leadership as reflected in mythology and religion of ancient times, and ending with a typological grouping that consists of post-modern ideas about leadership that challenge even the concept of leadership found in antiquity. Each of these categories will be developed more fully in the remaining chapters of the book. The typology ought to provide the reader with a broad view of the literature regarding leadership and administration in education and in other fields. The typology is centered around the development of an enunciative discourse in educational administration. While it is roughly chronological, tracing the history of ideas in any field does not yield definitive borders, and rarely shows clear demarcations. Ideas have their own sequence and evolutionary habits. They are notoriously interdisciplinary.

Perception Check and Applications

1. Constructing Alternative Typologies for Educational Administration

The typology utilized in this chapter was only one of a number of ways the literature in the field can be grouped. What other models and possibilities exist? What advantages or disadvantages do they possess over the one used in this chapter?

2. What Contextual Variables Centered Leadership in Educational Administration?

We have seen where the idea that an educational administrator was a "leader" amounted to a re-centering of the administrator as the "captain" of the educational ship. This re-centering and emphasis occurred most probably in the period between 1900 and 1925. Examine the historical, social, political, and economic trends during this time period to establish a *context* for this shift. What were the most likely trends to have triggered this change? Examine the sources for this period to see if, preliminarily, the data will support your determination.

3. Identifying the Progeny of Scientific Management

As a broad-based movement with large public support in the popular press, identify the ideological progeny of scientific management since it passed in the literature. On what basis did you identify these progeny? Which ones are dominant today and why?

4. Reviewing Plutarch's *Parallel Lives*

Plutarch was a Greek living in a Roman world. He described famous Greeks and Romans, side by side. If his purpose was not to engage in biography, what do you believe his real purpose was in using dual personages in two different cultures? Determine how to test your idea and comment on the results.

5. The Close Connection Between Behaviorism and Structuralism

Two metanarratives—behaviorism and structuralism—remain dominant in works regarding educational leadership and school administration today. Describe the close relationship between the two, conceptually and ideologically. Examine the various texts listed in the typology in these two categories. Could you reorder them? Propose a clearer delineation between the two metanarratives as a result.

6. The Identification of Critical Theory as a Metanarrative

The typology presents critical theory as a separate metanarrative. Advance a thesis that critical theory is not a specific typology at all, but simply a metanarrative which is either behavioral or structural, or a hybrid of both. How strong a claim can be made for this argument? In what ways can it be refuted?

7. Turning Leadership Inside-Out

Post-modern views of leadership are considerably "flatter" and more "bland" than traditional, heroic, leader-dominant, follower-passive concepts that have such strong and popular standing.

Comment upon the following situations and identify any aspects in which heroic leadership concepts were inapplicable or downplayed as they unfolded.

- the Persian Gulf War
- the Iran–Contra affair
- the Clarence Thomas confirmation hearings
- the efforts to find a vaccine for AIDS
- the creation of national curricular standards in education
- the tragedy of the space shuttle *Challenger*
- the L.A. riots of 1992

Key Chapter Concepts and Terms

androcentrism

Refers to "male" centered or dominated beliefs or sociocultural–political relationships. Androcentrism has its roots in antiquity—notably in Hebrew society—and is reflected in the Old and New Testaments. Androcentrism is also found in Greek mythology, philosophy, and writing, biological essentialism, and Freudian psychology.

anti-heroic leadership

Leadership that does not include the historical stereotypical "strong" personage who battles evil and hardship to persevere against them in ultimate triumph to remain a unique individual. Refers to a more faceless participation in an empowered group of colleagues.

climate

The result or outcome of the interaction between a leader and a group of followers. Leaders are typically seen as the sole initiators in most climate studies, with the followers conceptualized as responders. Climate studies reinforce the existing hegemony of authority in human organizations.

contingency theory

A view that leadership behavior is as much shaped by the interaction with the situation as by anything else. While behavior of the leader is important, it can only be understood by considering the context or situation the leader faces.

critical theory

A perspective derived from Marxism that includes the dialectical method (thesis, antithesis, synthesis) and insists that problems must be viewed in historical context to be fully understood. This means socioeconomic–political arrangements are considered part of the context, if not the most important part.

the doctrine of efficiency

An ideology that cheaper is better in most types of circumstances and based on a belief that any process, procedure, or product can be improved by finding the one best way to perform or construct it. Fundamentally anchored in the perspective of logical positivism.

executive

The embodiment of a general administrative officer, or *esecuzioni*, from the political philosophy of Nicolo Machiavelli (1469–1527), who acted on the notion of surprise in order to execute, and to impress subjects with the power of the office when its legal constraints had to be exceeded to compel obedience to the law. See Harvey Mansfield's (1989) *Taming the Prince*.

Father of Modern Management Theory

Generally, the Frenchman Henri Fayol (1842–1925) is considered the father of modern management theory. Fayol was the first to develop a list of general principles around which to view the role of management and to describe its general concerns and functions for an organization.

frame theory

Solving problems in organizations depends upon how one "frames" or structures a view of them. The view itself is believed to offer a variety of explanations to problems that may lend to their solution by changing lenses or frames.

general systems theory

Derived from biology, the concept that all systems engage in three activities: inputs, processing, and outputs. Outputs alter the inputs. Most systems function within a boundary. Interaction with the boundaries occurs through a mechanism called *feedback*.

intervention method

A procedure of conducting research in a human organization which is "scientifically" acceptable and which theoretically minimizes bias in its outlook and methodology. Those assumptions have been challenged as being naive by many qualitative researchers today.

the law of the situation

A management principle developed by Mary Parker Follett (1868–1933), who saw that administrative authority was not totally determined by hierarchical position, but by the competence required to engage in problem solving as well. Follett conceptualized management as a *social process*. In this perspective, she was considerably ahead of her time. Her views helped to establish the practice of OD, or organizational development.

leadership

A much-discussed word in contemporary times, often attached to failing enterprises or used to explain organizational shortcomings such as "the *lack* of leadership" or a *"failure* of leadership." From the word *lithan*, "to go" or the German, *leiten*, "to lead." Notions of leadership can be traced to antiquity, as well as to descriptions of leaders. Various metanarratives center, de-center, or re-center the concept of leadership from an individual, to an individual–group interaction, to contingent behaviors in specific settings, to group dynamics and organizational intervention methods. The concept has been called conceptually "flabby" by Spencer J. Maxcy (1991, p. 49).

mask of leadership

The concept that leadership involves both internalities and externalities, and that the act of leadership is properly politics and theatre simultaneously. The theatrical side of leadership is anthropologically contextual, local, and particular. To understand leadership, one must penetrate the "mask," i.e., the norms established by a culture which embody its expectations for leadership.

moral dimension of leadership

An expanded view of leadership which includes motivation, values, ethics, and beauty in discussing the act of leadership as a dynamic, interpersonal phenomenon rather than a marginalized, behaviorized, and sterilized set of externalities which are merely observable.

nuclear unit of the monomyth

The idea that most myths can be reduced to similar narratives, problems, and characteristics, irrespective of their culture or historical time period. Derived from Joseph Campbell's (1973) book, *The Hero with a Thousand Faces.*

the political "neutrality" of school administration

The idea that the office of school administrator is a largely technical office located in a meritocracy, and that the choices of the administrator must remain technical and never be "tainted" with politics. The establishment of school administration was the result of a political act, and the maintenance of the roles is a political decision. Questions of technical competence remain secondary. There are no "apolitical" roles in public education.

organizational theory

A metanarrative that explains what organizations are and do by comparing their internal and external functions, commonalities, and similarities without being concerned about the nature of the people who inhabit them as bosses or subordinates.

organized anarchy

The idea that in organizations with problematic goals, unclear technology, and fluid participation, the primary function of management is to sort problems into the right "garbage cans" rather than to solve them. Derived from a study of the college presidency by Cohen and March (1974).

rationality

When applied to people, the idea that humans were motivated by material gain and therefore motives were economic in nature, and when applied to organizations, tangible goals and objectives are the motivators.

school superintendent

From the Latin *superintentor,* which means "an overseer." Early school superintendents were often not permanent positions. In New York, the first superintendency at the state level was abolished after eight years and was combined with another office. City superintendencies were often abolished and re-established. Initially, the county superintendency was highly unpopular and only after several decades did it come to be accepted by the general populace.

typology

A classification system based on types, or a study of such a system. Used in this chapter to present and group the large variety of texts (usually books) relating to the idea of leadership.

References

American Association of School Administrators (1952). *The American School Superintendency.* Washington, D.C.

Argyris, C. (1970). *Intervention Theory and Method.* Reading, MA: Addison–Wesley Publishing Company.

Ayers, L. P. (1916). *School Organization and Administration.* Cleveland, Ohio: The Survey Committee of the Cleveland Foundation.

Barber, J. D. (1985). *The Presidential Character.* Englewood Cliffs, New Jersey: Prentice Hall, Inc.

Barnes, R .M. (1940). *Motion and Time Study.* New York: John Wiley & Sons, Inc.

Bem, S. L. (1993). *The Lenses of Gender.* New Haven: Yale University Press.

Bertalanffy, L. Von. (1968). *General System Theory.* New York: George Braziller.

Blau, P. M., and Scott, W. Richard (1962). *Formal Organizations.* San Francisco: Chandler Publishing Company.

Bolman, L. G., and Deal, T. E. (1991). *Reframing Organizations.* San Francisco: Jossey–Bass Publishers.

Burns, J. M. (1978). *Leadership.* New York: Harper & Row.

Burrowes, T. H. (1860). *Report of the Superintendent of Common Schools of Pennsylvania.* Harrisburg: A. Boyd Hamilton, State Printer.

Button, H. W., and Provenzo, E. F., Jr. (1989). *History of Education and Culture in America.* Englewood Cliffs, New Jersey: Prentice Hall.

Callahan, R. E., and Button, H. W. (1964). "Historical Change of the Role of the Man in the Organization," in D. E. Griffiths (Ed.), *Behavioral Science and Educational Administration.* Chicago: University of Chicago Press, pp. 73–94.

Campbell, J. (1973). *The Hero with a Thousand Faces.* Princeton, New Jersey: Princeton University Press.

Campbell, R. F., Fleming, T., Newell, L. J., and Bennion, J. W. (1987). *A History of Thought and Practice in Educational Administration.* New York: Teachers College Press.

Capper, C. A. (1992). "An 'Otherist' Poststructural Perspective of Educational Administration: A Case in Point: The Proposed Knowledge Base in Educational Administration." Unpublished paper presented at the University Council for Educational Administration, Minneapolis, Minnesota, 42 pp.

Cohen, M. D., and March, J. G. (1974). *Leadership and Ambiguity.* New York: McGraw–Hill Book Company.

Cuban, L. (1988). *The Managerial Imperative and the Practice of Leadership in Schools*. Albany, New York: SUNY Press.

Cubberley, E. P. (1914). *Rural Life and Education*. Boston: Houghton Mifflin Company.

Cubberley, E. P. (1916). *Public School Administration*. Boston: Houghton Mifflin Company.

Cubberley, E. P. (1929). *Public School Administration*. Boston: Houghton Mifflin Company.

Culbertson, J. A. (1988). "A Century's Quest for a Knowledge Base," in N. J. Boyan (Ed.), *Handbook of Research on Educational Administration*. New York: Longman, pp. 3–26.

Cyert, R. M., and March, J. G. (1963). *A Behavioral Theory of the Firm*. Englewood Cliffs, New Jersey: Prentice Hall.

Davis, H. (no date cited). *Plato's Republic*. New York City: Hinds & Noble Publishers.

Deal, T. E., and Kennedy, A. A. (1982). *Corporate Cultures*. Reading, MA: Addison–Wesley Publishing Company.

Derrida, J. (1976). *Of Grammatology*. Baltimore, Maryland: Johns Hopkins University Press.

Dutton, S. T. (1903). *School Management*. New York: Charles Scribner's Sons.

Dutton, S. T., and Snedden, D. (1908). *The Administration of Public Education in the United States*. New York: The Macmillan Company.

English, F. W. (1989–1990). "The Superintendent's Challenge: More Learning Time in Schools," *National Forum of Applied Educational Research Journal*, 2:1, pp. 24–33.

English, F. W. (1992). *Educational Administration: The Human Science*. New York: HarperCollins.

English, F. W. (1993, Spring). "A Poststructural View of the Grand Narratives in Educational Administration," in *Organizational Theory Dialogue*, SIG-AERA, William Foster (Ed.), pp. 1–4.

Estes, C. P. (1992). *Women Who Run with the Wolves*. New York: Ballatine Books.

Fiedler, F. E. (1967). *A Theory of Leadership*. New York: McGraw Hill.

Foster, W. (1986). *Paradigms and Promises*. Buffalo, New York: Prometheus Books.

Foucault, M. (1972). *The Archaeology of Knowledge* New York: Pantheon Books.

French, W., and Bell, C. H., Jr. (1973). *Organization Development*. Englewood Cliffs, New Jersey: Prentice Hall.

Freund, W., and Andrews, E. A. (1854). *A Copious and Critical Latin–English Lexicon*. New York: Harper & Brothers, Publishers.

Gadet, F. (1986). *Saussure and Contemporary Culture*. London: Hutchinson Radius.

Galbraith, J. (1973). *Designing Complex Organizations*. Reading, Massacusetts: Addison–Wesley Publishing Company.

Giroux, H. A. (1988). *Schooling and the Struggle for Public Life*. Minneapolis: University of Minnesota Press.

Gist, A. S. (1928). *The Administration of an Elementary School*. New York: Charles Scribner's Sons.

Grady, A. (1990). *The Man Who Discovered Quality*. New York: Penguin Books.

Grebanier, B. D., Middlebrook, S., Thompson, S., and Watt, W. (1957). *English Literature and Its Backgrounds*. New York: The Dryden Press.

Gribbins, R. E., and Hunt, S. D. (1981). "Is Management a Science?" in J. H. Donnelly, Jr., J. L. Gibson, and J. M. Ivancevich (Eds.), *Fundamentals of Management*. Plano, Texas: Business Publications, Inc., pp. 21–28.

Griffiths, D. E. (Ed.) (1969). *Developing Taxonomies of Organizational Behavior in Educational Administration*. Chicago: Rand McNally.

Gross, B. M. (1964). "The Scientific Approach to Administration," in D. E. Griffiths (Ed.), *Behavioral Science and Educational Administration*. Chicago: University of Chicago Press, pp. 33–72.

Halpin, A. W. (1966). *Theory and Research in Administration*. New York: The Macmillan Company.

Herzberg, F., Mausner, B., and Snyderman, B. B. (1959). *The Motivation to Work*. New York: John Wiley & Sons, Inc.

Hodgetts, R. M., and Kuratko, D. F. (1988). *Management*. San Diego, California: Harcourt Brace Jovanovich Publishers.

Howland, G. (1896). *Practical Hints for the Teachers of Public Schools*. New York: D. Appleton and Company.

Hoxie, R. (1915). *Scientific Management and Labor*. New York: D. Appleton & Co.

Immigart, G. L. (1988). "Leadership and Leader Behavior," in N. J. Boyan (Ed.), *Handbook of Research on Educational Administration*. New York: Longman, pp. 259–278.

Kaestle, C. F. (1983). *Pillars of the Republic: Common Schools and American Society 1780–1860*. New York: Hill and Wang.

Katz, D., and Kahn, R. L. (1966). *The Social Psychology of Organizations*. New York: John Wiley & Sons, Inc.

Keegan, J. (1987). *The Mask of Command*. New York: Elisabeth Sifton Books.

Kennedy, C. R. (1897). *The Oration of Demosthenes on the Crown*. Chicago: C. M. Barnes Company.

Kreisberg, S. (1992). *Transforming Power*. Albany, New York: SUNY Press.

Larue, G. A. (1975). *Ancient Myths and Modern Man*. Englewood Cliffs, New Jersey: Prentice Hall, Inc.

Lefkovitz, L. H. (1989). "Creating the World: Structuralism and Semiotics." In G. Douglas Atkins and Laura Morrow (Eds.), *Contemporary Literary Theory*. Amherst, MA: The University of Massachusetts Press.

Lehman, D. (1991). *Signs of the Times*. New York: Poseidon Press.

Lightfoot, S. L. (1983). *The Good High School*. New York: Basic Books, Inc., Publishers.

Likert, R. (1961). *New Patterns of Management*. New York: McGraw–Hill Book Company.

Lindeman, E. C. (1953). *Plutarch's Lives*. New York: A Mentor Book.

Lippitt, G. L. (1969). *Organization Renewal*. New York: Appleton–Century Crofts.

Livingstone, R. W. (1949). *Thucydides: The History of the Peloponnesian War*. London, England: Oxford University Press.

Mansfield, H. C., Jr. (1989). *Taming the Prince*. New York: The Free Press.

March, J. G., and Simon, H. (1958). *Organizations*. New York: John Wiley & Sons, Inc.

Massie, J. L. (1965). "Management Theory," in J. G. March (Ed.), *Handbook of Organizations*. Chicago: Rand McNally & Company, pp. 387–422.

Maxcy, S. J. (1991). *Educational Leadership*. New York: Bergin and Garvey.

Mintzberg, H. (1983). *Structure in Fives: Designing Effective Organizations*. Englewood Cliffs, New Jersey: Prentice Hall, Inc.

Nasaw, D. (1979). *Schooled to Order*. New York: Oxford University Press.

Neustadt, R. E., and May, E. R. (1986). *Thinking in Time*. New York: The Free Press.

Newlon, J. J. (1925). "Why Is Superintendence?" in *Proceedings*, pp. 657–664.

Nietzsche, F. (1956). *The Genealogy of Morals*. Translated by F. Golffing. New York: Anchor Doubleday.

Otto, H. J. (1954). *Elementary School Organization and Administration.* New York: Appleton–Century–Crofts, Inc.

Outhwaite, W. (1991). "Hans-George Gadamer," in Q. Skinner (Ed.), *The Return of Grand Theory in the Social Sciences.* New York: Cambridge University Press, pp. 21–40.

Owen, J. J. (1851). *The Anabasis of Xenophon.* New York: Leavitt & Company.

Payne, W. H. (1875). *Chapters on School Supervision.* Wilson, Hinkle and Company as cited in J. C. Almack (1933), *Modern School Administration.* Boston: Houghton Mifflin Company, p. 192.

Pohland, P. A. (1992, Spring). "Paradigm and Prospect: Educational Administration and Reform," in *UCEA Reform,* 33:2, pp. 4–8, 12–14.

Popper, K. R. (1968). *The Logic of Scientific Discovery.* New York: Harper and Row.

Potter, A., and Emerson, G. B. (1842). *The School and the Schoolmaster.* New York: Harper & Brothers.

Randall, S. S. (1844). *A Digest of the Common School System of the State of New York.* Albany, New York: C. Van Benthuysen & Co.

Rapaport, H. (1989). *Heidegger and Derrida.* Lincoln, Nebraska: University of Nebraska Press.

Ravitch, D. (1974). *The Great School Wars.* New York: Basic Books.

Reller, T., and Gilland, T. (1935). *The Origin and Development of the City School Superintendent.* Chicago: University of Chicago Press.

Richards, I. A. (1950). *The Wrath of Achilles.* New York: W. W. Norton & Company.

Rost, J. C. (1991). *Leadership for the Twenty-First Century.* New York: Praeger.

Rostand, E. (1923). *Cyrano de Bergerac.* B. Hooker (Trans.). New York: The Modern Library.

Senge, P. M. (1990). *The Fifth Discipline.* New York: Doubleday.

Sergiovanni, T. J. (1992). *Moral Leadership.* San Francisco: Jossey–Bass Publishers.

Shakeshaft, C. (1989). *Women in Educational Administration.* Newbury Park, CA: SAGE Publications.

Simon, H. A. (1945). *Administrative Behavior.* New York: The Macmillan Company.

Skinner, Q. (Ed.) (1991). *The Return of Grand Theory in the Human Sciences.* New York: Cambridge University Press.

Smith, S. C., Mazzarella, J., and Piele, P. K. (1981). *School Leadership.* Eugene, Oregon: Clearinghouse on Educational Management.

Stogdill, R. M. (1974). *Handbook of Leadership.* New York: The Free Press.

Thompson, J. D. (1967). *Organizations in Action.* New York: McGraw–Hill Book Company.

Thomson, S. D. (1992, January). "National Standards for School Administrators," in *The International Journal of Educational Reform,* 1, pp. 54–58.

Tyack, D. B. (1974). *The One Best System.* Cambridge, MA: Harvard University Press.

Webster's New Biographical Dictionary (1983). Springfield, MA: Merriam–Webster Inc., Publishers.

Webster's Seventh New Collegiate Dictionary (1972). Springfield, MA: G. & C. Merriam Company.

White, J. W. (1883). *First Lessons in Greek.* Boston: Ginn, Heath, & Co.

Wickersham, J. P. (1978). *Report of the Superintendent of Public Instruction of the Commonwealth of Pennsylvania.* Harrisburg: Lane S. Hart, State Printer.

Wood, M. (1985). *In Search of the Trojan War.* London, England: British Broadcasting Corporation.

ANCIENT TRACES AND HEROIC PORTRAITS

Pre-Scientific Views of Leadership

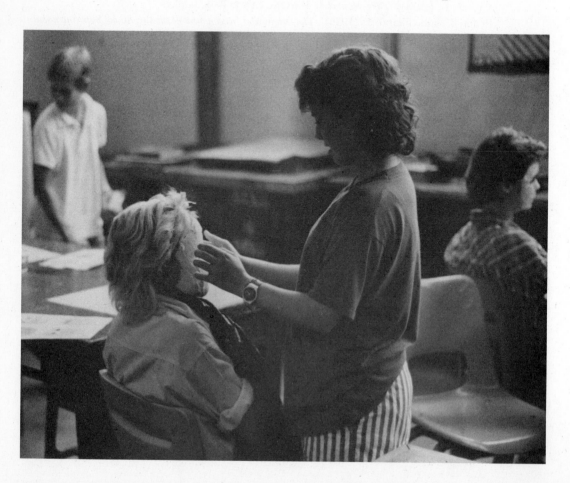

Educational administration is connected to a long tradition of leadership. This connection was made by Cubberley (1916) around the turn of the century. A view of leadership in educational administration is therefore part of the metaphorical mindset about generic leadership in Western culture. If school superintendents are described as "strong" in modern media metaphors, then their lineage can be traced to the earliest descriptors of leadership in Western history. This record enables us to consider the subject of leadership as a text, and involves hermeneutics and the hermeneutical tradition.

The concept of *text* goes beyond the written records themselves to include what Gadamer (1977) has called *wirkungsgeschichtliches Bewusstsein,* i.e., "consciousness that is effected by history" (p. 13). This is different from simply examining the historical record for what it says. That approach is far too narrow a tradition in hermeneutics. What Gadamer is talking about is to be aware of one's own mental life and consciousness, and of how one's own times have shaped one's thinking and responses when examining the past as reflected in the historical record. To do this requires a knowledge not only of twentieth century scientific traditions, but also knowledge of the artistic and historical traditions in which a text is inevitably embedded. Since some of twentieth century science *excludes* artistic and historical traditions (such as behaviorism), interpreting any text without that knowledge will mean understanding is very limited. Meaning is dependent upon understanding. The potential full range of interpretations is much narrower than if one was aware of these larger contextual forces. Enlarging understanding to include such knowledge is the concept of the hermeneutical circle of Dilthey (see Rickman, 1986, p. 10). It also includes the knowledge that language itself is a living mechanism and "has a teleology operating within it" (Gadamer, 1977, p. 13).

A **teleology** is an explanation of the past and the present in terms of the future. It comes from the Greek *telos* which means end, or completion (Runes, 1984, p. 331). Using language to think about and describe the past means that knowledge of the world is built up in a structured way that may not altogether fit the same world using a different language in a different time. Hermeneutics involves the whole of human experience, leaving little aside—including awareness of the living language that is the means and the mirror to describe that experience.

Where does one begin to study leadership of the past? We can take a clue from Gadamer (1977) who says, "If one acknowledges hermeneutics to exist wherever a genuine art of understanding manifests itself, one must begin if not with Nestor in the *Iliad,* then at least with Odysseus (p. 22). Homer, the Greek writer–poet, exercises a continuing influence on thinking about leadership in modern times (see Saracek, 1968). These two sources—the *Iliad* and the *Odyssey* of antiquity—engage and inform the Western mindset in defining the concept of leadership. It was the Oracle of Delphi that advised the Greek philosopher Zeno to "take on the complexion of the dead," or to study ancient authors (de Grazia, 1989, p. 27). These ancient sources are critical in order to comprehend what *leadership* means in the Western tradition.

It ought to be acknowledged that beginning with these ancient sources, a definite **Eurocentric** version is being re-centered in this quest. Intellectual and cultural traditions intertwine to produce a perspective unique to time and place. The Eurocentric view is rooted in ancient Greek cultural and intellectual traditions. These are not viewed as better or worse than others, as for example, Afrocentric perspectives (see Asante, 1990, pp. 8–11) rooted in ancient Egyptian writings. Eurocentric (in this case, Greek) views are the place where American intellectual interiors can be traced historically to their major literary and historical wellsprings.

Tracing this heritage shows the continuing influence of Greek thinking on contemporary life. However, even this lineage is being challenged today. Asante (1990) proffers that the Greeks were the intellectual children of the Egyptians (who were Africans) because Thales, Pythagoras, Oenopidus, Eudoxus, and Plato all studied in Egypt (p. 65). More is being learned about these connections and the possibility of re-centering Western views about leadership to be more than Greek. With more thorough study and analysis in time, as for example Martin Bernal's (1987) book, *Black Athena* (which also documents the Greek–Egyptian cultural and linguistic linkages as African), a more panoramic view of Western culture may emerge. There is nothing sacreligious about such reinterpretations. They happen all the time. In the words of Nietzsche (1956):

> The whole history of a thing, an organ, a custom, becomes a continuous chain of reinterpretations and rearrangements, which need not be causally connected among themselves, which may simply follow one another . . . [This] is a sequence of more or less profound, more or less independent processes of appropriation, including the resistances used in each instance, the attempted transformations for purposes of defense or reaction, as well as the results of successful counterattacks (p. 210).

Meaning is fluid and always renegotiable. The leadership construct in Western thinking is itself the product of such transformations. This book is part of that process in educational administration.

HOMERIC HEROES AND HEROINES: WESTERN PORTRAITS OF LEADERSHIP

Western leadership is centered around the concept of a **hero** or **heroine.** *Hero* comes from the Greek *heros,* meaning a real or legendary figure—usually a warrior—of great strength, courage, or daring. It is from literature that the West's heroes are found in the *Iliad,* the great epic poem by Homer who is alleged to have written it in the eighth century B.C. (Fagles and Knox, 1990, p. ix).

The *Iliad* is the story of the Trojan War, a struggle between the inhabitants of Troy (a rich, walled city on the coast of Asia Minor adjacent to the Hellespont—a passage which connects the Black and Aegean Seas), and the Achaeans (dwellers of the Bronze Age Greek city–states). It is thought that Homer drew upon a rich storehouse of stories about the fall of Troy in his time. The *Iliad* draws upon the events that occurred in a few weeks of the tenth year of the siege of the city (Wood, 1986, p. 19). The historical cause of the war may have been economic in that Troy commanded the passageway of commerce, exacting tribute for safe travel. Members of the Greek citty–states may have decided to put an end to the paying of tribute to Troy by sacking Troy.

The literary cause of the war was a woman—Helen, wife of the Spartan King, Menelaus—who ran away with Paris to Troy. Paris was one of 50 sons of Priam, King of Troy. On a point of honor, Menelaus organized an army to retrieve his abducted queen.

The characters in the *Iliad* are rich, complex, and very much flesh-and-blood humans. It is within this panoply of conflict that the heroic precepts of leadership are described in this great epic poem—the cornerstone of Western literature, and the forge and anvil in which the word *leader* was shaped into present times. All who followed Homer, including Alexander the Great, Cicero, and others assessed themselves to the shadows of the heroes of the *Iliad*.

The *Iliad* builds to a climax with the duel to the death between the greatest Trojan warrior—Hector—and the greatest Greek warrior—Achilles. These two meet in final combat on the plains below the walled city. All of Homer's listeners understand who will be the loser.

While Achilles will triumph, it is Hector who is the lasting hero of the *Iliad*. Hector is a man of peace who fights for his country even though he fully comprehends that Troy will be leveled and that he will die in its fall. He understands his own son will perish and his wife will be taken into slavery. With all of this foreknowledge, he stands as the foremost Trojan leader against the Greeks for as long as possible to stave off the inevitable disaster.

Achilles is not so much a leader as he is a great warrior. He has chosen to come to Troy understanding that in this decision, he too will perish. For most of the fight, Achilles remains in his tent, brooding over an insult to him by a fellow Greek—Agamemnon. He only casts his anger aside when his friend, Patroclus, is killed wearing his armor. Achilles is known as a problem character—i.e., he is a great but flawed person. It is precisely these conditions that make a character interesting to an actor who might portray a person in a play or film.

For example, the veteran Western actor, Clint Eastwood was attracted to a character he played in the film *Unforgiven* (1992). Says Eastwood:

> The character I play, William Munney, is an old outlaw who is tired of his way of life. Like some other men I've portrayed, he's a male fantasy figure. I like him. He's strong. But he has weaknesses, and that's what drew me to him. Actually, that's true of most of the characters I've played. I like and admire just about all of them, but each is flawed in some meaningful way (p. 4).

So Achilles is the problem character of the Iliad. He never comes to understand himself in his sulking depression. Achilles is a barbarian. Hector, on the other hand, is the tragic character—the valiant figure who fights in spite of a lost cause. Hector is the civilized figure, the protector of his people, the man they need to keep fighting. He fully understands the necessary role he must play in the conflict. Hector's mother Hecuba called to him to take a rest from the fighting, and bade him drink some honey wine. Hector replied:

> Don't offer me mellow wine, Mother, not now—you'd sap my limbs, I'd lose my nerve for war. And I'd be ashamed to pour a glistening cup to Zeus with unwashed hands. I'm spattered with blood and filth. How could I pray to the lord of storm and lightning? (Fagles and Knox, 1990, p. 204)

Hector's wife urges him to leave the front ranks and to command the Trojans from their high walls, thereby abandoning his role as leader. She reminds him of their small son, and of her own love for him. He responds:

> All this weighs on my mind too, dear woman. But I would die of shame to face the men of Troy and the Trojan women trailing their long robes if I would shrink from battle now, a coward (Fagles and Knox, 1990, p. 34).

After many valiant battles in which the Trojans, led by Hector, drove the Greeks to the beaches and their ships, Achilles returns to the fray with revenge in his heart for the loss of his comrade—Patroclus. The Trojans are slain in numbers and flee to the walls of Troy. Hector alone waits at the Scaean Gates of the city. He refuses to hear the pleas of his mother and father to come into the city. He contemplates retreating, but cannot stand to hear the criticism he knows will come from some of the Trojan warriors.

Finally, in the moment he faces Achilles alone, he falters and runs before the Trojan ramparts, hoping that the spear-throwers on the walls will hit Achilles. But Achilles cuts him off at the corners. Three times they circle Troy.

In the end, Hector gathers his courage and stops. He says to Achilles:

> No more running from you in fear, Achilles! Not as before. Three times I fled around the great city of Priam—I lacked courage then to stand your onslaught. Now my spirit stirs me to meet face-to-face. Now kill or be killed! (Fagles and Knox, 1990, p. 549)

In the exchange of spears, Hector's weapon glances off Achilles' shield. As he closes in on Achilles with his sword, Achilles rams his spear through Hector's throat without severing the windpipe. Hector asks that his body be returned to Troy for a proper burial. Achilles scorns him. After Hector's death, he pierces his tendons near the ankles with rawhide and lashes his body to his chariot. In full view of all the Trojans, he drags Hector's body in the dust around the city for all to see.

This great saga not only marked the beginning of Western literature, but it also created the concept of the "hero" in the Western mind. The image and flavor of bravery and determination were emboldened in the picture of Hector trying to save his city–nation before a superior adversary. In this respect, the two combatants of the Trojan War find parallels in the American Civil War, where the enraged Ulysses S. Grant, with superior numbers and weapons, eventually overwhelmed the Confederate Hector—Robert E. Lee—and devastated the South.

The *Iliad* is also a fine example of the application of hermeneutics. In dealing with the expurgations of the *Iliad*, Murray (1924) comments:

> It is certain that the poet [Homer] is representing with conscious art a past age of heroism and chivalry. Naturally, therefore, he excludes from it not only what is low and modern, but also a good deal that was really ancient, but indicated the squalor and brutality of the past, rather than its chivalry (p. 122).

Both heroes and the gods were cleansed in subsequent versions of the *Iliad*. Cases of incest are covered up. Battles fought between combatants never include barbarism, despite the fact that in some earlier versions Hector was dragged alive behind Achilles' chariot. Prisoners are never tortured or mistreated. Such occurrences have been expurgated from the *Iliad* of Homer (pp. 125–126). Homer's past never was the present (Murray, 1924, p. 120). So the definition of heroic behavior can be considered only partially true, if we mean that it actually represented what happened in the Trojan War. The *Iliad,* like many other stories, is a patient and idealistic reconstruction of events.

THE UNIVERSALITY OF THE HERO: UNLOCKING THE HUMAN PSYCHE

The **epic hero** has many faces and exists in many races and civilizations. Joseph Campbell (1968) spent a lifetime examining the internality of the heroes and gods of human civilization. Inner themes unite the external faces that seem so different in time and place. Campbell finds parallels in the lives of Buddha, King Arthur, Osiris, the Arabian Nights' Prince Kamar al-Zaman, the Navajo Spider Woman, and the Holy Ghost. He calls them the "monomyth."

The internalities of human dreams and needs are deep in the species' psyche. A hero is one who goes forth to an adventure, crosses the threshold of the story, endures tests, and returns to the world to help the rest of humanity.

The crossing of the threshold occurs in a **primal battle,** as in the case of Hector and Achilles, or death and dismemberment as with the Egyptian god Osiris, crucifixion as in the story of Jesus, or being swallowed by a whale as in the case of Jonah. In the full cycle, the hero encounters the supreme test—a dragon, a monster, a puzzle, death, a transformation—and is himself transformed. He then returns to humanity with the magic potion, elixir, powers, vision, strength, eternal life, or becomes divine himself.

This eternal cycle is called mythology, but Campbell (1968) has shown us that, "mythology, in other words, is psychology misread as biography; history, and cosmology" (p. 256). Campbell illustrates his themes by combining myths into patterns revealing that the function of these stories "is to serve as a powerful picture language for the communication of traditional wisdom" (p. 256).

This traditional wisdom, from ancient to modern, teaches that all form is a manifestation of a single source. Though it appears through human senses as fractured or disparate, it is a unity. Science calls this source *energy.* Traditional wisdom calls it *God.* The inner view of such things is, says Campbell (1968), what Jesus was referring to when he said in Luke 17:21, "behold, the kingdom of God is within you" (p. 259).

What Jesus meant, says Campbell (1968), is that man's superconscious became his unconscious in the Biblical "Fall" from God's grace. The world, as represented in sensory data, is illusory and even false. The capability of perceiving it more holistically can only be attained in bringing the unconscious back to full awareness. This is redemption (p. 259). Thus, mythology is the thread which shows the introversion of the mind back to itself through the unconscious.

It is this fundamental inversion that creates heroes as symbols in the visualized human world. The hero is the formal face of the introverted human spirit calling for contemplation, action, courage, and valorous deeds in the pursuit of that which is good and pure. Within this introversion lies the leader–follower dichotomy and its unification. Followers make leaders possible. And all leaders are followers of those that follow, i.e., they understand that in order to lead, one must let himself/herself be followed, and in this process the leader is led (while leading).

In her best-selling book, *Women Who Run with the Wolves*, Clarissa Pinkola Estes (1992), a Jungian analyst and cantadora (storyteller) uses various female stories to show that every woman is trying to reconnect with *the wild woman*. This female archetype is the instinctual mother who understands and is at home with the life/death/life cycles of all living forms. Reality is to be found in the interior of the mind as opposed to externalities. Estes discusses the concept of the "heroic mother" as one who possesses "some very fierce qualities, qualities that, in many cultures, are considered masculine and . . . [are] expressly forbidden" (p. 176). The *Iliad* represents one example of such feminine suppression.

The *Iliad*, as a story of the City of Troy, has been proven by archaelogical excavation, to have occurred. It is, however, interwoven with other stories that have been shown to be classic myths of other ages. For example, the major female figure—Helen—is the subject of other legends. In these legends, Helen is seen as a "swan child." She is always being carried off by a ravisher. Murray (1924) explains that as a Spartan bride (Helen was the queen of Sparta), it was a customary ritual to be carried off as a part of the marriage ceremony itself (p. 205). In some Greek cities, Helen was visualized as the marriage goddess, and her image was regularly carried off in the Feast of Tonaia (Murray, 1924, p. 205).

It would be a mistake to believe that the Western world with its high science has abandoned the images of Homer emblazoned in its unconscious so long ago. The psychic need for heroes and heroines has never left us. In a penetrating analysis of modern monomyths, Jewett and Lawrence (1988) show that technology has enabled the monomyth to survive and grow. They perform an analysis of the TV series *Star Trek* as the archetypal Homeric heroes in space. The superhuman hero is supplied in the role of Mr. Spock, who is half human and half Vulcan. Spock has innate capacities that exceed humans. He has superior strength and intelligence. He is immune to certain diseases and is able to perform mathematical calculations that exceed contemporary computers. Spock also is supremely rational, except in rutting season. As Jewett and Lawrence note, the success of many missions is Spock's ability to rigidly repress his sexual feelings. Women are attracted to him, and to Captain Kirk of the Starship Enterprise. However, in order to be considered superheroes, sexual engagements are denied, in much the same way the Greeks refused to engage in sexual intercourse when besieging Troy (see Murray, 1924, p. 133). Indeed, the repression of sexual drives—a Greek ideal based on cultural misogyny—has persisted through the late nineteenth century in the writings of Frederich Nietzsche who scoffed at the idea that a "real philosopher" would never be married (Golffing, 1956, p. 242).

Star Trek has developed scores of fanatic followers. The series is almost a cult. Other American monomyths are *Rocky* and *Rambo* played by Sylvester Stallone. *Star Wars*, perhaps the most popular film series of all time, was replete with monsters, heroines and heroes, dueling with light sabres, and battling the "dark side" of the "force."

Far from liberating Western minds from the need to have their psychic needs fulfilled, technology has been utilized to fill the gap, creating new archetypes of heroes and heroines. Homer would be amused and right at home among them.

The need for real-life heroes lives on in the image of Marine Colonel Oliver North swaggering before the TV cameras, posing as the archetypal hero while defying and lying to Congress, or in the followers of Ross Perot and his aborted campaign to become president on a third-party ticket. There is a persistent longing for heroes and for heroic leadership which is very much alive today.

MILITARY OFFICERS AS MODELS OF LEADERSHIP

Heroic leadership and the ideal of heroism are deeply implanted in the Western mind. The earliest sources were pictures of military leaders and military expeditions, whether it be the excursions of Alexander the Great as he meticulously plotted his outnumbered army's victory over Darius at Gaugamela, or the dazzling technology and strategy of H. Norman Schwarzkopf's famous "Hail Mary" tank thrust around Saddam Hussein's left flank in Desert Storm, some 2000 years later.

In the case of Alexander the Great, Plutarch (Lindeman, 1953) tells us that he kept a copy of Homer's *Iliad*, edited by Aristotle, under his pillow next to his dagger (p. 168). On his way to Asia Minor, Alexander had to stop at Troy and make an offering at Achilles' tomb, running around the pillar of the tomb naked, as was the custom (p. 174).

Alexander was the epitome of heroic leadership, plunging into the battle in front of his troops in deep phalanx formation, engaging the opponent face to face, and sharing the dangers his *yspaspisti* (infantrymen) faced. Alexander's models were the characters in the *Iliad* (Keegan, 1987, p. 35). Another world military figure was also influenced by the *Iliad* and the exploits of Alexander. Napoleon himself had a copy and favored the tales of Achilles (Bernal, 1987, p. 185).

The military commander is the living persona of the image of heroic leadership, and it is no accident that the first President of the United States was also its Revolutionary War hero–general, George Washington.

To inspire men in combat, military commanders have resorted to various devices to accentuate the right to lead. As John Keegan (1987) analyzed Alexander the Great—the Western world's first exemplary military leader—he found in his leadership a planned theatricality anchored in ceremony and deeds. Keegan asserts that Alexander's **coups d'theatre** were brilliantly timed and costumed. They were elaborately staged on and off the battlefield.

Keegan accounts for two that have lived into the stream of Western consciousness: his cutting of the Gordian Knot and the taming of Bucephalus. In the cutting of the Knot, he refused to follow all the others who tried to untie it. He simply took his sword and chopped it off. A dramatic act that illustrated his "leadership style," to use modern terminology. In the taming of the magnificent horse, Bucephalus—a stallion no one could ride—Alexander noticed he was afraid of his own shadow. He therefore pointed the horse into the sun, mounted him, and rode off.

Keegan notes that Alexander wore battlefield outfits that marked him unmistakably to his soldiers: a helmet polished so brightly it reflected the sun, jeweled armor and flowing capes. Alexander's heroics are legendary: He was wounded eight times, four of which were minor, three quite serious, and one almost terminal. The most serious of his wounds came from arrows inflicted in sieges of cities.

The eccentricities of dress of commanders have passed into modern times in the distinctive cap and corncob pipe of the U.S. General Douglas MacArthur, the pearl-handled six shooters on the hips of George S. Patton, the colorful berets of the British General Bernard Montgomery, or the cocked hat and goggles of his crafty German opponent, Erwin Rommel, the "Desert Fox."

The **mask of command** in these ancient traces which run so deep in Western minds includes calculated and planned events, rituals, oratory, and carefully staged scenes that can be considered a form of theatre. The leader creates an image that is systematically exposed to the followers, and that comes to be distinctive.

The traces of the heroic are still strong ingredients in the public mind in modern times. Newspaper editorials that call for "leadership" are almost always a longing for "heroic" models which can be laid at the feet of Homer and the Walls of Troy.

For a very long time, the mask of command has been a lost concept in the study of leadership, first to the idea that "traits" can be divorced from the leaders and the times in which they were displayed, and secondly in the patina of behaviorism that is simply expanded trait theory. The ancient writers of history did not fall into such bogus "scientific" traps, nor did the playwrights or poets. In their artistic creations, leadership was understood and portrayed *in context*.

Perhaps the most negative aspect of Western leadership as heroic is the enshrinement of metaphors that are androcentric. It is one thing to wonder what the face that launched a thousand ships could have looked like, but it's another to imagine Helen of Troy as a superintendent of schools, corporate executive, or as president of the United States. The real "Trojan horse" of leadership is the one-sided dimensionality of it as exclusively male or **gender exclusive.** The suppression of women in the *Iliad* has been noted by Homeric scholars (Murray, 1924, p. 134). Homer apparently practiced the notion voiced by Pericles, "that a woman's fame is to be as seldom as possible mentioned by men, either for praise or blame" (Murray, 1924, p. 135). That posture excludes half the population from being considered leaders, and it forces women to become "like men" to be considered "tough enough" to command. The doubled-edged sword for women has always been that when they exhibit courage and decisiveness (male characteristics in battle), they are derided as "pushy" or "unladylike." The stereotype of the "lady" as unheroic has meant that women are placed in a double bind in being considered leaders: If they act like so-called men they are ridiculed; if they act like so-called women they can't be leaders. This prejudice is rooted in antiquity and reflected in Homer as well. A study of the life of Joan of Arc will amply demonstrate the difficulties women face. The prejudicial barriers that only a saint could overcome in the Middle Ages continues into the present, and is now called the "glass ceiling" (Lelyveid, 1992). Less than 3 percent of the 6502 *Fortune 500* company positions were held by women in 1991. At the current rate, it will take 450 years to attain parity with males in executive positions (Associated Press).

As women serve in greater numbers than ever before in the U.S. military, the debate about whether or not they are "fit" for combat grows more intense, despite the fact that at least one female served in the Continental army as a soldier, was wounded, and was honorably discharged (see Freeman and Bond, 1992), and some 400 women managed to get into the Union army in the Civil War when physical exams were often not given (Tschanz, 1992, p. 33). How many died in combat is unknown. Examples of courageous women in battle are to be found in many cultures, Western and Eastern, as for example, the case of World War II Russian air ace Lydia Litvak, "the White Rose of Stalingrad" (Strobridge, 1986).

Lydia was barely five feet tall, a diminutive blond woman who fought with an exclusive all-male elite fighter squadron. She was shot down twice, wounded as many times, and was credited with 12 "kills," which made her an ace. Her plane was adorned with a large white rose, which meant she was recognizable to the enemy as a distinctive personality. Her prowess as a fighter pilot was earned when she fought and won a 15-minute duel to the death dogfight with a German ace credited with 20 kills (p. 61). She was elevated to the position of flight commander and led male pilots to battle. She mysteriously disappeared when attacking a German bomber squadron. She was jumped by eight German fighters who knew she was the flight commander.

Lydia Litvak created an "image" as a leader in the same way many male leaders have done. She wore distinctive attire, including an unusual logo on her fighter plane. She was in front of men and led by example. When her male lover crashed his plane into the ground teaching another pilot how to dogfight, she neither cried nor spoke. Nobody ever accused Lydia Litvak of (1) not being a woman, or (2) not being "tough enough."

The other legacy from Greek literature and leadership cast in military terms is the idea that not only were women inferior, but also the repressed idea that there might be psychosexual orientations *between* cultural gender polarizations. Heroes were always "real men," despite the fact that Greek warriors were, if not homosexual, often bisexual. In fact, the Sacred Battalion of Thebes was almost entirely composed of men–boy lovers (Tannahill, 1980, p. 91). The persecution of gays and lesbians in contemporary times as weird or queer traces its intellectual origins to gender polarization in Western literature. What is different about contemporary polarization is that it has been embodied in law, religious and educational institutions, and the mass media (Bem, 1993, p. 81).

Military heroes also have sexual orientations that differ from approved cultural stereotypes, whether they be Alexander the Great, Lawrence of Arabia, or Philippe I, Duc D'Orleans (Wallace, Wallace, Wallechinsky, Wallace, 1981, pp. 362, 371).

THE LEGACY OF PLUTARCH: PORTRAIT PAINTER OF MEN OF ACTION

Perhaps the oldest legacy of leadership portraits in the Western world belongs to Plutarch, a Greek biographer who lived between 46 and 119 A.D. Plutarch studied in Athens and traveled in Rome. He wrote *Parallel Lives* in which he contrasted famous Greeks and Romans.

The purpose of writing *Parallel Lives* using both Greeks and Romans was to place the two civilizations on the same plane, even though the majesty of Greece had long since been eclipsed in the Empire of Rome. The Romans had a high regard for all things Greek, and Plutarch took advantage of this proclivity (Scott-Kilvert, p. 9).

Reading Plutarch today, one encounters the kind of strong narrative tradition that all good biographies possess. But Plutarch was interested more in probing his characters than in simply describing them. In contemporary jargon, he included "the warts" as well as the commendations, awards, and illustrious accomplishments of his famous personae. It was Plutarch's mastery of detail—his use of rich anecdotes and stories—that set him apart from his contemporaries. He was, according to Scott-Kilvert, "a social historian" (p. 9).

Plutarch utilized what modern writers such as Thomas Sergiovanni (1992) have called **mindscapes** (p. 8). A mindscape is a tacitly held mental picture about how things work in the world. In this sense, as a moral painter of humans, Plutarch was thoroughly modern. For Plutarch held that the purpose of his work was to "bring out the moral pattern in a hero's career, the movement from virtue to vice" (Scott-Kilvert, p. 16).

Plutarch sketched his characters in terms of their personalities, and he employed the ethical standards of a person's private life as the benchmark for his or her public decisions. In this, he echoed Sergiovanni's (1992) delineation of moral authority as a source for leadership, or **moral leadership**—i.e., a "form of obligation and duties derived from widely shared values, ideas, and ideals" (p. 31).

It was to this ideal that Plutarch spoke when describing Pericles (Scott-Kilvert):

> Moral good, in a word, has a power to attract towards itself. It is no sooner seen than it rouses the spectator to action, and yet it does not form his character by mere imitation, but by promoting the understanding of virtuous deeds it provides him with a dominating purpose (p. 171).

Plutarch has been criticized for his moral stance, however (see Whittemore, 1988, p. 26). The ideals of private life conduct are not always transferable to public life, the latter presenting situations where administrative decisions must be made in an arena of competing interests and groups instead of choices between black and white, and where each may be considered legitimate instead of correct or incorrect (Scott-Kilvert, p. 16). This standard was illustrated in his portrait of Aristides when he said of him, "Aristides was scrupulously fair in his private dealings and relations with his fellow-citizens, but in public affairs he often followed whatever policy his country had adopted, recognizing that this must involve a good deal of injustice on occasions" (p. 128).

It is Plutarch's humanity, his sense of drama, his understanding of the *theatre* of leadership, combined with his "power . . . to epitomize the moral grandeur of the ancient world" (Scott-Kilvert, p. 17) that inspired Shakespeare and Montaigne, and that provide the modernity and freshness to *Parallel Lives* today. Indeed, this text transcends nearly all behavioral "scientific" studies in its power and scope because Plutarch was "convinced that a portrait which reveals a man's character and inner qualities possesses a far greater beauty than one which merely reproduces his face and physical appearance" (Scott-Kilvert, 1960, p. 139). Plutarch was aware of potential bias in his descriptions when he noted in a presentation of the life of Cimon who was accused of incest with his sister Elpinice:

> When an artist has to paint a face which possesses fair and handsome features, we demand that he should neither exaggerate nor leave out any minor defect he may find in it, since in the first case this would make the portrait ugly, and in the second destroy the likeness (p. 139).

The only modern equivalent in education close to Plutarch is perhaps Sara Lawrence Lightfoot's *The Good High School* (1983) in which she describes several school principals—warts and all.

When Plutarch compared two lives as he did with Demosthenes and Cicero, his values were clearly revealed. While he found both to be great orators, Demosthenes' oratory "was without embellishment and jesting, wholly composed for real effect and seriousness" (Davidow, 1936, p. 402). The Roman Cicero's oratory was filled with mockery, "jests and facetious remarks, with a view to the advantage of his clients, he paid too little to what was decent" (p. 403).

Demosthenes never bragged about himself, remarks Plutarch, "but Cicero's immeasurable boasting of himself in his orations argues him guilty of an uncontrollable appetite for distinction" (Davidow, p. 403). Such an appetite has been documented by modern scholarship independent of Plutarch when Shackleton Bailey (1971) noted of Cicero that he possessed an, "ever-driving hunger for prominence" (p. 22).

It is clear that Plutarch believed Demosthenes morally superior on these grounds when he wrote, "It is necessary, indeed, for a political leader to be an able speaker; but it is an ignoble thing for any man to admire and relish the glory of his own eloquence" (p. 401).

Plutarch combined a set of values with observations. His sources were extremely varied and thick. Plutarch's morality guided his selection of anecdotes, as well as the priority he placed on them. He weighed the overall character of his person and commented:

> It is difficult . . . To represent a man's life as entirely spotless and free from blame, we should use the best chapters in it to build up the most complete picture and regard this as the true likeness. Any errors or crimes, on the other hand, which may tarnish a man's career and may have been committed out of passion or political necessity, we should regard rather as lapses from a particular virtue than as the product of some innate vice (Scott-Kilvert, 1960, p. 139).

Plutarch was aware of how hard it is to discern the truth when he said, "how thickly the truth is hedged around with obstacles and how hard it is to track down by historical research" (Scott-Kilvert, p. 185).

Plutarch's approach in using biography was quite modern. For example, Kofodimos (1990) at the Center for Creative Leadership in North Carolina described how biography could be used to understand managerial behavior and personality. In setting forth guidelines for developing biographies, Kofodimos advocates using multiple perspectives and multiple methods, combining research and service in a kind of "action research" mode (pp. 13–17). Plutarch utilized all of these guidelines, with perhaps more emphasis on oral than written sources.

Plutarch may be said to be the first scholarly biographer in the Western tradition. Leadership and the trials and problems encountered with leading were behind the Greek tragedies of Sophocles, who portrayed the life of Oedipus Rex (the character who lives on in Freudian psychology as the prototype for the "Oedipus complex," where the first sex object for a young male is his mother; the "Electra complex" is a similar situation for daughters and fathers).

Virgil's *The Aeneid* and Livy's *History of Rome,* which contains a portrait of Hannibal, are also sources of the ancient world's conception of leadership. They have laid a cornerstone in the Western mindscape which is still firmly in place today. There are few portraits of women as leaders in these times. One of the rarest is the story of Boudicca, Queen of the Iceni, a Celtic tribe of eastern England, who led an unsuccessful rebellion against the Romans in about 60 A.D. (Smith, 1989, pp. 8, 61–64).

LEADERSHIP IN THE MIDDLE AGES: WARS, FAITH, KNIGHTS, AND LADIES

The period between the Fall of Rome (450 A.D.) and the emergence of the late Italian Renaissance (1500 A.D.) is commonly referred to as the "Middle Ages" (Cantor, 1991, p. 17). Like other periods of human history, the times were filled with images of leadership.

The Middle Ages saw climactic battles between European armies and those of invading Mongols, Turks, Berbers, and Arabs. In 732 A.D., a Moslem army led by Abd-er-Rahman thrust deep into the heart of France, pausing at Poitiers, some 60 miles away from Tours. The Moslems crashed into an army raised by Charles Martel, and in the ensuing battle, swift Moslem cavalry tried to break a heavily armed Frankish phalanx arrayed Roman style on high ground. At a propitious moment, the Frankish infantry turned from defense to offense and nearly enveloped the enemy. Arab resistance was broken and they panicked and fled back through Spain (Niderost, 1988, pp. 35–41). Charles Martel was the grandfather of Charlemagne, first King of the Franks and later Emperor of the Holy Roman Empire.

Charlemagne would later form an army, and campaign against the Moslems in Spain. It was such a thrust and ensuing journey home, that another legend was created in the minds of men and women regarding heroic leadership (Luquines and Smyth, 1952).

As Charlemagne's army went through the Pyrenees Mountains in 778 A.D., his baggage train and rear guard were set upon by Basques. The guard was headed by a French Knight—Roland. A great epic poem was written about Roland's force, wiped out to the last, who died protecting Charlemagne's army. "The Song of Roland" became the equivalent of the *Iliad* to Europeans. It was sung by nobles and military men for hundreds of years, including William the Conqueror of England in his efforts to motivate his troops at the Battle of Hastings.

The poem recounts the attack of the Basques and how one by one the French knights fall. Roland is left alone and wounded. He falls and is set upon by a Saracen. He kills him with his horn and staggers to his feet.

Roland feeleth his eyesight reft,
Yet he stands erect with what strength is left;
From his bloodless cheek is the hue dispelled,
But his Durindana [his sword] all bare he held.
In front a dark brown rock arose
He smote upon it ten grevious blows.
Grated the steel as it struck the flint,
Yet it brake not, nor bore its edge one dint.
"Mary, Mother, be thou mine aid!
Ah, Durindana, my ill-starred blade,
I may no longer thy guardian be!
What fields of battle I won with thee!
What realms and regions 'twas ours to gain
Now the lordship of Carlemaine!
Never shalt thou possessor know
Who would turn from face of mortal foe,
A gallant vassal so long thee bore,
Such as France the free shall know no more.
(Translated by John O'Hagan as cited in
Grebanier, Middlebrook, Thompson and Watt,
1957, pp. 1033–1038.)

The conflagration between Christian and Moslem came to a head in the Crusades. Between 1096 and 1270 A.D. Christian forces were in continuous battle with Moslems in an effort to capture the Holy Land and its capital of Jerusalem (see Grousset, 1970).

The Crusades are filled with pictures of heroic leadership, from the First Crusade when the figures of Godfrey of Bouillon—duke of Lower Lorraine—came upon the scene. Godfrey was tall, blond, and of legendary strength. He was a devout believer, gentle and humble. His inner strength matched with his physical prowess enabled him to be a moral leader. After the conquest of Jerusalem, Godfrey's peers elected him head of state. He refused to take title or wear a crown, believing that the Lord only wore a crown of thorns, and the only true monarch of the Holy City was Jesus himself (Grousset, 1970, pp. 32–33). On the battlefield, Godfrey was fearless and gave no quarter. Once when Arab princes came to pay him homage they found him in his tent reclining on straw. Amazed that the Christian leader was in such a state of poverty, without guards or carpets, they remarked of their observation aloud. Godfrey responded by reciting Scripture: "Man must remember that dust he is, to dust he shall return" (Grousset, 1970, p. 35).

The Third Crusade matched the forces of Conrad of Montferrat, Philip Augustus, and Richard the Lionhearted against Saladin. Even Hollywood has found the Crusades too alluring to ignore.

Of notable importance were the actions of the Moslem chieftain, Saladin. The Crusaders were to learn of this crafty, wise, and chivalrous leader of their enemy. Once Saladin was approached by a Christian woman who came to his camp and groveled in the dust. She lay prostrate before him and sobbed for her child carried away by Moslem night raiders. Saladin ordered the child returned. When he learned the infant had already been sold into slavery, he used his own funds to unite mother and offspring (Grousset, 1970, p. 181).

Once in the heat of battle, Richard the Lionhearted so impressed the Moslems with his courage and strength, that he was sent a horse by them through the carnage, because it was not acceptable to them that such a king would have to fight on foot. When Richard fell ill, Saladin sent him peaches and sherbets from the mountain snow of Mount Hermon (Grousset, 1970, p. 196).

When at last Jerusalem fell to the Turks in 1244 A.D., a French King, Saint Louis, "took the cross" and vowed to recapture the Holy City. He organized an expedition, landed in Egypt, and fought his way off the beaches to a city near Cairo called Mansura. There the battle was joined for real, and the King—his forces divided on either side of the Bahr as-Saghir canal—found himself outnumbered and encircled. Chronicles of this battle recount that without the personal example provided by the King ahead of his cavalry, the entire force would have been lost. When at last the foot soldiers of Louis' army made it across the canal by devising a pontoon bridge, the Franks prevailed on the battlefield.

We see Saint Louis later, his army racked with typhus, dysentery, and Spanish influenza, cut off from supplies and reeling under famine, surrendering to the Moslems. Threatened with death, Saint Louis was resolute and stoic. His personal example again impressed his captors who ransomed his entire army instead of putting them to the sword. The agreement ended the battle, but maintained Christian power in Syria. Saint Louis stayed for four years as an able administrator, and put the kingdom in order (Grousset, 1970, p. 256).

The Crusades read as an extended *Iliad,* with individual battles and great heroes on both sides. Instead of Troy, Jerusalem was the walled city of prize. It was conquered several times, and fell into the control of both sides, each of whom considered it a holy city of worship. Today it remains a contested piece of earth with not-so-chivalrous stories being recounted between Israeli police and military units battling Palestinian *intifadeh* in their homes and the streets of the occupied territories (Beyer, 1992, p. 49).

THE UNPARALLELED HEROIC LEADER: JEANNE D'ARC

No account of the Middle Ages would be complete without examining the life of Joan of Arc—*La Pucelle d' Orleans*—the "Maid of Orleans." Joan's story is unique and heroic. Barbara Tuchman (1979), the historian whose best-selling book, *A Distant Mirror,* chronicled the Middle Ages, commented:

The phenomenon of Jeanne d'Arc—the voices from God who told her she must expel the English and have the Dauphin crowned King, the quality that dominated those who would normally have despised her, the strength that raised the siege of Orleans and carried the Dauphin to Reims—belongs to no category (p. 588).

No great leader ever contradicted the personal characteristics of Homeric heroes more than Joan of Arc. An adolescent female from common, peasant heritage, she was unschooled and no great beauty, but succeeded in convincing male-dominated monarchical society that she could lead an army in a direct assault against one of the strongest English fortresses of the area, and carry the day for France. Joan never held command rank. Yet she made her generals stop swearing, and forbade the usual camp women from following the army. When the time came for the attack, she insisted on no ruse tactics, but a straightforward assault on the strongest part of the English citadel. She was always more than a military leader. She had become a spiritual leader in a nation thirsting to retrieve its national soul and pride.

The life of Jeanne d'Arc was a mere 19 years (1412–1431), the period of her leadership but three years. In what must be considered a very short life, she recast and reconstituted the soul of a nation to evict its invaders and unite itself physically in 36 months. In this feat she must be considered the consummate *transformational leader* (Burns, 1979, p. 36).

There is no surviving painting, sketch, portrait, or image of Jeanne d'Arc made in her time. Her most famous biographer, Victoria Sackville-West (1936), culled the evidence and found that Jeanne was most likely short and stocky, far from the Ingrid Bergman Hollywood caricature of the silver screen. Jeanne most likely had black hair, was swarthy, and by contemporary standards, rather homely looking. Sackville-West says, "Many men and women who had known her in her youth came forward later to testify to her moral character, to her early avocations, to the personal impression she made on them, to the affection and respect with which they regarded her, but not a single one mentions even as a passing comment that she was pretty" (p. 3).

So Jeanne d'Arc was no French femme fatale, not even passably pretty. She was a short, sturdy peasant girl with brown eyes who wore armor for days without taking it off, and rode 3000 miles on horseback, often having little sleep on her travels. What did she offer France in this country's hour of need?

Victoria Sackville-West claimed for Jeanne d'Arc "the genius of personality":

She did possess the power to accomplish what she had undertaken. Her courage and conviction were superhuman. They were of the quality which admits no doubt and recognizes no obstacle. Her own absolute faith was the secret of her strength (p. 356).

Here Sackville-West recognizes the value of a moral leader, one that Plutarch has already noted in his statement that "Moral good has the power to attract towards itself" (Scott-Kilvert, p. 171).

While Joan was female, poor, uneducated, and homely, she nonetheless adopted the mask of command. Perhaps instinctively she understood that her armor had to be unblemished and plain. Her own flag standard with the holy name of Jesus set against a field of lilies was recognizable by the troops (Banfield, 1985, p. 14). In her own way she was different, and she was heroic. She dressed as a man.

She preferred the company of soldiers. She was fully steeped in the lore of chivalry. Her selection of a sword remains wrapped in mystery. It is still listed as one of her "miracles."

When Jeanne was brought armor and her standard she accepted them. But she declined the sword she was offered. Instead, she instructed her attendants to go to the church of St. Catherine at Fierbois and dig up a buried sword. No one had ever heard of a sword buried at this church. Following her orders they found a sword with five crosses. It was said to originally have been used by Charles Martel against the Saracens at Poitiers in 732 (Sackville-West, 1936, pp. 144–145). This incidence increased Jeanne's prestige as a leader and reinforced her psychological hold on the troops. It is evident that she understood the secrets of the mask of command, and the coups d'theatre it required. Another incident also reinforced her command authority in that she prophesied her own wounding at the battle of Orleans. Jeanne was wounded by an arrow which sank some six inches into her shoulder at Orleans. Jeanne's prophecy was repeated by her confessor, Paquerel (Sackville-West, 1936, p. 374).

Jeanne was not a woman posing as a man, but a woman, with a woman's voice and upbringing, who abandoned most feminine ways to lead soldiers into battle. She wept easily, and she wept for friend and foe. She had few false pretenses, and was of simple and straightforward demeanor with a superhuman faith in her own destiny and mission. Victoria Sackville-West summarized Jeanne d'Arc's persona when she said, "From beginning to end, she is all of a piece" (p. 354).

English influence in France was nearly eliminated in the decisive battle at Castillon outside Bordeaux in 1453 where the French defeated an English force lead by John Talbot, Earl of Shrewsbury (Tuchman, 1979, p. 592). Charles VII, the Dauphin now King, became at last the ruler Jeanne d'Arc believed he could be, and initiated a re-examination of the Maid of Orleans' life which was to result in her canonization as a Saint in 1920—489 years after Jeanne had been burned at the stake as a heretic, "relapsed apostate [deserter from faith], and idolater [one who worships a false god]" (Banfield, 1985, p. 82). One of Jeanne's "crimes against God" was the wearing of a man's clothes to which she answered at her trial, "These clothes do not burden my soul. As for women's clothing, I shall not put it on until it pleases God" (Banfield, 1985, p. 83).

Jeanne's crossover into a man's world, where she became a leader for all time, reflects the dominant gender hegemony that was hardening at the same time as her rise and fall. Male hegemony crystallized when church officials and the nobility came to terms over power. The church prevailed over the nobility's relationships with many women in adulterous relationships or concubinage by imposing the rules of monogamy on the nobles. The nobles ultimately consented to this imposition because it increased their power over their vassals and serfs. This new "system," which punished Jeanne d'Arc by burning her alive at the stake, was the new man's world. And the women? Historian Georges Duby (1983) confesses:

> It all added up to a solid system. But amid the clamor of all these men asserting what they had done or wanted to do, we must not forget the women. Much has been said about them. But how much do we really know? (p. 284)

Even as Jeanne d'Arc creates a heroic portrait of leadership that few men have ever surpassed in a lifetime, let alone three years, she was relegated to an anomaly. Making her a saint cemented her legend as an eccentric and an aberration of the medieval period. In this male act of "honor," Jeanne was recognized and summarily sealed away like a fragile China doll in the glass case of history, forever the exception instead of an emulative exemplar empowering women to take up leadership in earthly affairs. Since few women ever see themselves as saints, they come to believe that in order for a woman to lead men, she must be a saint—and after all, there was only one Jeanne d'Arc.

Like Jeanne's voices from God, women's voices in leadership have largely been ignored, suppressed, or exceptionalized by men. Those traditions began with Homer and were solidified in the Middle Ages. The sole female voice of the medieval period—Christine de Pisan—wrote extensively of the double standard imposed on women in military warfare and other famous women. But her work was read only by nobles and in no way compared to more popular male writers. Her last work—written in a convent at age 54—was a poem dedicated to Jeanne d'Arc (Tuchman, 1979, pp. 218–219).

SUMMARY

This chapter presented a starting point in the Western mindscape, or text, for the concept of leadership. All traces lead back to Homer's *Iliad*. In this epic poem, which was deeply etched in Greek and Roman minds, these two civilizations defined leadership as androcentric. Feminine voices were ignored or suppressed. These traditions have continued into modern times and are epitomized in the "glass ceiling," i.e., the invisible barrier that prevents women and minorities from rising to the top of bureaucratic pyramids that are dominated by white males.

Homeric leadership emphasizes courage under stress and hardship. Leadership in good times cannot be heroic. Heroic leadership is the outcome of individual courage under adversity. Heroic leadership is centered on individual acts of bravery and perseverance which are public and become coups d'theatre. The leader acts, dresses, and creates a distinctive public face in the process. Great political and military leaders develop such faces, from Winston Churchill's cigar and "victory" sign to Jeanne d'Arc's personal flag standard with Jesus on a field of lilies, and her mysterious sword with five crosses.

Coups d'theatre connect the leader to the hidden symbols that link emotions to psychic energy, and thought to real actions in the human world. Leaders—either instinctively or through education—come to understand that for humans to achieve great things under adversity, they must come to believe in special causes and circumstances, otherwise, their actions are simply ordinary. Extraordinary accomplishment by everyday people requires extraordinary purposes, causes, reasons, and beliefs.

Behind the symbols and public persona of leaders lie eons of psychic expressions, etched in story, myth, drama, and folktales, that reveal the interior of human life. It is to this interior that leaders reach for sustained psychic energy, which is

transformative in nature. The leader is thus the lifeline to heroism to his or her followers, creating the image that extraordinary accomplishments require extraordinary leaders. Leaders are quite ordinary in most human activities. It is to their own
interiorities that they come to realize what must be presented externally to those
that they lead. They come to grasp the manifestations that will externally link their
interiority to their followers' interiorities. This is the critical linkage between the
leaders and the led. Moral leadership that is centered on spiritual gain, as opposed
to physical/temporal gain, has since Homer's Hector, Plutarch's Aristides, the
Crusades' Godfrey of Bouillon, and France's Jeanne d'Arc, been the psychic well-
spring of empowerment and accomplishment in the Western world. The inner
yearnings of humans in contemporary times have not abated for leaders with these
insights, as the heroes and heroines of the silver screen and television attest.

The ancient traces of Western Homeric heroes run deep into the psyche of
contemporary culture. Whether leadership that is bureaucratic and organizational
can ever be "heroic," and satisfy such psychological cravings, remains to be seen.
The continuing call for leadership in education, commencing with the political
tract, *A Nation at Risk* released in 1983, created a national "Trojan War" for education by enciting principals and superintendents to play "a crucial leadership role in
developing school and community support for the reforms we propose" (p. 32).
The mindscape of Homeric leadership is served up as the antidote for the collapse
of the competitive economic position of the United States in the world.

The "call to arms" tone of *A Nation at Risk* is reminiscent of that of Pope Urban
II preaching the necessity for the First Crusade to wrest Christendom's capitol—
Jerusalem—from the infidel Islamic rulers in June of 1095. To date, no educational
leader like Godfrey of Bouillon has mobilized an army to lead America to its previous preimminent position in the world following World War II. Furthermore, it is
unlikely education will ever see a Godfrey of Bouillon, given the essential tasks of
providing organizational leadership in the nation's schools. A distinctive kind of
"unheroic" leadership is called for on that front. Thus, a basic mismatch is established in the mind of the public and politicians calling for leadership, and the actual tasks involved in effective school administration. The popular mindscape of leadership is both heroic and masculine. It needs emergencies and crises to put on its
"public" face and to engage in coups d'theatre. Effective day-to-day educational
administration is simply not heroic in the Homeric tradition.

William Manchester (1992) reframed this idea of heroic leadership when
speaking of the feats of Magellan. He wrote:

> The hero acts alone, without encouragement, relying solely on conviction and his own
> inner resources. Shame does not discourage him; neither does obloquy. Indifferent to
> approval, reputation, wealth, or love, he cherishes only his personal sense of honor,
> which he permits no one else to judge (p. 288).

A principal or superintendent is often alone and makes decisions on occasions
in which few are privy to the full range of facts and circumstances. There are no
galleries full of onlookers who will understand and applaud, and there is sometimes much pressure to make a popular, but poor decision. On these occasions, the
real stuff of leadership is made. In such unheroic moments, real heroism flickers.

To the outside world, it is never revealed—sealed in a silent vault of the faceless bureaucracy.

Perception Check and Applications

1. Sketching Your Favorite Hero/Heroine

Examine your own heroes or heroines. Who are they and why have you selected them? Compare them to Homeric heroes. Are they different or similar? Is it hard to imagine a hero or heroine that does not resemble Homeric ones?

2. Leadership as *Coups d'Theatre*

Accept for the moment that leadership involves certain coups d' theatre. Select your favorite hero or heroine and examine his or her life/career to determine if he or she exhibited a kind of public face along with coups d 'theatre. If he or she did, what kind of acts or symbols were utilized? If not, how did your leader's public face become known?

3. Jeanne d' Arc and the Attractive Female

Western literature and mindscapes are filled with portraits of women and their physical attributes. The physical attractiveness of women has partly been as a "sex object" to men.

Biographers of Jeanne d'Arc universally have noted that she was never even called "pretty." What does such a comment denote? In what ways is this significant or not significant in dealing with the life of Jeanne d'Arc? You may wish to review the role of women in the middle ages in Barbara Tuchman's, *A Distant Mirror* (1979, pp. 204–220).

4. Heroic Leadership in Education

Reread the 1983 "call to arms" in *A Nation at Risk* published by the National Commission on Excellence in Education. Find the parallels between Homer's *Iliad* or the Crusades to crises and the request for heroic leadership to rectify the evils of the times. Speculate on the causes as to why this message was framed in this context by the writers, and the type of response that would meet this "need."

5. The Dangers of Heroic Leadership

Heroic leadership requires that adversity be demonstrated. What kind of adversity would exist for the typical school principal or superintendent in educational administration, that would be the equivalent of classical travails? Rent the film *The Principal* starring James Belushi and Louis Gossett, Jr. (1987) and utilize it as a starting point in your analysis.

Key Chapter Concepts and Terms

consciousness as text

The idea that mindscapes or mental images are formed within human consciousness and can in turn be envisioned as a kind of "text."

coups d'theatre

The concept that leadership requires "public acts" by which leaders become known and famous. Such acts are intended to be motivational and symbolic of the leader's power to lead.

epic hero and primal battle

An examination of epic poetry, mythology, and folktales indicates that they are narratives of the human *interior,* revealing deeply felt psychic needs of the human soul. Mythology is really psychology dressed up as history and literature (Campbell, 1968 and Estes, 1992). Therefore, battles are primarily camouflaged contestations between the conscious and unconscious, libido, ego, and id.

Eurocentric history

The view that history began with the Greeks and included only white people of European ancestry. A view that ignores or diminishes the contribution of other peoples, races, and religions to the Western tradition. The Afrocentric view recenters history around the establishment of the Egyptian civilization as African—not Asian or Arabic—which predated Greek civilization.

gender exclusivity

As it pertains to the image of leadership, the concept that only men, or women who act and/or look like men, can be leaders. Defining leadership solely in terms of male roles, customs, dress, and assigned characteristics.

hero/heroine

A specific human or mythical character who engages in great deeds and valor in order to accomplish a great or worthy end. A person who engages in superhuman effort, deeds, or accomplishments against great odds. To this end, heroes require adversity and great evils in order to be compared to everyday actions. Heroes are therefore defined by the situations in which they find themselves. All heroes are contextually configured.

the mask of command

The idea that leaders have to construct a "public face"—based on accomplishments and distinctive dress and accoutrements—to extract above-average human performance from mere humans. The "face" is a mask that appeals to the interiority of the followers, but does not reveal the real interior of the leader.

mindscapes

A term used by Thomas Sergiovanni (1992) to describe an often tacitly held mental image about how things are or ought to be in the "real" world.

moral leadership

The focus of leadership that centers on ideals and values dealing with ethical principles, spiritual longings, religious revelations, or psychic needs, and that empowers rather than controls or enslaves the led. Moral leadership was recognized, notably by Plutarch, as the best motivator of leaders in antiquity.

teleology

An explanation of the past and the present in terms of the future which is created by a design of nature. A study of the evidences of nature or explanations of ends from nature.

References

Asante, M. K. (1990). *Kemet, Afrocentricity and Knowledge.* Trenton, New Jersey: Africa World Press, Inc.

Associated Press (1991, August 26). "Women hold 2.6% of top Fortune 500 Jobs." *Lexington Herald–Leader*, p. A3.

Banfield, S. (1985). *Joan of Arc.* New York: Chelsea House Publishers.

Bem, S. L. (1993). *The Lenses of Gender.* New Haven: Yale University Press.

Bernal, M. (1987). *Black Athena.* New Brunswick, New Jersey: Rutgers University Press.

Beyer, L. (1992, August 31). "Deadly Force." *Time*, 140:9, pp. 49–50.

Burns, J. M. (1979). *Leadership.* New York: Harper and Row.

Campbell, J. (1968). *The Hero with a Thousand Faces.* Princeton, New Jersey: Princeton University Press.

Cantor, N. F. (1991). *Inventing the Middle Ages.* New York: William Morrow and Company, Inc.

Cubberley, E. P. (1916). *Public School Administration.* Boston: Houghton Mifflin Company.

Davidow, L. S. (1936). *Plutarch: Lives of Illustrious Men.* Reading, Pennsylvania: The Cuneo Press, Inc.

de Grazia, S. (1989). *Machiavelli in Hell.* Princeton, NJ: Princeton University Press.

Duby, G. (1983). *The Knight, the Lady, and the Priest.* New York: Random House.

Eastwood, C. (1992, August 2). "We Need to Challenge Ourselves." *Parade*, pp. 4–5.

Estes, C. P. (1992). *Women Who Run with the Wolves.* New York: Ballantine Books.

Fagles, R., and Knox, B. (1990). *The Iliad.* New York: Penguin Books.

Freeman, L., and Bond, A. H. (1992). *America's First Woman Warrior.* New York: Paragon House.

Gadamer, H. G. (1977). *Philosophical Hermeneutics.* D. L. Linge (Trans. and Ed.). Berkeley, California: University of California Press.

Golffing, F. (1956). *Friedrich Nietzsche: The Genealogy of Morals.* New York: Anchor Doubleday.

Grebanier, B. D., Middlebrook, S., Tompson, S., and Watt, W. (1957). *English Literature and Its Backgrounds.* New York: The Dryden Press.

Grousset, R. (1970). *The Epic of the Crusades.* New York: Orion Press.

Jewett, R., and Lawrence, J. S. (1988). *The American Monomyth.* Lantham, Maryland: University Press of America.

Keegan, J. (1987). *The Mask of Command.* New York: Elisabeth Sifton Books.

Kofodimos, J. R. (1990). *Using Biographical Methods to Understand Managerial Behavior and Personality.* Greensboro, North Carolina: Center for Creative Leadership.

Lelyveid, N. (1992, August 12). "'Glass Ceiling' Remains in Place," Associated Press. *Lexington Herald–Leader,* p. B5.

Lightfoot, S. L. (1983). *The Good High School.* New York: Basic Books, Inc.

Lindeman, E. C. (1953). *Plutarch's Lives.* New York: A Mentor Book.

Luquines, F. B., and Smyt, N. A. (1952). *The Song of Roland.* New York: The Macmillan Company.

Manchester, W. (1992). *A World Lit Only by Fire.* Boston: Little Brown and Company.

Murray, G. (1924). *The Rise of the Greek Epic.* London: Oxford University Press.

National Commission on Excellence in Education (1983). *A Nation at Risk.* Washington, D.C.: United States Department of Education.

Niderost, E. (1988, December). "Peak for Moslem Tide," in *Military History,* 5:3, pp. 35–41.

Nietzsche, F. (1956). *The Genealogy of Morals.* F. Golffing, (Trans.). New York: Anchor Doubleday Books.

Rickman, H. P. (1986). *Dilthey: Selected Writings.* Cambridge, England: Cambridge University Press.

Runes, D. D. (1984). *Dictionary of Philosophy.* Totowa, New Jersey: Rowman & Allaneld.

Sackville-West, V. (1936). *Saint Joan of Arc.* New York: The Literary Guild.

Sarachek, B. (1968). "Greek Concepts of Leaders." *Academic Management Journal,* 11, pp. 39–48.

Schackleton Bailey, D. R. (1970). *Cicero.* New York: Charles Scribner's Sons.

Scott-Kilvert, I. (1960). *Plutarch: The Rise and Fall of Athens.* London, England: The Folio Society.

Sergiovanni, T. J. (1992). *Moral Leadership.* San Francisco: Jossey–Bass Publisers.

Smith, R. B. (1989, April). "Queen of Rebellion." *Military History,* 5:5, pp. 8, 61–64.

Strobridge, T. R. (1986, December). "White Rose of the Skies." *Military History,* 3:3, pp. 14–17, 61.

Tannahill, R. (1980). *Sex in History.* New York: Stein and Day Publishers.

Tschanz, D. W. (1992, July–August). "A Graver Threat than Rebel Bullets: Infectious Disease and the Union Army." *Command,* Issue 17, pp. 33–37.

Tuchman, B. W. (1979). *A Distant Mirror.* New York: Alfred A. Knopf.

Wallace, I., Wallace, A., Wallechinsky, D., and Wallace, S. (1981). *The Intimate Sex Lives of Famous People.* New York: Delacorte Press.

Whittemore, R. (1988). *Pure Lives.* Baltimore, MD: The Johns Hopkins University Press.

Wood, M. (1986). *In Search of the Trojan War.* London, England: British Broadcasting Company.

Chapter
6

SCHEMERS, POPES, AND PRINCES

Protoscientific Portraits of Leadership

159

The ancient and medieval worlds were filled with glittering personalities of saints, kings, popes, apostates, and state crafters. In the year 1469, following the climax of the Hundred Years War between France and England, an Italian statesman who would become the author of several political works that would qualify as the first protoscientific studies of administration and leadership was born.

Niccolo Machiavelli was no armchair academic, musing on the political problems of his times from the lofty confines of the medieval university. He earned his practitioner knowledge of statescraft by serving in the high court of equity in Florence, and as secretary to the Florentine Executive Council for 14 years. In this capacity he traveled on diplomatic missions to Germany, France, and the other Italian cities and states (Merriam–Webster, 1983, p. 635). Machiavelli was privy to the most intimate of political thoughts and plots of his times. As Max Lerner (1950) has noted, "He met the movers and shakers of the world" (p. xxvi). He was on hand representing Florence when France's Louis XII declared that even if he lost everything, he would not evacuate Italy and bow to Pope Julius II's efforts to reunite that fractured nation of quarrelsome city–states (Tuchman, 1984, p. 95).

Machiavelli lost his position when the Medici came to power and established a long line of powerful popes who were more interested in temporal pleasures and accomplishments than in saving souls. Some even had mistresses and illegitimate children. Machiavelli was implicated in a plot against the Medici, and was imprisoned and tortured by the rope (strappado). He finally left public service, retiring to his home to write poetry, plays, and political tracts that have endured since the Renaissance. He died in 1527.

Machiavelli was an embittered moralist, particularly in the escapades of the popes when they invited foreign troops onto Italian soil. He observed the actions of ecclesiastical officials and commented that, "the nearer people are to the Church of Rome, which is the head of our religion, the less religious are they" (Tuchman, 1984, p. 112). Another discerning eye on the affairs of Rome was a devout Catholic monk who visited the City of Saints from the German city of Erfurt in 1510. He was shocked by what he experienced there. His name was Martin Luther (Bainton, 1977, p. 41).

In Machiavelli's short 57 years on earth, he lived in a tumultuous time when wars, intrigue, shifting alliances, corruption, and brutality were repetitively displayed amid enduring artistic and literary triumphs. It was after all Pope Julius II, the same pontiff who forged alliances with the French, who took a young Michelangelo into his service to paint the Sistine Chapel in the spiritual heart of the Vatican.

THE RAUCOUS RENAISSANCE

It was during this time in Italy that the leaders of the house of Lodi were burned alive in the public square in Bologna, and in the same city an enraged husband discovered his wife had enjoyed sexual affairs with his prince and threw her alive from one of the turrets of his castle. The cuckolded spouse also murdered two of the prince's brothers. In return, the husband's entire family was butchered and sliced—men, women, and children alike—and their body pieces hung by the joints and paraded through Bologna's streets (Plumb, 1961, p. 15).

Another tale involved the Madonna of Forli, mentioned in four of Machiavelli's political works. The Madonna's husband was killed by assassins, and she and her children were taken captive by them. Unable to convince the fortress gatekeeper to open the doors to her captors, she persuaded them to free her to gain entrance. Once inside, she mounted the ramparts and spit in their faces, crying out that she would extract a sanguine revenge upon them. She then lifted her skirts and bared her genitals to prove she could conceive more children and the ones they held hostage were insignificant. The assassins were terrified and fled (de Grazia, 1989, p. 135). Machiavelli was an envoy to the Madonna's court and knew her courage well. He would also know her ultimate fate—to be bound in chains, a victim of Cesare Borgia's military triumph years later (Roeder, 1933, p. 147).

The Renaissance was a period of human history unlike many others. While great emphasis was placed on spiritual faith, at the heart of Christendom this was a facade to the decadence of the times. A new emphasis on materiality and wealth emerged, giving rise to the ambitions of greedy popes and princes. Pontiffs were power players in the seizure of cities and fielded their own armies during these times.

MACHIAVELLI: A REPUBLICAN AT HEART

Machiavelli is often criticized as a schemer, an evil brooding genius who spoke mostly of the darker side of humanity, its foibles, and avarice. He was officially blacklisted by the Church, and directly attacked by monarchs and their nobles in the seventeenth and eighteenth centuries. The reason is not hard to discern. He was of the secular world and disdained the corruption of the clergy. He was a thorough republican at heart. For a time, Florence had been a republic. He was well suited to understand this form of government's strengths and weaknesses.

The nineteenth century found Machiavelli apropos. What the Renaissance Florentine had been describing in his times was the *realpolitik* of the emergence of the modern nation–state. Machiavelli's books described the centralization of power required to create such a political entity. Max Lerner has described Machiavelli's works as **the grammar of power** (Lerner, 1950, p. xliii).

All around Machiavelli were the vices and villains of the Renaissance that liberally sprinkle his two most important works—*The Prince* and *The Discourses*. His contribution was to describe them without fanfare, foggy idealism, pomposity, or moralistic preaching. Machiavelli's contribution was the *naked realism* he brought to the topics of administration and leadership.

Machiavelli's was a discerning eye. This man who had stood before popes and princes, led military campaigns, written about the art of war, settled the peace when Florence conquered Pisa, and loved lustily in the courts into which he was sent with intellectual women, was a student of power and passion. The full spectrum of human foibles and regency were the wellsprings of his continuing education.

Machiavelli's works were important from at least two important perspectives: (1) they were the first to step back from individuals and personalities embedded in moralistic stories to try to establish generalizations or principles based upon historic data and real world experience, and (2) his viewpoint on leadership led to the creation of the modern-day office of **the executive** (Mansfield, 1989) and contemporary concepts of realpolitik. Machiavelli's Italian city–states' squabbles and sieges were to be the context in which such leaders as Germany's Frederick the Great, Bismarck, and Hitler, France's Napoleon, Cardinal Richelieu, and Clemenceau, Italy's Mussolini, and Russia's Lenin and Stalin were to be pupils who learned the grammar of power from the crafty Florentine. Max Lerner summarizes Machiavelli's influence:

> A reading of *The Discourses* should show that his thinking fathered many movements, democratic as well as dictatorial. The common meaning he has for democrats and dictators alike is that, whatever your ends, you must be clear-eyed and unsentimental in pursuit of them, and you must rest your power ultimately on a cohesive principle (1950, p. xliii).

Ironically, the contradiction in Machiavelli's works is the unadorned realism he brings to his topic, and yet these often chilling penetrations into a flesh-and-blood world are tempered with an equally burning moral outrage. Machiavelli was obsessed with the idea of *virtue,* particularly of leaders in public office (Whittemore, 1988, p. 61).

Machiavelli's intellectual world is one that is filled with evil and virtue, vice and purity, carnality and asceticism, and gentleness and ruthlessness. Machiavelli, the Christian, finds the real Christian world—especially that of the church and its clergy—disgustingly immoral and corrupt. He has negotiated with them far too much and for far too long not to know their most intimate vices. In his world-class comedy *Mandragola,* he tells his audience to be cautious about going into the confessional because "these priests are worldly wise, astute; and it is understandable, because they know both our sins and theirs" (de Grazia, 1989, p. 111).

MACHIAVELLI'S MORAL OUTRAGE

Machiavelli understood the difference between interiority and exteriority in human affairs. He once wrote, "I laugh, and my laughter is not within me; I burn, and the burning is not seen outside" (Manchester, 1992, p. 100).

Machiavelli cannot condemn without having some concept of virtue and goodness in his mind and heart. These ideas constitute his morality—his sense of right and wrong, of purpose, priorities, honor, love, charity, and appropriate action. His observations, perceptions, counsel, and caveats are laced with his indignation at the world as he found it implicitly compared to the world as it should be. This tension in Machiavelli is central to understanding his works. He is telling the reader "like it is," all the while wishing it wasn't that way at all. He admires Saints Francis and Dominic. He honors Peter and David because they choose to confess directly to God without going through the clergy. He draws upon the Scriptures, particular sections of Samuel, Paraleipomenon, Luke, and the Psalms in formulating *The Prince* (de Grazia, 1989, p. 111). This was a man who knew his Bible well. While Niccolo Machiavelli has been identified as the supreme evil—particularly as personified in Shakespeare's Iago in *Othello*—in real life Machiavelli's morality is what provides the sting to his observations, the irony to his advice, the compassion to his temperment, and the idealism to his humanity. Far from being the "objective" scientist of the worst and best of his times, he worked hard to shed his illusions, to see the world as he swam in it, and to dispense advice accordingly. But this advice was always wrapped in the context of his persona, his religious and moral beliefs, his patriotism, and his times.

Machiavelli's morality was anchored in the idea that most men were inherently evil. Good men were few and hard to find. Good men had to pay attention to evil since the majority of men were enamored with it.

THE PREDICAMENT OF LEADERSHIP: THE PEOPLE ARE FICKLE

The predicament of leadership for Machiavelli was to be found in his Republicanism, which held forth that the people were the final arbiters of whether a leader was good or not. Yet the people were mostly corrupt themselves. Despite the commonality of evil among the people, and their propensity to engage in it, they could recognize the goodness in a leader. Such qualities were used by the people as an *image of conduct*—a standard by which a leader is measured and judged by them. This meant that the people carry in their minds principles of right and wrong. The qualities that the people thought important in Machiavelli's morality were: *compassion, word keeping, sincerity, humaneness,* and *piety* (de Grazia, 1989, p. 294).

The standards of judging adequate leadership were, according to our Florentine secretary, to be found in the people, not in law, Scripture, or Canon. The people, however, while capable of recognizing these qualities, were most often not possessing of them in any great abundance.

The leader was therefore confronted with a dilemma if he was to step in front of the people and try to point them in a direction based on their image of him or his own inner beliefs that assumed these were usually compatible. What if these were not compatible? What if the truth simply did not fit the situation? (There were plenty of times in Machiavelli's career when leaders and their peoples were interested primarily in greed, vice, destruction, sloth, pride, cruelty, deceit, and word breaking). What if the situation required one or more of these?

In *The Prince*, Machiavelli contrasted this position as follows by suggesting that:

> A man who wishes to make a profession of goodness in everything must necessarily come to grief among so many who are not good. Therefore it is necessary for a prince, who wishes to maintain himself, to learn how not to be good, and to use this knowledge and not use it, according to the necessity of the case (p. 56).

The discontinuities between the "image" of the leader and the people's own weaknesses were readily apparent to Machiavelli. He had witnessed how the people turned on their leaders when their vices and self-interests prevailed and drove them from office. The idealism of the people was always sacrificed to their short-range needs and vices. Their leadership requirements for an office holder were always compromised.

THE LEADER'S STRATEGIC RUSE: THE MASK OF VIRTUE FOR THE COMMON GOOD

In resolving this dilemma, Machiavelli turned to a higher principle—**the common good** (de Grazia, 1989, p. 307). This concept consisted of creating a desired condition to which and by which all other acts could be judged moral or immoral. The common good was the preservation of the state and the continuation of a unified and faithful people.

In formulating this "higher principle," Machiavelli could then contextualize any single leadership act. For example, the case of fraud. Fraud was, in the abstract, the mark of an evil and dishonest leader. Yet in war, fraud is considered a virtue, particularly if it results in victory.

Machiavelli's notation has been underscored in most wars where leaders attempt not only to deceive the enemy, but to deceive their own people as well. In the recent Persian Gulf War, the Bush administration repeatedly denied reports that they were trying to kill the Iraqi leader, Saddam Hussein, even when two specially designed bombs were dropped on a command bunker believed to be housing him. *U.S. News and World Report* (1992) commented:

> The taxpayers who bore the burden of the cost of Desert Storm were told of virtually none of the battles of the war, where they were fought, or how tough they were (p. 413).

That same source commented on the fraud of the Bush administration in going to the United Nations to circumvent having to deal with Congress over the war. This move was designed to put a damper on the domestic political problems the war would have caused, while cloaking it in a call for strengthening the powers of the United Nations. In fact, "the Bush administration's reliance on the United Nations has been highly selective" (p. 414).

The dissonance between the qualities of the leader and those desired or sacrificed by the leader's people require the development of a mask, something de Grazia (1989) has called "the rhetoric of imposture" (p. 295). In Machiavelli's own words:

> It is not, therefore, necessary for a prince to have all the above-named qualities, but it is very necessary to seem to have them. I would even be bold to say that to possess them and always observe them is dangerous, but to appear to possess them is useful (Machiavelli, *The Prince,* 1950, p. 65).

Men are easily deceived because they believe what they see. Machiavelli warns that men judge more by their eyes than their hands, "for every one can see, but very few have to feel. Everybody sees what you appear to be, few feel what you are, and those few will not dare to oppose themselves to the many" *(The Prince,* 1950, pp. 65–66).

It is because the people are so gullible, so apt to be swayed by appearances, so driven by their immediate short-term ends, that leaders must don a mask and espouse the five virtues: mercy, faith, integrity, humanity, and religion. But the leaders themselves must understand that these virtues are a mask, and that competent statescrafting involves acts which transgress the same virtues, committed for the common good.

Machiavelli therefore envisions the acts of leadership as neither good nor bad per se, but whether or not they were put to good use. The norm of "good use" is whether or not the leader is able to maintain the state, and maintain a well and unified people.

By these same standards, Machiavelli would most certainly have frowned on John F. Kennedy's deliberate lie about his health when running for president of the United States. He declared that he was "the healthiest candidate for president in the country" (Altman, 1992, p. C12). Kennedy denied that he had ever suffered from Addison's disease, when he had been taking the adrenal hormone cortison to combat its effects for a long time.

The President's brother—Robert Kennedy—publicly declared that his brother John "does not now nor has he ever had an ailment described classically as Addison's disease." The statement was duplicitous in that it hung on the words "described classically," since Addison believed the adrenal glands were destroyed by tuberculosis. After the Kennedy assassination, the family objected to an autopsy since it would have disclosed what medical experts later found, that "no adrenal tissue could be found at Kennedy's autopsy and that his body showed the effects of long term hormonal replacement therapy" (Altman, 1992, p. C12). If Kennedy had disclosed his ailment he might have lost a close election to Richard M. Nixon at the time.

What Machiavelli's works broached was the dilemma that absolute moral principles, or any absolute principles for that matter, must be considered but be flexible tools in the arsenal of the able leader in order to keep her or his eyes on the end. Such means are never in themselves absolute or inflexible. This is a kind of tangled and tortured morality, but it was the world Machiavelli inhabited. Sometimes the lamb had to become a lion in order to survive. Survival is the ultimate end. It is to this end that Machiavelli inverted the so-called Golden Rule, expressed by Jesus in Matthew 7:12, "Do unto others as you would have them do unto you." Machiavelli stripped this idea of its adornment and ideal; i.e., treating others as your ideal of how you would wish to be treated would frame the guidelines for their behavior. In this parable, the imagery of a standard is imposed by the one to receive the treatment on the person giving it.

Machiavelli eschewed such idealism as clouding the eyes of students of the real. In transmitting *The Prince* (1950) to Lorenzo the Magnificent he confessed:

> I have not sought to adorn my work with long phrases or high sounding words or any of those superficial attractions and ornaments with which writers seek to embellish their material (pp. 3–4).

The Renaissance Florentine changed the Golden Rule in statescraft to "Do unto others before they do unto you" (see de Grazia, 1989, p. 299). In this transposition, Machiavelli leaves out the idealistic imposition of behavioral guidelines of how a person would wish to be treated, focusing on how he or she would most likely treat them were they in a position of authority.

This Machiavellian twist of the Golden Rule was used in modern times by none other than Winston Churchill when he rose on August 16, 1945, in the House of Commons to defend the decision to drop the atomic bomb on Japan.

In response to critics who charged that the bomb should not have been used against the Japanese (do unto others as you would have them do unto you) he argued, "Six years of total war have convinced most people that had the Germans or Japanese discovered this new weapon, they would have used it upon us to our complete destruction with the utmost alacrity" (Cannadine, 1989, p. 281) (do unto others as they would do unto you). Machiavelli turns his moral code on the idea that one must first take actions against one's enemies before they would harm you. The harm you do to them is simply what they would have done to you had they been able to do it (de Grazia, 1989, p. 301).

Machiavelli also mused on whether it is better to be loved or feared by one's people. He chose feared. His reasoning is rooted in his observations of the strife and wars to which he was privy. If a leader is loved, observed Machiavelli, when inconveniences arise, the people will be quick to compromise their obligations because they will act in their own self-interests. On the other hand if the leader is feared, people who are afraid of punishment are more apt to be reliable in times of stress. Love does not provide the same bonds as fear, at least in civic matters. Machiavelli's data were everywhere around him. Like an umpire at a baseball game, he simply called the pitches as he saw them. The modern reader is confronted with the question, "Are the people really that unreliable and selfish?"

Consider an educational example reported by a superintendent of schools in Louisiana, Ronald Perry, reported in the September 23, 1992, issue of *Education Week*. Superintendent Perry came from Pennsylvania into a school system that was functioning on a deficit budget. School personnel had functioned on salary reductions. The entire system had burned up a $10 million dollar surplus in four years.

With community help, Superintendent Perry passed a property-tax hike and an increase in the sales tax. He went outside the school system to contract for maintenance and operations, which resulted in a 32 percent savings the first year and 4 percent reduction in utilities.

Within three years these policies had accrued an $8 million dollar surplus, despite the fact that salary improvements averaging 52 percent were provided to all personnel and the size of the staff was increased by 5 percent.

Working on achievement, Superintendent Perry increased pupil attendance to between 97 and 98 percent, reduced dropouts by 75 percent (the lowest in the state), and raised achievement test scores. The school district was recognized as a "beacon light" by the governor and state superintendent.

The membership of the board changed, however, and with it came a different set of priorities. When at last the board began to undo the policies that resulted in these remarkable improvements, the superintendent could see that his contract would not be renewed so he resigned to take a professorship at a college. At the last tally, district revenues had increased by 17 percent, but the system was again running a deficit of $2.3 million dollars. Superintendent Perry concluded his chronicle by quoting John Dewey, "Familiarity breeds contempt" (*Education Week*, p. 36). He could have just as well quoted Machiavelli who spent some time observing the delusions of the people of his times, and who noted in *The Discourses* (1950):

> first, that the people often, deceived by an elusive good, desire their own ruin, and unless they are made sensible of the evil of the one and the benefit of the other course by some one in whom they have confidence, they will expose the republic to infinite peril and damage. And if it happens that the people have no confidence in any one, as sometimes will be the case when they have been deceived before by events or men, then it will inevitably lead to the ruin of the state (p. 247).

Machiavelli was also aware of the priest reformer Savonarola, ruler of Florence, who was finally hung and burned at the stake, and observed, "it is easy to persuade them [the people] of a thing, but it is difficult to keep them in that persuasion" (de Grazia, 1989, p. 296).

STANDARDS OF DETERMINING MORAL LEADERSHIP

Machiavelli used two standards in determining the morality of leadership. First, it was necessary to form some concept of a person's most private thoughts to grasp his or her intent or purpose. Second, it was requisite to have some record of their actions. Working between the two (Machiavelli was a student of history and read voraciously), it was possible to appraise the morality of leadership.

Machiavelli thus formed a context for judging leadership. By reading history, he developed a longer view of context than the immediate. He also sought to extrapolate lessons from history because he did believe history repeated itself, or at least was similar through time because "all peoples are and ever have been animated by the same desires and the same passions" (*The Discourses*, 1950, p. 216). Without this critical assumption, writing a book that included both observation and advice would be *absurd*. Without similarities or patterns, advice, as well as education, is useless and much of the motivation to study history would be erased.

With the idea that events are similar, Machiavelli examined the actions of a leader in context by seeking to understand what the leader believed he or she was doing and thus finding the key to that person's perceptions. In this, he emulated Theseus, who penetrated the secret of the ancient Cretan labyrinth, slew the Minotaur lurking there, and extricated himself from the impenetrable maze with a thread.

In his times, the thread that was Machiavelli's method for unlocking human motivation and action was the criterion of "well used," as it related to attaining the ultimate aim of the common good. These were really multiple criteria, and data were derived from a variety of sources and interwoven into a description or narrative which formed the base for *The Prince* and *The Discourses*. Machiavelli's methods, however, were those of the playwright. Machiavelli wrote an exceptional comedy of human foibles—*Mandragola.* In a play, the author simply provides characters and voices to a narrative or story that illustrates her or his understanding of events. Characters often assume positions of varying points of view within a discourse. Characters and themes are laced together within a sequence of temporal events in order to reveal the outcomes and consequences of human thought and action. A play's audience comes to conclusions about the characters based on what the characters say and then do. An audience uses the same data base as Machiavelli employed. Statescraft involves acting, ritual, and pomp (the visible), as well as intrigue, spying, contrivance, deceit, and fraud (the invisible). The only difference between a play and the real thing is that a play is the contrivance of the playwright. The world represents multiple contrivances. Machiavelli was a great sifter of contrivances. His genius was being able to gather a great deal of information of all different kinds, get a bead on the characters, the plots, the motivations, and the aspirations of the principal parties, and piece together courses of actions, probabilities, and potentialities. It is within this stream that he learned to forge well by understanding the human currents of the world, the obvious qualities of the surface of the water, and the deeper streams pursing below.

Machiavelli used the river analogy to explain whether he believed human choice mattered at all. He confessed in *The Prince* that he believed humans were simply swept up by events beyond their control at times. In more reflective moods, however, Machiavelli said that fortune or God, whatever one chose to call it, designed events and determined all things. This view would be *determinism,* i.e., the idea that all facts can eventually be related to laws that govern actions and events. Like so many before and after him, Machiavelli was revolted at the idea; he said, "Nevertheless, that our free will may not be altogether extinguished, I think it may be true that fortune is the ruler of half our actions, but that she allows the other half or thereabouts to be governed by us" *(The Prince,* 1950, p. 91).

Fortune was like a river, mused Machiavelli. Sometimes the river was wild and raging, sweeping all in front of it after torrential rains. At this particular time, the river devastated all that stood in its way. Yet at other times, by constructing dykes, dams, canals, and waterways, people could direct the river's different levels and keep it within boundaries. In this respect, the world was *indeterministic,* i.e., responsive to human will and choice. Morality requires choice. Humans cannot be moral if they have no choices. Morality exists when men and women can choose between good and evil. Moral codes exist on the presumption of some free will.

PORTRAITS OF PRINCES: THE MODERN MACHIAVELLI

Machiavelli is very modern. All one has to do is to substitute the word *leader* for *prince,* and the Renaissance man is reborn as a prophet in our own times. Take the case of a world villain such as Saddam Hussein of Iraq. As the nations of the world grappled with Saddam's moving of military forces to the Kuwaiti borders in September of 1990, the Western military powers struggled to understand this complex leader. Instead of Machiavelli's sharp eye, judgment of character, and personal observation of an opponent in his own court, the Central Intelligence Agency commissioned several psychological profiles to be developed on the Iraqi leader. The Israelis also developed one (see *U.S. News and World Report,* 1992, p. 151). A psychological profile represents an attempt to gain access to the inner person who is making decisions. The **interiority** of a person is essential to understanding perception and motivation. Then behaviors and actions can be judged not only by external standards imposed by the observers, but also by an understanding of what the leader thinks he or she is accomplishing, and by how the leader has responded in similar past events.

In *The Prince,* Machiavelli writes about those leaders who attain their positions by villainy. He discusses two examples—Agathocles of Sicily and Oliverotto da Fermo. Both men rose to power by deceit in which they gathered together their political enemies and had them killed.

Saddam Hussein employed the same ruse more than once. Machiavelli presented the consequences of attaining office by such methods. In Agathocles' case, Machiavelli observes, "It cannot be called a virtue to kill one's fellow citizens, betray one's friends, be without faith, without pity, and without religion; by these methods one may indeed gain power, but not glory" (p. 32).

In the case of Oliverotto da Fermo, Machiavelli noted that he had been strangled by Cesare Borgia by deceit. Both men lived under the constant threat of overthrow because of their atrocities. Machiavelli noted that if atrocities are to be used, they should occur *all at once* and not be repeated again. "Whoever acts otherwise, either through timidity or bad counsels, is always obliged to stand with knife in hand, and can never depend on his subjects, because they, owing to continually fresh injuries, are unable to depend on him" (p. 35).

Strobe Talbot (1992) of *Time* magazine observed that Saddam Hussein still ruled by fear in Iraq, or in Machiavelli's words, "with knife in hand," and that his subjects were uneasy and restless. The prospects of a coup were increasing against the leader's life (p. 49). One of the longest chapters in *The Discourses* concerns the nature of conspiracies. Machiavelli treated the subject with the full powers of his reading of history and his experience in world affairs.

As the United States learned in the case of Saddam Hussein, conspiracies most often fail. Machiavelli warns that for a leader (prince) there is no greater misfortune than to have a conspiracy formed against him. If the conspiracy succeeds, the leader is killed. If it is crushed, the leader is dishonored. It is, in modern jargon, a "lose–lose" situation.

Conspirators have to be on the same plane or nearly so as the leader, warns Machiavelli. The simple reason is that they must have access to the leader without suspicions being aroused. He notes from history that Philip of Macedon was assassinated by a person of near equal rank—Pausanias—when he was surrounded by a thousand armed soldiers. Assassins are also those who have been so rewarded by their leader that they have nothing other than the office of the leader itself to which to aspire. Machiavelli warns:

A prince, then, who wishes to guard against conspiracies should fear those on whom he has heaped benefits quite as much, even more than those whom he as wronged (p. 415).

There are several motives for conspirators. Revenge is a powerful motive, says Machiavelli, and men who have had their possessions taken, their honor transgressed, or even more powerful—the honor of their wives violated—constitute a likely band of potential malcontents.

The other motive for conspirators is their love of country, and their desire to rid it of a tyrant. Machiavelli observes that this is the most important motive of all for assassination, "his [the leader] being hated by the mass of the people" (p. 411).

Then, as now, Machiavelli shows that conspiracies are most often foiled in the initial stages. If the planners exceed three or four persons, the odds are greatly enhanced that the plot will become known through "treason, imprudence or carelessness" (*The Discourses,* 1950, p. 418). In order to ensure success and not to court perfidy "is not to afford your associates in the plot any time to betray you; and therefore you should confide your project to them at the moment of its execution, and not sooner" (*The Discourses,* 1950, p. 418).

In warning leaders about conspirators, Machiavelli advises them not to threaten their subjects. If the leader has his subjects executed, plots die with them and they cannot return from their graves to carry them out. But threats work against the leader issuing them by providing people with an "alternative of having either to destroy you or perish themselves" (*The Discourses,* 1950, p. 423). Such threats are counterproductive.

So, Saddam Hussein continues in office as of the writing of this book. He has put down many conspiracies—the latest being in September of 1992, when he executed a hero of the 1980–1988 war with Iran—Major General Abdul Wahid Shanan al-Rabat, and 30 other military officers who were believed to be organizing political opposition to the Iraqi leader (Associated Press, October 4).

THE CONTEMPORANEITY OF MAKING WAR

"The chief foundation of all states, whether new, old, or mixed, are good laws and good arms," observed Machiavelli (*The Prince,* 1950, p. 44). A leader defends his possessions with his own army or with mercenaries. Mercenaries were to be avoided because a leader using them "will never stand firm or sure, as they [mercenaries] are disunited, ambitious, without discipline, faithless, bold amongst friends, cowardly amongst enemies, they have no fear of God, and keep no faith with men" (p. 45). Machiavelli concluded that "no prince is secure without his own troops" (*The Prince,* 1950, p. 52).

Niccolo Machiavelli's early works saw the publication of a book called *The Art of War.* Machiavelli was heavily involved with military affairs. He raised and trained troops, planned and executed field military maneuvers, and had intimate knowledge of weapons and tactics. He was a strong advocate of the use of native militia as troops, advising that "the best armies that there are are those of armed populations [native citizens] . . . [nothing] can stand in their way except armies similar to them" (de Grazia, 1989, p. 383). Machiavelli's insistence on infantry rather than cavalry and a politically active army of native citizens was the doctrine followed in the formation of the People's Army of Vietnam (PAVN).

PAVN followed Machiavelli's concept that citizen soldiers were the most formidable force against invaders. In addition, PAVN used citizens as spies, porters, laborers, and recruiters. The doctrine of PAVN was centered in their concept of *Dau Tran,* which meant that war meant a total struggle for the entire nation together with a "complete commitment of moral and material resources, which together creates the higher spirit necessary for ultimate victory" (Miranda, 1992, p. 19). It was this principle that formed the will and political longevity to defeat the French, United States, and Red Chinese armies in successive battles. In the 1990s, PAVN is still considered by military experts to be "the most potent military force in Southwest Asia" (Miranda, 1992, p. 19).

THE OFFICE OF THE EXECUTIVE

As Florentine Secretary, Machiavelli practiced some of the duties embodied in today's executive. In fact, a prince was an executive in Renaissance contextual terms. Distinguished national scholar Harvey C. Mansfield, Jr., of Harvard (1989) attributes the formation of the modern executive or *esecuzione* to Machiavelli.

The foundations of this role—now nearly universal in every country on earth—are rooted in law. But law alone cannot compel men to be good because men are evil by nature. In *The Discourses* Machiavelli (1950) writes, "Men act right only upon compulsion; but from the moment that they have the option and liberty to commit wrong with impunity, then they never fail to carry confusion and disorder everywhere" (pp. 117–118).

Machiavelli, avers Mansfield, appropriated the Christian concept of "God's will" to the executive to perform retributive deeds with force. In this public display of force, the laws are given credibility because men will not obey unless they are fearful. Thus, behind all laws lies a special kind of "extra" legal persuasion provided by force, or the threat of force to compel obedience to the law itself. It is the power of execution that is compelling, and the capability to do it swiftly in a surprise move that lies behind executive power.

There is a strange paradox involved in formulating "good" laws. The perceived force of the executive must be capable of going beyond the law to execute it. This power is vested in surprise. We use words like *decisive* and *energetic* to capture the spirit of suddenness in an effective executive's actions (Mansfield, 1989, p. 142). Suddenness requires secrecy or there is no surprise. "Executive session" means "without the public present" in nearly all school board meetings. So secrecy is part of effective executive action. An effective "executive secretary" is one who acts in secret. *Secret* is the base word for *secretary* (Mansfield, 1989, p. 145).

The effective executive is *uno solo,* alone and taking the power unto himself or herself; he or she is responsible not to some principle, but to the outcomes or effects of his or her actions. The idea is to work back from effects to the actions taken by the executive functioning alone (Mansfield, 1989, p. 148). It is to Machiavelli that executive accountability, power, extra-legal authority, decisiveness, and fear can be attributed. The modern corporation president, superintendent of schools, hospital executive director, university president, governmental agency, and bureau director are simply Renaissance princes in contemporary dress. They all owe their offices to the insights, ruminations, cogitations, frustrations, and career of an extraordinary fifteenth-century Florentine secretary. Moral leadership requires immoral, or extra-moral, actions by one person. What Machiavelli understood was that behind every successful executive is the shadow of a tyrant. This idea was firmly grasped by Lincoln who, when polling his cabinet on an issue, asked for all of the ayes and raised his hand. Virtually everyone else said "nay." Observed Lincoln, "the ayes have it" (see also Wills, 1992).

Machiavelli's basic belief in the evil spread among the majority of men, and the observation that in order for the prince to do good he must be cautious, even duplicitous, is reflected in the imbalance between the powers of the executive found in governmental/corporate life, and the desire of others to be included as partners in the developmental decision process. While few understand why this power imbalance is present, it is certainly felt, and in some cases, is resented. It remains to be seen whether executives can continue to be solely accountable when their capability to act decisively and alone has been compromised in such ideas as site-based management, parents as partners, teacher councils, and the like. Without the possibility of surprise and secrecy, it is doubtful that executive action can be decisive. It is much more apt to be perceived as plodding and uninspiring, and it is unlikely that those who do the criticizing understand the real reasons for the perceptions, i.e., that the *esecuzione* has been recast into a bureaucrat (English, 1992).

Niccolo Machiavelli's works were directly blacklisted by Pope Paul IV and the Church sometime after his death in 1557, even though the Church used Machiavellian arguments to justify its excursions and massacres in conducting religious wars (Lerner, 1950, p. xxxix).

Machiavellianism particularly intrigued Tudor England, where there are some 400 references in Elizabethan literature to the Florentine secretary's works (Lerner, 1950, p. xxxix). Yet the paradox is that few Englishmen ever read Machiavelli. Instead, they read about him through a French book that attacked him—Gentillet's *Anti-Machiavel*. *The Prince* was not translated into English until 1640—some 36 years after the supreme Machiavellian figure (or so it seemed to the English) had come across Shakespeare's Globe Theatre in *Othello* in the human form of Iago. Since Shakespeare died in 1616, he only knew of Machiavelli by way of Gentillet's criticism of him.

THE GREAT BARD AND PORTRAITS OF LEADERSHIP

Iago, one of the three central characters in Shakespeare's *Othello* (written in 1604), is the bard's re-creation of Machiavelli. *Othello* is a complex play. It consists of the tensions, doubt, love, sex, race, and tragedy between a white Italian woman, Desdemona; her lover, husband, and commanding general of the armies of Venice, Othello, who is African; and Iago, Othello's ensign in his command.

Othello is a great general and is highly respected. Yet, because of his racial and cultural differences, he is isolated from the larger, white, Venetian society. Despite the respect the Venetians owe him, they frown upon his marriage to a lovely, white

Venetian woman. The black–white, male–female connection represents one of the most continuing sexual and racially inflammatory issues of our time. The threat to white men posed by black men who covet their women is a continuing undercurrent in Southern American culture, the principle cause of the practice of lynching, and the rise of the Ku Klux Klan who practiced it. At least a third of all lynchings in the South were motivated by suspicions of rape (Hair, 1989, p. 175).

So Shakespeare is exploiting not only psychological but also sexual antagonisms in *Othello*. The deadly triumvirate in the play revolves around Iago's playing on Othello's fears that Desdemona has been sexually unfaithful to him with his lieutenant, Cassio. Iago continually, and increasingly aggressively, exploits his general's inner fears that he has become a cuckold, resulting in Othello murdering the woman he loves.

Iago is evil incarnate. Critics over the years have been unable to fathom his motivations, his baseness, his diabolical destructiveness. Shakespeare has elevated Iago to a kind of supreme Machiavellian superdevil who takes on metaphysical properties of pure embodied evil (Rackin, 1978, p. 71). Iago is the schemer—a convinced cynic—a despiser of happiness and idealism in any form. The frequent animal metaphors in his lines lead one to speculate that he really sees nothing but animal lust and depravity in the world. He tells Desdemona's father of what the wedding night was like between his daughter and Othello in the lines, "Even now, now, very now, an old black ram is tupping [copulating with] your white ewe." Later, Iago says, "I never found man that knew how to live himself. Ere I would say, I would drown myself for the love of a guinea hen [promiscuous female], I would change my humanity with a baboon" (Rowse, 1988, p. 1823).

Walker and Wilson (1960) quote a passage by Lytton Strachey that Shakespeare faced a dilemma with the three characters. If Iago had secretly loved Desdemona himself, then the audience would feel some sympathy for him. This would reduce the focus on Othello and his weaknesses, and prevent the enormity of the tragedy. To maintain great empathy with Othello, to elevate the suspense and prevent the cloaking of the irony of good being twisted by evil, Shakespeare gave Iago no motive at all. Iago has no interest in sex himself. He is unhappily married. He is a practiced malcontent. Shakespeare's Iago is conceived as demonic, and the horror that unfolds is perceived by the audience as "purposeless, profound, and terrible" (p. xxx).

Shakespeare's plumbing the depths of human interiority accounts for his greatness. He explored the most inner motivations and actions in the leaders he portrayed on his stage. Grebanier, Middlebrook, Thompson, and Watt (1957) noted that, "Not even the most 'modern' of psychological novelists has been gifted with Shakespeare's insight into the workings of the human spirit" (p. 471).

Shakespeare was not university educated, but was firmly grounded in Latin and Greek authors—among them Homer, Aristotle, Seneca, and Plutarch. He also was well-read in the Italians—notably Boccaccio, Petrarch, and Cinthio (Giraldi), the latter providing him the source material for *Measure for Measure* and *Othello*. The structure of Shakespeare's early plays also matched Greek and Roman models (Rackin, 1978, p. 11). Shakespeare appears to have taken the Greek concept of

hamartia to heart. This idea means something like "the tragic flaw" of great people (Rackin, 1978, p. 48). So many of his leaders exhibited hamartia: Hamlet, King Lear, Othello, Macbeth, Julius Caesar, Antony and Cleopatra, and Coriolanus.

AN EXPOSÉ OF EVIL: THE TRIAL OF KING LEAR

Perhaps the Shakespearian play that Niccolo Machiavelli would have most appreciated is the Bard's greatest tragedy, *King Lear*. In this drama, Lear is literally blinded, but he has been blind all along. In his bumbling, he acts kindly to deceivers and betrayers, and humiliates and banishes those who love him the most. He systematically destroys good in the world for very rational reasons. In the end, he awakes to his terrible decisions and faces what he has done.

King Lear pays a steep price for his hamartia—his character flaw. He drives his only daughter who loves him, Cordelia, away in a fit over whether she would love him above all others. When she professes her love, but says that half of it would be to her husband, Lear compares her to her sisters who have falsely sworn they love only Lear. Lear banishes his only true servant—the Earl of Kent—who nonetheless comes back in disguise to continue to serve his blind monarchical master.

Slowly, Lear comes to comprehend the disaster he has created. He recognizes the falsity of social rank as it is expressed in clothes, so much so that near the end of the play he strips away his own clothing to stark nakedness, finally proclaiming, "A man may see how this world goes with no eyes" (Rowse, 1988, p. 1933). Lear's realization was that the falsity of images clothes present is now seen by the blind king, "Robes and furr'd gowns hide all."

Throughout the play, Lear probes the meaning of life and the mysteries it presents: "When we are born, we cry that we have come to this great stage of fools," he muses (Rowse, 1988, p. 1933). Later, when he learns of the demise of his only true daughter, Cordelia, he confronts the finality of death:

Had I tongues and eyes, I'd use them so
That heaven's vault should crack. She's gone
for ever!
I know when one is dead, and when one lives,
She's dead as earth (Rowse, 1988, p. 1946).

In the face of folly and the unrelenting envelopment of death, Lear compares human life to other forms: "Why should a dog, a horse, a rat have life, And thou [Cordelia] no breath at all? Thou'lt come no more, never, never, never, never, never" (Rowse, 1988, p. 1947).

Many themes criss-cross this tragedy: loyalty and disloyalty, and loyalty that is disloyalty and disloyalty that is loyalty; two views of nature as either brutal and unrelenting, or as gentleness and the higher arts unique to humankind; fashion and foppery compared to simplicity and honesty; measurement and rationality versus intuition and paradoxical honesty (Rackin, 1978, pp. 86–106). Against these themes stands the ultimate totality of death, "never, never, never, never, never" to return to life again.

Shakespeare was a conventional thinker. His morals were conventional. Most likely he was Catholic (Harrison, 1948, p. 6). His genius was his universality and his gift for expression within a morality that did not make judgments, except within the plots and twists of his characters who were identifiable to Elizabethans and their times. In his holding up the mirror of life to his audiences, he reflected their feelings, aspirations, outrages, sentiments, and vices in such a broad manner as to still be relevant over 300 years later, despite the fact that the language expressions of the Elizabethans require ever greater notation to understand the bard.

What Shakespeare brought to a study of leadership were the following concepts:

1. Leadership Is a Moral Act and Represents Choices in Situ.

Any judgment of leadership involves reviewing a leader's choices in context, not out of context. Loyalty may be a good thing, but sometimes a loyal subordinate can give colored advice because of his or her own sentiments which are not helpful in determining a proper course of action. Shakespeare, like Plutarch, relied on the position of Aristotle on morality when the philosopher said, "Character is that which reveals moral purpose, showing the kinds of things a man chooses or avoids" (Whittemore, 1988, p. 97).

2. Morality Requires a Center or an Anchor.

Moral acts require some centering of values. Such centerings represent the masts of ships with sails against the decisions that are made about direction. Such centerings may be deistic or atheistic, but require differentiation and coherence to guide choices. Morality is more than one choice, but infinite choices do not quantitatively qualify, singly or in sum, as moral or immoral.

3. Choice Involves Discrimination and Boundaries.

Choice occurs within boundaries and can only exist where there are alternatives. These alternatives stand between boundaries. On a short-term basis, the boundaries may represent something quite mundane, to court solvency or insolvency in financial decisions. On a broader scale, the choices may invoke a larger dimension of life and life hereafter, between Heaven or Hell, good or evil, peace or damnation. Whatever the case may be, the matter is characterized as greater in magnitude than the immediate.

4. Choice Involves Judgment, Which Is a Matter of Studying Human Interiority.

Leadership emanates from the human interior and sometimes manifests itself externally. Leadership is first and foremost the study of the human interior—the mind, perceptions, beliefs, motivations, aspirations, fears, and weaknesses of those who make decisions. Observation (of externalities) must be wedded to understandings of purpose (internalities) in order to comprehend the nature of leadership. Action must be attached to intent in context in order to grasp the act of leadership. We must not only understand *what,* but *why.*

5.   Moral Decisions Are Determined by Their Consequences.

Decisions cannot be moral in the abstract or in advance. Moral decisions are those that can only be judged by their results. Results can be determined both on the short-term basis and on the longer term. Favorable results "match" the values held in the "centering" process. Moral decisions possess an externality at this point. They are capable of being judged by others compared to the standards or values held by the leader, or by those the leader is alleged to represent, and by the leader himself or herself and his or her own interior value clusters. On occasion these may not match—i.e., a leader may act upon his or her own values that may appear contradictory to observers. Only time can provide the ultimate contextual claimer or disclaimer as to whether or not leadership is effective—i.e., desired results were obtained.

Questions regarding morality are timeless. Therefore, they always remain modern. John Wareham (1991), an internationally known executive headhunter, indicated how a leader might come to better understand people. He explained that a leader should read great plays and novels. "For, becoming a good judge of people entails being able to feel what they feel—and the writer's art is to evoke these very emotions in you. Shakespeare was onto the ideas Sigmund Freud made famous long before the Viennese professor himself" (p. 222). Wareham notes that becoming analytical about people requires perusing material that involves judgment. Morality is the heart of judgment.

MARTIN LUTHER: PORTRAIT OF AN APOSTLE OR APOSTATE?

History has recorded few individual consciences that have been as troubled as Martin Luther's. This diminutive Augustinian monk and son of a miner was the ideal catholic friar. Devout, pious, contrite, and humble, he rose to challenge the authority of the pope and the Roman Catholic establishment over a matter of conscience. His was the true story of interiority which could not be salved by tradition. Luther searched directly for God through the Holy Scriptures. He refused to be quieted by authority, fear, retribution, or excommunication.

During Martin Luther's examination at Worms before the German Diet, when his entire faith was on trial, he was asked pointedly by Johann von der Ecken, a representative of the Archbishop of Trier:

How can you assume that you are the only one to understand the sense of scripture? Would you put your judgment above that of so many famous men and claim that you know more than they all?

Luther's audacity in challenging 1000 years of Roman Catholic authority and tradition individually was simply an example of what every Protestant faith professes:

Unless I am convinced by Scripture and plain reason—I do not accept the authority of popes and councils . . . my conscience is captive to the Word of God. I cannot and I will not recant anything, for to go against conscience is neither right nor safe (Bainton, 1977, p. 144).

This response, as the Roman Church fully understood, was the defense of virtually every heretic it ever prosecuted, some of whom it later canonized.

Martin Luther's leadership was the result of an intense internal conflict. As an Augustinian friar, Luther was the model Catholic monk. The thing that set him apart from his fellow monks was his passion to be at peace with God. Luther pursued every traditional Church avenue and remedy possible in this endeavor. In performing his first Mass, he was suddenly paralyzed by the thought that he was in Communion with the Divine Majesty. "And shall I, a miserable little pygmy say 'I want this, I ask for that'? For I am dust and ashes and full of sin and I am speaking to the living, eternal and the true God" (Bainton, 1977, p. 30).

Luther never believed that he was good enough, holy enough, or contrite and humble enough to face God directly. His regimen in the monastery never provided the inner peace he sought. He confessed so often and with such intensity that his confessor once exclaimed, "If you expect Christ to forgive you, come in with something to forgive—parricide, blasphemy, adultery—instead of all these peccadilloes" (Bainton, 1977, p. 41).

Luther was trapped in a logical paradox regarding confession. In order to be forgiven, sins had to be confessed. Sometimes a human cannot recognize or remember all of his or her sins. If they cannot be remembered or recognized, they cannot be confessed, and hence a sinner cannot be forgiven. Luther could find no way out of this dilemma. His confessions searched his childhood for every nook and cranny of fault, and still he lay awake at night probing for clues in his memory of sins he had committed.

Luther's very logical mind considered whether God was moved at all by human problems. After all, God was the Master of the Universe. How could He be concerned at all with the trivialities of human life? If, therefore, as Master of the Universe, God had a choice about whether to be concerned or not concerned, and sometimes was or was not responsive, then God had to be capricious. If God were capricious, and even if a man had led a perfect life, there was still the problem that he might not be redeemed in the eyes of God.

On the other hand, if God were so powerful that everything in life was permanently fixed so that there were no contingencies, no possibilities at all, then man had no free will to decide between good and evil; thus, some men were already cast into the roles of heretics, nonbelievers, sinners at birth because they were predestined to be "losers." How could God, the Master of the Universe, hold some men in such contempt when it was decreed that they would be evil all along? This indeed was a terrible punishment for those who tried to be redeemed, but never could be redeemed. How could God be considered to be *just* when these sinners never had a chance?

Luther struggled between determinism and indeterminism. He eventually selected near complete determinism, writing, "God "foresees, foreordains, and accomplishes all things by an unchanging, eternal, and efficacious will. By this thunderbolt free will sinks shattered in the dust" (see Manchester, 1992, p. 176).

His inner integrity would not let him take easy solutions, and his agony shook his interiority in a horrific angst.

The monastery leaders finally determined that for Luther, who had demonstrated such earnestness, integrity, and dogged pursuit of the dilemmas of faith, should pursue an advanced degree in the Scriptures at Wittenberg University. Luther was to become a doctor of theology. His reading of the Scriptures not only clarified his problems of doubt, but also laid the foundations for his challenge to the medieval church itself, and ultimately spawned a theological revolution called the Reformation.

At the university, Luther was imbued with the traditions of argument by reason, logic, and facts. This tradition of scholarship was to be internalized so well that he ultimately refused to be convinced by anything else. Luther's apostasy was rooted in the classical traditions of the Church, which had been borrowed in its appropriations of the writings of the ancient Greek philosophers and their Roman translators. The reconciliation of the ancients with Christian faith had been attained by Thomas Aquinas—the great Dominican teacher. Aquinas was the accepted translator of Aristotle.

With Luther's logical mind and his dogmatism regarding his unrelenting search for logical answers, he became a doctor of theology and became supremely educated in Biblical writing. It was upon this hermeneutical base that he challenged the practice of papal indulgences. He was not the first to do so. At least four others prior to Luther had gone to their deaths questioning indulgences (Manchester, 1992, p. 150).

The Roman Church had begun the practice of issuing pardons for sins in advance of their being committed, for a fee. Called indulgences, these official pardons could totally forgive sins or reduce the time a soul spent in purgatory by thousands of years. Indulgences were used to construct St. Peter's in Rome. They were used by those who purchased their offices from Rome as a way to recompense their own pocketbooks. So, once installed as a Bishop, indulgences could be sold with Rome's permission to finance a variety of projects, including repairing buildings or making war.

It was this practice, later conceded by the Roman Church to be in error, that Martin Luther challenged. As the sale of indulgences touched upon Luther's territory, in disgust he nailed on the church door 95 arguments called *theses* and written in Latin, for debate. Luther's scholasticism, his reading of Scripture, and his logical mind were deeply embedded in this attack on the accepted papal practice.

Luther argued that papal indulgences could not erase guilt. Contrition is an individual matter with God, argued Luther. The pope could only remove conditions that he controlled on earth. The pope, therefore, could not offer an individual soul redemption. This occurred in the sacrament of penance. Luther contended that the pope had no treasury of credits to transfer to a human by which his or her time in purgatory could be reduced. Purgatory was run by God, not the pope.

Then, by using logical deduction and extension, Luther commented that if the pope did indeed control credits in purgatory, why did he not let everyone out to demonstrate Christian love and forgiveness? To sell indulgences to those who could afford it was to perpetuate avarice, a practice the Church opposed.

In another extension, Luther posed the situation that it was far better to give to the poor than to purchase an indulgence. Buying indulgences created a false sense of religious security and posed a barrier against charity. Using Scripture, Luther wrote, "Did Christ say, 'Let him that has a cloak sell it and buy an indulgence'?" (Bainton, 1977, p. 63). Although Luther's 95 theses were aimed at provoking learned debate in church circles only, they were quickly translated into German and circulated widely. The rock had been thrown into the pond. The ripples could not ever be recalled. The Reformation had begun.

Let us review the five principles of leadership described and exemplified in Shakespeare's dramas, and apply them to the life of Martin Luther.

1.   Leadership Is a Moral Act and Represents Choices in Situ.

The morality of Martin Luther, his piety and faith, his contrition and humility, his search for God and the "right" path to God, are well-established in his life's work. The act of nailing the 95 theses on the church door was a moral act. In fact, the act meets every one of the definitions of *moral* in the dictionary as: (1) of or relating to principles of right and wrong in behavior, (2) expressing or teaching a conception of right behavior, (3) conforming to a standard of right behavior, (4) sanctioned by or operative on one's conscience or ethical judgment, (5) capable of right and wrong action, (6) probable though not proved, (7) of, relating to, or acting on the mind, character, or will (Webster, 1972, p. 550).

Luther's act of nailing his arguments on the door was an expression of his morality and his anger at the practices which he believed contradicted the Scriptures and the Church doctrine. The Church later agreed. In this act Luther declared that the Pope could err because he was human. If the Pope could err, so could the Church. The judgment regarding whether Luther's act was moral *in the context* in which it occurred is affirmed by nearly everyone who has studied it. At the time, many believed it was an act of apostasy against a morally sanctioned practice.

2.   Morality Requires a Center or an Anchor.

Morality represents a cluster of values and more than one choice. Throughout his life Luther wrote many books—mostly concerning religious matters or interpreting Scripture, but also some on government. His basic anchor was Scripture—mostly the theology of Paul. This was Martin Luther's anchor for everything else he did. Luther resolved the conflict of man's relationship to God by accepting the viewpoint of Paul—that only by faith could a human come to understand the nature of God through Christ. Because logic failed him, Luther came to understand that the mysteries of God cannot be rationally explained. It is simply not logical that Christ (who was perfect) should stoop to accept humanity's sins and die for them in a most painful and slow death. To develop this faith, one does not achieve anything. One comes to understand that faith is a gift.

Luther's acceptance of Paul's belief system hinged on a Greek word in Biblical hermeneutical scholarship that had two meanings: justice and justification. The first meaning had to do with adherence to the law as a matter of enforcement. The second had to do with a judge being able to commute a sentence, change the conditions of sentencing, and redeem a defendant or prisoner. It was in this duality that Martin Luther resolved his logical answer to the relationship of man to the Almighty. While humans might be forever damned, the sentence could be commuted to enable redemption (Bainton, 1977, p. 49).

3. Choice Involves Discrimination and Boundaries.

Martin Luther had a choice to make. He could have remained silent. He could have argued behind closed doors. He could have remained securely within the Church and not faced any risks. He lessened the risks by first making his public outcry in Latin. When the 95 theses were translated and became public, he could have recanted. He was fully aware of what the Church did with convicted heretics, and the shadow of the stake and death by fire were ever before him. He chose to stay the course. This man had wrestled with the fires of Hell and his own quest for Divine Forgiveness made his earthly problems appear small.

4. Choice Involves Judgment, Which Is a Matter of Studying Human Interiority.

Along with Martin Luther's choices, his firmness and bravery (two externally based characteristics of leaders) can be explained by understanding his interiority and his intense personal struggle with standing right before God. Luther was consumed with this struggle. Others might speak of the Devil; Luther actually saw the Devil (Manchester, 1992, p. 139). His conscience would provide him no rest. The logic of his mind swept away unconvincing arguments. It was because of his own inner and uniquely individual pursuit of what was "right" that his interior beliefs became hardened. They became the "rock" of his ship in the external world. It was Martin Luther who wrote the words and the music to a Protestant hymn that is still sung today, "A Mighty Fortress Is Our God" (Manchester, 1992, p. 137).

The battle over heresy is one of interiority. It involves a questioning of beliefs, reasons, interpretations, and, ultimately, actions. While some of Luther's observations were not original, his act of publicly engaging in them, and his logic in pursuing extensions of those beliefs in proposing reforms of the sacraments and religious practices, coupled with unrest in the world of the laity, produced a unique human movement called the Reformation. Even the great Erasmus had shrunk before this task.

5. Moral Decisions Are Determined by Their Consequences.

It is perhaps on this criterion that Luther's initial act of outrage encountered criticism. Luther's insistence on his own reading of the Scriptures along with his hermeneutical interpretation of them as primary, and his refusal to accept any argument that was not centered in Scripture or argument derived from them, produced a schism in Europe that was never to be repaired.

Luther's act of nailing his theses on the church door, although in context a moral one, led to abuses he did not foresee. Certainly the influence of one great Church ameliorating the squabbles between the emerging nation–states was lost forever.

If Luther could interpret Scripture and act individually on his beliefs, so could and so did others. The revolt of Thomas Muntzer, who interpreted Scripture that the true believers should slay the ungodly with the sword, produced a massacre of thousands of peasants, as well as Muntzer, who was killed as he fled the massacre.

Luther was later to assent to the persecution and deaths of the Anabaptists in Germany, on the grounds that their refusal to accept oaths of loyalty to the state constituted sedition and was punishable by death. Luther participated in the repression of others who followed him, and who utilized the same methods: scriptural interpretation and human reason. Christianity was thus forever split into rebellious and sometimes warring cults and sects that continue into present times.

Perhaps what Luther did not anticipate was that Lutheranism became the vassal of the nation–states. Having no independent army, when religious or secular insurrections arose, Luther countenanced putting them down by the sword in the name of social order. Lutherans therefore reinforced the socioeconomic hierarchy of the times, and became subservient to national power exercised by national governments. Protestantism therefore became the vehicle of hegemony exercised by the privileged over the peasants. Many of the peasants believed at first that Protestantism was going to provide a change in their socioeconomic condition. Such beliefs were brutally crushed by the sword and the stake by Protestant leaders themselves. Luther was prominent among them.

There can be no denying that Luther's first act of moral outrage was justified. His later decisions and acts, centered around the same moral cluster of values, however, remain debatable. Luther made every man a priest, and every woman a nun. In so doing, he unleashed the potential for acts of destruction, desperation, and demagoguery to be committed in the name of idiosyncratically defined religion. Many were founded on unschooled scriptural interpretation by readers with little understanding of linguistic nuances and problems of translation from one language to another. The concept of inerrancy with Scripture is totally ignorant of linguistic paranomasia that dooms any attempt at language finality to futility, and with it any measure of absolute, eternal truth that assumes a linguistic form. The nature of language itself dooms determinism.

A CRITIQUE OF MORALITY AS THE LOCUS FOR LEADERSHIP

One of the most penetrating examinations of human morals and ethics was undertaken by the German philosopher Friedrich Nietzsche (1844–1900) in *The Genealogy of Morals,* completed in 1887 (Golffing, 1956). In tracing the roots of morals, Nietzsche found them to be very much class based and aristocratic. It was from the aristocrats and nobility that such values as *good* and *virtue* were used. In fact, Nietzsche asserts that in German, the word *schlecht* (bad) and *schlicht* (simple) were used as synonyms (Golffing, 1956, p. 162), revealing that the despised oppositional values found in morals were given to commoners and the lower classes of people.

Nietzsche found that the Megarian poet—Theognis, of the Greek aristocracy—utilized the word *esthlos,* which meant "one who is, who has true reality, who is true" (Golffing, 1956, p. 163). Moral terms as opposites were then appropriated by the upper class to refer to themselves. In several historical appropriations, the lower classes who were politically weaker and oppressed (the Jews and Christians) reversed these distinctions and made their own positions appear virtuous. Suffering, torture, pain, poverty, and weakness then became the supreme oppositional values to *bad,* or *evil.* The rich and powerful became the enemies. The Jews and early Christians then reversed their political and social positions by declaring their status next to God. "All good things have at one time been considered evil; every original sin has, at some point, turned into an original virtue," says Nietzsche (Golffing, 1956, p. 249).

Nietzsche's analysis reveals that human morals were always steeped in oppression and that "ethics has never lost its reek of blood and torture" (Golffing, 1956, p. 197). Morals require the development of a conscience and the acquisition of guilt. Neither of these is possible without the assault of one person or class upon another over time. In a somewhat shocking exposition, Nietzsche declares that, "No act of violence, rape, exploitation, destruction, is intrinsically 'unjust,' since life itself is violent, rapacious, exploitative, and destructive and cannot be conceived otherwise" (Golffing, 1956, p. 208).

Morality, according to Nietzsche, is simply the twisting of one set of oppositional values into the most desired and treasured by those in power. Ethics represent an appropriation of these binary opposites originally by force, and then by the development of a guilty conscience rooted in pain.

Any discussion of moral leadership must also include the basis of defining morals and of who benefits from them. This theme was displayed in the timeless works of art in the Rennaissance period of European history. Leadership is never a neutral act. It inevitably takes sides in the continuing conflicts and tensions between those who govern and those who are governed.

SUMMARY

The Renaissance and Reformation were filled with leaders, real and fictional, who continue to influence us in modern times. The period produced thoughts, ideas, plays, and books that could be called protoscientific—i.e., they were "like" science, and in many ways exceeded what science has produced, even in modern times, to an understanding or description of leadership.

The Renaissance and Reformation were times in Western history when the most important aspects of life were part of the interior. Religion was the centerpiece of daily routine, and thoughts of the hereafter were always in the present—front and center.

Western concepts of leadership and the dilemmas of leadership were framed by powerful forces and writers. These were set into moral frameworks where questions regarding proper action and proper thought were uppermost in the minds of readers, leaders, and audiences.

Prescient writers and thinkers such as Machiavelli and Shakespeare penetrated the secrets of leaders and followers, pursuing themes and revealing insights that are still profoundly relevant.

The call today for renewed moral leadership in educational administration (see Sergiovanni, 1992) on a secular basis attempts to avoid the problem of centering morality on or around religious principles or values—something that would have been declared heresy several hundred years before. To be completely moral, one must come to grips with all of the questions faced by Machiavelli, Shakespeare, and Luther. The issues and answers have historically been centered in religion. "Right" action follows "right" thinking. A completely secularized morality is likely to be shallow, temporal, and convenient, and to be abandoned in times of stress. Lasting morality requires a harder rock upon which to stand. To date, any such attempt at morality in educational administration stands on a base of clay. Early pioneers in educational administration tried to switch "objective science" for morality. This has proved unworkable in dealing with moral issues or in understanding very much about leadership.

In America, the separation of church and state with the dominance of the state is a distinct consequence of the Reformation, and the long shadow of Martin Luther. American schools have been shrouded in basic Protestantism, so much so that Catholics were driven from the system to found their own schools (Tyack, 1974, p. 105). Protestant Bible reading in them was not declared unconstitutional until 1963 (LaMorte, 1990, p. 36), and continues in many schools despite the legal caveats to cease and desist. The U.S. Supreme Court's rationale regarding the exclusion of Bible reading in the schools reflects the schism wrought by Martin Luther in Christianity itself. "The secular state is advanced because it respects the conscience of every minority," wrote Justice William O. Douglas (1966), "it assures those who happen to make up the majority that the coercive power of government will not be used in their name to violate the conscience of any minority" (p. 35).

The dilemma of using a strictly defined morality in modern organizational life is that many points of view can be considered moral; therefore, there is more than one correct position. This situation presents the school administrator with a multi-morality that is complex, and eschews absolutism as a prerequiste to effective practice (see Lane, Corwin, Monahan, 1967, p. 303).

The problem of morality in educational administration had been thought to be solved by declaring the discipline "scientific," and eliminating the need for morals altogether. The criticism of such an approach—that it was fooling itself and its adherents—is the subject of the next chapter.

The basic character of American education owes almost its total code of morality to Martin Luther, a man who personally thought he saw the Devil. Another American also supposedly observed the Devil. A friend once remarked that "he saw fiends and other horrid shapes distinctly as with his bodily eyes, and was obliged to use the utmost force of his will to keep from screaming" (Mann, 1937, p. 17). The founder of American public education, Horace Mann, was reared in very basic Calvinism in Massachusetts. To Mann, "a physical hell was a living reality, as much so as though I could have heard the shrieks of the tormented, or stretched out my hand to grasp their burning souls" (Mann, 1937, p. 14). While Mann later modified many of his early Calvinistic views of childhood, the sculptor of public education in America had a clear concept of good and evil, right and wrong. Schooling and morality merged into the social good he perceived was to be obtained by attendance in public schools.

Perception Check and Applications

1. Who Was the Real Prince?

It is widely believed that Cesare Borgia, bastard son of Pope Alexander VI, was the actual model for Machiavelli's *The Prince*. Examine the life of Cesare Borgia and compare it to the advice Machiavelli provides in *The Prince*. Where are the parallels? Render a decision as to whether or not Borgia—the Prince in real life—was Machiavelli's *The Prince*.

2. Lincoln and the Rhetoric of Imposture

Machiavelli describes the dilemma that any leader faces as the necessity to be what an audience wants one to be, though not necessarily what one might be. Now read this description of President Abraham Lincoln by Garry Wills (1992):

> What should not be forgotten is that Lincoln was himself an actor, an expert raconteur and mimic, and one who spent hours reading speeches out of Shakespeare to any willing (and some unwilling) audiences (p. 36).

Consider the life of Abraham Lincoln and construct one or more scenarios in which Lincoln may have donned the mask of imposture in presenting his face to the electorate.

3. Leadership as a Moral Act

Take any great world leader who was not foremost a religious personage admired for advancing humankind in a secular way, and construct a picture of the cluster of values that shaped his or her morality. What connection is there to religious beliefs? What kinds of questions did that person's belief system answer? What questions were left open or unaddressed? Is it possible to exercise moral leadership in a secular enterprise?

4. Shakespeare's Morality

From one of Shakespeare's tragedies, select a major or a pivotal figure, and construct a portrait of that person on the five criteria discussed in the chapter:

- Leadership is a moral act and represents choices in situ.
- Morality requires a center or an anchor.
- Choice involves discrimination and boundaries.
- Choice involves judgment, which is a matter of studying human interiority.
- Moral decisions are determined by their consequences.

5. Defining the "Common Good" in Educational Administration

Right actions or means involve constructing some idea of the "common good." Define the "common good" in educational administration. Then draft a board policy that would include it and give at least three examples of situations where it would be useful in decision making that would include either student rights, collective bargaining, religious activities, or prayer in school.

6. Portrait of a Failure: Jan Hus

While Martin Luther was a success in fostering religious reform in Europe, Jan Hus was not. Hus was the first national Czech patriot who was burned at the stake for, among other things, challenging the sale of papal indulgences. Find out about the life of Jan Hus. Compare it to Martin Luther's. Both were professors. Both were excommunicated and continued preaching. Both rose on a tide of nationalism of the peasants. Why was one a success and the other a failure?

7. Leadership, Morality, and Absolutism

Once Protestantism began its rise in the Reformation, it reverted to practices that were as authoritarian and destructive as any under Catholic rule. Analyze why and under what conditions morality leads to absolutism. Under what conditions is morality not prone to absolutism?

8. Portrait of an Explorer: The Feat of Magellan

Obtain any good account of the circumnavigation of the earth by Ferdinand Magellan (1519–1521). It took a resolute leader to achieve this feat. The voyage also reveals Magellan's *hamartia* in his death in the Philippines. A very readable account is William Manchester's (1992) "One Man Alone," (pp. 223–292) in his book, *A World Lit Only by Fire.*

Key Chapter Concepts and Terms

the common good

The "end" and ultimately most important objective for a leader. Actions taken by a leader are always judged against this standard. A separate action is neither good nor bad, but it depends upon whether or not this condition has been met.

the executive

An officeholder equivalent to a prince in Machiavelli's time. The executive acts on behalf of the law, and to make the law effective, must exceed the law. A decisive executive is one who acts by surprise, in secret.

exteriority

The aspects of leadership that are visible: actions, behaviors, declarations, commentaries, speeches, conversation, gestures, and facial or body expressions.

the grammar of power

The idea that there is a structure to the formation and use of power based on theory.

hamartia

A Greek concept that means a great person may have a flaw, even a very minor one, that under the proper circumstances causes their undoing.

interiority

The aspects of leadership that account for how a person behaves but are hidden: values, motivation, perceptions, feelings, etc.

the predicament of leadership

A Machiavellian concept that a leader cannot depend upon a people for support because they are ultimately corrupted by evil. Knowing this, a leader must appear to the people as possessing virtue in order to retain their support, but must also have the capacity to act virtuelessly if necessary.

References

Altman, L. K. (1992, October 8). "Pathologists Confirm John F. Kennedy Had Serious Illness," New York Times News Service as it appeared in the *Lexington Herald–Leader*, p. C12.

Associated Press (1992, October 4). "Hussein Executes War Hero, Other Officers, Envoys Say" in *Lexington Herald–Leader*, p. A9.

Bainton, R. H. (1977). *Here I Stand: A Life of Martin Luther*. New York: New American Library.

Cannadine, D. (1989). *Blood, Toil, Tears and Sweat*. Boston: Houghton Mifflin Company.

de Grazia, S. (1989). *Machiavelli in Hell*. Princeton, New Jersey: Princeton University Press.

Douglas, W. O. (1966). *The Bible and the Schools*. Boston: Little, Brown, and Company.

English, F. W. (1992, January). "The Principal and *The Prince:* Machiavelli and School Leadership," *NASSP Bulletin*, 76: 540, pp. 10–16.

Golffing, F. (1956). *Friedrich Nietzsche: The Genealogy of Morals*. New York: Anchor Doubleday Books.

Grebanier, B. D., Middlebrook, S., Thompson, S., and Watt, W. (1957). *English Literature and its Backgrounds*. New York: The Dryden Press.

Hair, W. I. (1989). "Lynching," in *Encyclopedia of Southern Culture*, C. R. Wilson and W. Ferris (Eds.). Chapel Hill, North Carolina: The University of North Carolina Press, pp. 174–176.

Harrison, G. B. (1947). *Shakespeare*. New York: Harcourt, Brace, and Company.

LaMorte, M. W. (1990). *School Law*. Englewood Cliffs, NJ: Prentice Hall.

Lane, W. R., Corwin, R. G., and Monahan, W. G. (1967). *Foundations of Educational Administration*. New York: The Macmillan Company.

Lerner, M. (1950). "Introduction" to *The Prince* and *The Discourses*. New York: Random House.

Machiavelli, N. (1950). *The Prince*. L. Ricci (Trans.). New York: Random House.

Machiavelli, N. (1950). *The Discourses*. L. Ricci (Trans.). New York: Random House.

Manchester, W. (1992). *A World Lit Only by Fire*. Boston: Little, Brown and Company.

Mann, M. P. (1937). *Life of Horace Mann*. Washington, D.C.: National Education Association.

Mansfield, H. C. (1989). *Taming the Prince*. New York: The Free Press.

Merriam–Webster (1983). *Webster's New Biographical Dictionary*. Springfield, Massachusetts: Merriam–Webster Inc., Publishers.

Miranda, J. (1992, September–October). "The PAVN and TET" *Command*, 18, pp. 16–29.

Perry, R. J. (1992, September 23). "Do Reformers Survive?" *Education Week*, 12:3, p. 36.

Plumb, J. H. (1961). *The Italian Renaissance*. New York: Harper and Row.

Rackin, P. (1978). *Shakespeare's Tragedies*. New York: Frederick Ungar Publishing Co.

Roeder, R. (1933). *The Man of the Renaissance*. New York: The Viking Press.

Rowse, A. L. (1988). *The Annotated Shakespeare*. New York: Greenwich House.

Sergiovanni, T. J. (1992). *Moral Leadership*. San Francisco: Jossey–Bass.

Talbott, S. (1992, September 28). "Iraq: It Could Be Even Worse," *Time*, 140:13, p. 49.

Tuchman, B. W. (1984). *The March of Folly*. New York: Ballantine Books.

Tyack, D. B. (1974). *The One Best System*. Cambridge, MA: Harvard University Press.

U.S. News and World Report (1992). *Triumph Without Victory*. New York: Random House.

Walker, A., and Wilson, J. D. (Eds.) (1960). *Othello*. Cambridge, England: Cambridge University Press.

Wareham, J. (1991). *The Anatomy of a Great Executive*. New York: HarperCollins.

Webster's Seventh New Collegiate Dictionary (1972). Springfield, MA: G. & C. Merriam Company.

Whittemore, R. (1988). *Pure Lives*. Baltimore, MD: The Johns Hopkins University Press.

Wills, G. (1992, October 5). "Dishonest Abe," in *Time*, 140:14, pp. 41–42.

Wills, G. (1992). *Lincoln at Gettysburg*. New York: Simon and Schuster.

Chapter 7

THE SEARCH FOR SCIENCE AND SYSTEM

Continuing Reform and the Gospel of Efficiency

Reprinted by permission: Tribune Media Services.

The rise of leadership positions in education that occurred in the United States around 1800 was followed by the creation of stable bureaucracies that depended upon persons to manage, control, and direct them. In this sense, organizational boundaries and offices preceded the establishment of formal preparation programs to prepare people to occupy them.

In the development of America, our predecessors exhibited a proclivity to institutionalize many social functions, among them schools, asylums, reformatories, and penitentiaries (see Cremin, 1080, p. 373). The creation of these institutions revolved around ideas pertaining to a new secular morality in the name of efficiency. These forces were pitted against the obvious corruption within the cities that affected schools. The nation began to feel the twin forces of the population shift to the cities from the agricultural countryside, and the flood of immigration that began to be felt across the Eastern seaboard. Boards of education were notoriously large and cumbersome, staffed with scores of committees filled with grafters, schemers, pork barrelers, and "keepers of groggeries, who can hardly write their own name" (Ravitch, 1974, p. 88). Their inefficiency was well known. One administrative reformer caustically noted that because of the standing committee system which was in place in the Springfield, Massachusetts public schools late into the twentieth century, it took six months to decide to acquire a piano (Strayer, 1933, p. 9).

AMERICAN EDUCATION'S MARTIN LUTHER: HORACE MANN

The American educational system was engineered by early reformers, among them a dashing lawyer from Dedham, Massachusetts named Horace Mann. The "father of American public education" was described by his contemporaries such as Ralph Waldo Emerson, Nathaniel Hawthorne, William Ellery Channing, Jared Sparks, and Theodore Parker as, "charming, witty, a great orator, a spellbinding conversationalist, a man of vision gifted with a quicksilver mind, a magnetic attractiveness and an unlimited capacity for work" (Tharp, 1953). Mann's life stretched over two centuries—the last of the eighteenth to the mid-nineteenth. In a remarkable 63 years (1796–1859), he recast the spiritual and physical form of American public education into present times.

Horace Mann's childhood was harsh. As he remembered it, life consisted of work and churchgoing (Tharp, 1953, p. 19). Mann's church inculcation was the sternest of spiritual immersions. The family's pastor was none other than New England's Nathaniel Emmons, a pure Calvinist who preached the total depravity of humankind. Emmons taught that some human souls were born damned, and that God took delight in their eternal suffering and damnation. These were the "Lost Souls" of God (Mann, 1937, p. 13).

Two deaths of people very close to Horace Mann were instrumental in developing the fabric of his morality and life's work. The first was his brother's death by drowning. At the funeral, when he heard Dr. Emmons preach about the unconverted and their wickedness (suggesting that this revered sibling was possibly one of God's damned), Mann rebelled at this concept being applied by insinuation to his innocent sibling. Over a period of time, Mann came to believe in a God of Love, a God who took care of the true believers and rewarded those who kept to His Word. Mann believed that justice would triumph in the end because God could permit no other ending for the righteous.

These beliefs were swept away in the death of his first wife, Charlotte, daughter of the president of Brown University, Asa Messer. Charlotte's death brought Mann face-to-face with his view of a loving God. How could a loving God permit a human so full of compassion and zest for life to die? The death of his beloved spouse fully exposed the nakededness of his belief in a moral universe—one ruled by a loving and divine force.

Mann pondered that perhaps there was no God in the universe, and that this was the reason for his personal loss. He ultimately rejected this notion, and assumed a more personal sense of guilt about his tragedy. He came to believe that he had been enamored of ambition for power and material things such as fine clothes and furnishings in his home. He came to accept his wife's death as a form of punishment by God for his frivolities, and he returned to the God of his child-hood who valued "modesty, simplicity, sobriety and kindness" (Messerli, 1972, pp. 163–180).

Horace Mann became a crusader of reform because for him, it represented a reconciliation of his life to a concept of morality in his personal universe. He turned his attentions to the poor and their sufferings. In the words of his second wife—Mary Peabody Mann (1937)—one sees this reworking of his fundamentalist Protestant upbringing:

> Education, religious and political freedom, then, were the watchwords of his life and action. All collateral evils would vanish if these things could be established. In one sense, he cannot be said to have sacrificed himself to them; for he identified himself with them, and cared little for any thing else. To work for them was his happiness. All culture, all living, that could be transmuted into material for their advancement, were dear to him, if they were not to be monopolized by the few at the expense of the many; for there was nothing beautiful or of good repute which was to be selfishly appropriated. He wished every child of God to be so situated as to lay hold of the means of self-improve-ment; and with sledge-hammer and battle-axe he would beat down the obstacles, if they did not yield to the arguments of love and truth and justice (p. 61).

It was clear that Horace Mann's life was firmly shaped by the hand of Martin Luther's personal turmoil. The deeply felt losses of his brother and his wife shook him to his moral core. Mary Peabody Mann, his second wife, described his personal reconciliation and new mission: "When he looked upon the inequalities of human condition, he saw that it was the consequence of man's not using worthily his God-given gifts; and that the stimulus of acting for the good of each and all caused these gifts to become divine in their proportions" (p. 61). Horace Mann's personal salva-tion was to be his life's work and explain why he turned away from a profitable career in law to assume the position of secretary to the Massachusetts State Board of Education in 1837. From this "bully pulpit," Mann launched the drive for free public education as a personal moral crusade. The loss of his powerful and influen-tial seat as President of the Massachusetts State Senate was envisioned by him as a personal sacrifice for doing God's work on earth as a martyr to the "principles of truth and duty" (Messerli, 1972, p. 246).

Based on his Calvinistic upbringing, Mann's cosmological views were rather simple. There was good and there was evil. There were no other hues to his moral universe. Mann championed the cause of temperance in Massachusetts. He supported total abstinence of all alcoholic beverages, despite the fact that at one time he had enjoyed an occasional glass of wine.

It was in his pursuit of a completely temperate society that he came to see that the common man would not always do what was right. The common man had to have guidance from "an ethical elite" (Messerli, 1972, p. 214). The common man's weaknesses required the presence of the law to enforce morality (a point expressed by Machiavelli in his writings centuries before—see Chapter 6).

Mann's personal theology was also to embrace the writings of Henry Lord Brougham (1778–1868), one of the founders of the *Edinburgh Review* who in his *Discourse of Natural Theology* claimed that miracles and revelations had no place in a true religion. Validity in religious doctrine must be centered on scientific proof (Messerli, 1972, p. 244). Mann accepted this idea, and put it to use in his writings about improving public education for the poor. In the process, he set a powerful example for the use of data in his divine cause, mixing science and secularism in a fertile soil. This new ground was eventually to produce a hybrid in which science, research, and efficiency became a purely secular religion, shedding any overt sectarian trappings, but a religion nonetheless in its core. It is what could be called **scientism,** where objectivity is paraded as a virtue in which its innate subjectivity is hidden.

Mann's public reports as Secretary to the Massachusetts State Board of Education were filled with facts gathered by questionnaire. His law background was of immense help in constructing arguments based on the evidence he mustered. In his very first *Annual Report,* he was able to show that in reality, Massachusetts had no "system" of education at all (Messerli, 1972, p. 284).

The method of gathering data by survey and using it to come to conclusions over a great range of topics, set the stage for the later development of the *school survey* (Sears, 1933, p. 220). The school survey was to become the exemplar of the new "science" of education. It was to be employed as the fuel of the efficiency movement in American public education. It became the embodiment of the scientific method, and it provided the rationale for the development of a cadre of experts who alone knew how to apply it. It was upon this base that the professionalization of educational administration was established in American education (see Spring, 1986, pp. 222–235).

Mann was thoroughly smitten with the Prussian educational system. He found its principles of order appealing. His praise and sponsorship lifted it from its Teutonic absolutistic environment, and set it firmly down on Puritan soil. He never saw the ahistorical paradox in transplanting an institution supporting tyranny to the ground trod by the Minutemen or those who dumped British tea in Boston Bay that ignited a revolution (Messerli, 1972, p. 298).

Mann's social views were conservative. He was a Whig who eschewed extreme social protest. Although he favored absolute temperance, he sought to maintain distance from the Abolitionists. He was a backer of railroad legislation and monied interests while he served in the Massachusetts Senate (Katz, 1968, p. 35). He wrote in his journal, "Agitate, agitate, agitate—but nevertheless, in a proper way and for a good cause only" (Messerli, 1972, p. 284).

Perhaps Horace Mann showed what type of reformer he really was when in his *Seventh Report* he was challenged by the Boston School Masters. They wrote a 150-page diatribe against Mann and his ideas such as teacher training, the use of Prussian educational methods, and his recommendation to eliminate corporal punishment in the schools. The School Masters insisted that children were evil and they had to be taught to obey God's Will with the rod.

Mann not only answered their charges, but he succeeded in getting some of his friends to run for the Boston School Committee as well. Upon their election, they developed printed, standardized tests and without warning, would turn up at a school and administer them to the children. All of the testing was performed on the same day in the same subject to paralyze the opposition, and to prevent them from talking to one another or in sharing the tests. The results showed that the School Masters were incompetent. In addition to releasing four from duty, many more were transferred from their schools. The writers who summarized the test results also recommended the appointment of a superintendent and a principal with assistants at each school (Messerli, 1972, pp. 412–420). The educational administrative bureaucracy was about to be established.

Horace Mann's crusade for free public schools for the masses was based on his religious and moral views that: (1) laws were necessary to compel people to do that which was proper and right (his work with temperance had convinced him of this), and (2) that large masses of children could be educated in schools so that evil could be eradicated from the larger society. Mann even confessed, "that schools will be found to be the way that God has chosen for the reformation of the world" (Messerli, 1972, p. 441).

In Mann's public schools, Bible reading was required. Schools were God's places on earth. Of course, it was Protestant Bible reading that was encouraged. The holy scriptures of the Catholics, Hebrews, or any other faith were not considered appropriate.

Horace Mann's mind was one of an absolutist. His biographer—Jonathan Messerli—observed that, "Rarely did Mann exhibit a humility in the face of complex or irreconcilable social controversies. His was a rigid and occasionally arrogant security, built upon a set of simplistic moral laws, but all the more brittle and tenuous because it could not tolerate ambiguities, imponderables, or the plurality of contradictory 'truths'" (p. 432). Mann's work helped create school bureaucracy to control his educational system. It laid the intellectual framework for the rapid rise of the efficiency expert in education. Another of his legacies was the set of expectations he created in the minds of the public and their elected representatives—i.e., that the public schools could be the mechanism to purify society of its evils. Such gargantuan promises have never been able to be kept, eventually leading to calls for the disestablishment of the schools via site-based management (an extreme form of de-centralization), parental choice of schools both public and private, and vouchers to combat school monopoly.

Michel Foucault (1972) has said that, "in our time, history is that which transforms *documents* into *monuments*" (p. 7). Horace Mann's school reports were the major defining agents for the contemporary apparatus of schooling in the United States. His moral views became their discourse—the way people think and speak about the schools. This was "what was being said in what was said"—i.e., the special context of the statements by Mann to the larger society (Foucault, 1972, p. 28).

The discourse about schooling is still heavily laced with the morality of Horace Mann—both by the critics and the defenders of the public schools. Both defend the schools as moral agents. The critics attack that schools have not transformed society. The defenders still believe that with proper support and some internal modifications, the schools can be more morally effective. The underlying premises remain inviolate, set into relationships involving the institution, "economic and social processes, behavioural patterns, systems of norms, techniques, types of classification, modes of characterization" (Foucault, 1972, p. 45).

These relationships comprise the web, the immanent rationality of the objects contained within a discourse. Discourses lead to practices as lived examples of beliefs. Horace Mann created teacher training institutions. His new system required a different form or preparation of teachers. He prescribed teaching methods based on his observations of Prussian schools.

Mann was neither a deep nor an original thinker. He simply capitalized on what he knew. Brought up in Calvinistic traditions, his moral world was very simplistic. Inculcated as a lawyer, he learned a kind of logic and argumentation based on facts. As a barrister and Massachusetts senator, he practiced oral delivery in social settings. He grew up immersed in a web of discourse that he simply extended. His pragmatism revealed that he came to understand that mass education was indeed possible. He overestimated its salutary effects. He underestimated the extent of hegemony it would require to manage within the existing ideas of political control dominant in New England at the time.

The most obvious form of this control was the school district organization pattern, which was taken to the West in the mental baggage of the settlers as they trekked through the Great Plains and on to the California coastline. The result was the multiplication of the local board of education and appointed superintendent dyad that was cloned from East to West and remains dominant today within the larger state-controlled educational machinery. The concept of the school superintendent was another ancestral concept of Mann's time. Cuban (1988) has indicated that prior to its use for schools, it was employed to denote the bishop of a Methodist church in the United States. He traced its heritage to the 1560s in Europe, and found that the managers of the factories on the Eastern seaboard were also called superintendents (p. 111). The amalgam of religion and industry are antecedents to the top administrative post in American education.

THE RISE OF SCIENTISM IN SCHOOLING

Tracing the development of the history of ideas is never a clear-cut operation. Foucault (1972) says that in doing so, one confronts an "uncertain object, with badly drawn frontiers, methods borrowed from here and there, and an approach lacking in rigour and stability" (p. 136). The problem with tracing the development of ideas is that it is extremely difficult to fix boundaries and to establish limitations. "The history of ideas is concerned with all that insidious thought, that whole interplay of representations that flow anonymously between men," observes Foucault (1972, p. 137).

The establishment of common schools—their regulation, grouping them into systems, the development of normal schools in which the new common school-teacher was prepared, the battle between the Boston school masters, and the state as represented by Horace Mann—prepared the intellectual soil for the rise of public school administration in American public education.

The rhetoric of school administration was to be found in the discourse of moral Calvinism reformed with the trappings of Henry Brougham's de-miraclized and nonrevelatory "scientific religion" in which proof consisted of the "facts" garnered to support logical argument. The intellectual triumvirate that was to emerge revolved around three words: science, research (embodied as the scientific method), and efficiency (as calculated by an efficiency expert). Often, these three words were used interchangeably. The odd mixture that emerged may be called *scientism,* a discourse that was cloaked in old world morality and the new world of science, but that lacked the rigor to challenge its own shroud between the world it believed was "out there" and its suppositions about how one was to discover the "truth" about what was really "true."

This intellectual discourse's final expression was to be found in mid-twentieth century logical positivism, and its pure form of analysis—first in behaviorism and later in total quality management (TQM). Despite modern protestations to the contrary, it was, and remains, a secularized religion: floating on suppositions it does not recognize, insisting on divisions between object and subject that have collapsed, believing as an article of faith in an "out-there" world that is subjectively defined everywhere and idiosyncratically described in particularistic human linguistic heritages that are anything but universal. The interplay of assumptions, tactics, and beliefs contiguous to overall strategy is called a *doctrine* in military circles (Eldridge, 1992, p. 32). The label represents a mixture of belief, culture, traditions and technological applications. Similarly, Horace Mann's approach could be called a doctrine.

The distillation of Mann's moral educational and managerial views were slowly absorbed by the nation's new educational ruling class of city and state school superintendents. These were "philosopher–educators" rather than the scientific managers, and they reigned in the time period 1865–1900 (Callahan and Button, 1964, pp. 73–76). It was to these men that Raymond Callahan lamented their demise from the educational scene in his classic critique, *Education and the Cult of Efficiency* (1962), which called the rise of scientific management in education an "American tragedy" (p. 244). While Callahan's treatise has been challenged by Berman (1983), and Cuban (1988) has shown that there was a strong efficiency movement already underway in educational administration prior to the rise of scientific management, no one can doubt that educational administration became dominated by the model of corporate leadership first observed in factories. The result in educational administration was a situation that "produced men who did not understand education or scholarship," and who, when questioned about their academic preparation for their jobs, indicated that the most important fields to study were finance first and public relations second (Callahan, 1962, p. 260).

The men in the time period between1865 and 1900—the philosopher–educators—were E. E. White, W. N. Hailman, and Francis W. Parker. They were more concerned about developing the individual talents of students, and not of aping industrial cost studies (Callahan and Button, 1964, p. 74).

They were to be replaced with a new breed such as William Torrey Harris and William H. Payne, who although inclined toward pragmatism and science, were still philosophers. In fact, Harris was a world-renowned Hegel scholar (see Leidecker, 1946, p. 548) and editor of the *Journal of Speculative Philosophy*—the nation's first modern scholarly publication devoted to philosophy (Button and Provenzo, 1989, p. 158). Payne was superintendent of schools of Adrian, Michigan, and is credited with developing one of the first textbooks in educational administration (Callahan and Button, 1964, p. 75).

Scholars do not agree with the demarcation lines separating the last of the philosopher–educator school leaders, and the rise of the corporate executive role model in school administration. For example, David Tyack (1974) conceded that Harris, "was probably the outstanding intellectual leader in American education in the years between the death of Horace Mann in 1859 and the emergence of John Dewey as spokesman for the new education at the turn of the twentieth century" (p. 43). Yet Tyack was critical of Harris for his penchant for organization and system. Tyack quotes Harris from his 1871 report to the St. Louis Board of Education:

> The first requisite of the school is ORDER: each pupil must be taught first and foremost to to conform his behavior to a general standard. . . .The pupil must have his lessons ready at the appointed time, must rise at the tap of the bell, move to the line, return; in short go through all the evolutions with equal precision (p. 43).

Educational historian Michael Katz (1971) proffered the position that the role of William Torrey Harris, as National Education Association President and later the fourth U.S. Commissioner of Education, was to lower the level of public expectations for the public schools established by Horace Mann and his followers. Katz observed that the writings of Harris and others were devoid of the passion and devout predictions by Mann that the public schools were God's answer to the reformation of society. Instead, Harris and his followers insisted that the purpose of schooling was to bring order and discipline into society, so that "there is little police-restraint on the part of the constituted authorities" (p. 94). Katz believes that Harris' generation of administrators decided their overarching mission was to preserve the system that had begun with Mann. This posture supplanted Mann's goal which focused on children (p. 95). Harris' generation of school leaders engaged in "the transformation of expectations" of the public schools by downgrading missionary zeal and moral expectations as their framework, and focused instead on the bureaucratic benefits of public school systems for society at large. The second generation of administrators had come to realize that Mann's promises for the public schools could not be attained.

A very similar transformation occurred in the capability of the medical profession to deal with insanity (Foucault, 1973). The rise of psychiatry and the role of asylums in housing the insane, bear a striking resemblance to those of public schools. The role of the asylum shifted from one of confinement and separation, to a religious and moral one where the asylum became a religious order without religion. Patients became not adults, but innocent children. In this process, madness was never cured, it was simply controlled.

Originally, psychiatrists made bold promises that their ministrations would cure insanity. Later, when this proved illusory, they became the administrators of asylums. Foucault asks some penetrating questions about the practice of psychoanalysis that run parallel to those of teachers and administrators in bureaucratic school systems:

> The doctor . . . remains the key to psychoanalysis. It is perhaps because it did not suppress this ultimate structure, and because it referred all the others to it, that psychoanlaysis has not been able, will not be able, to hear the voices of unreason, nor to decipher in themselves the signs of the madman (p. 278).

School administrators and teachers in bureaucratic systems have rarely challenged the efficacy of their own roles as necessary in organized education. Administrators particularly, are in charge. The public schools have proven themselves incapable of transforming our society. Indeed, they merely reproduce it—inequities and all (see Bowles and Gintis, 1976). Organized groups of administrators and teachers continue to search for clues to realize the promises of Horace Mann with themselves as the centerpieces of the search. As in the case of psychoanalysts in curing insanity, this assumption may be the major obstacle to any improvement in mass educational systems. Existing roles in existing systems freeze the system from being fundamentally changed. The peculiar brand of science that came to fruition in educational administration showed itself over time to be falsely objective, often where its "research" simply restated logical tautologies as "findings."

EARLY SCIENTISTIC VIEWS OF LEADERSHIP

To crack the enigma of leadership, early thinkers who considered themselves scientific tried to isolate and identify the types and specific traits that would mark a leader as someone special. What was apparent to these early scholars was a human being's capacity to lead a mob or crowd. The early work of Le Bon (1897) and later by Conway (1915) were centered on the ability to lead a crowd. Conway believed that there were three types of crowd leaders. The first inflamed a crowd into acting on his or her agenda. This leader was a crowd-compeller. The second leader somehow sensed what a crowd wanted and expressed it. This leader was a crowd-exponent. The third type of leader, the crowd-representative, simply expressed the already formed opinions of his or her followers.

The work of Bogardus (1918) was predicated upon there being at least four types of leaders. They were autocratic, democratic, executive, and reflective. The rise of the testing movement in education was paralleled by the development of personality theories. These theories were based on early positivistic methods of investigation in science which included: observation of people in group situations, situations in which choice or voting for leaders was present, nomination or selection by qualified observers, rating and testing of people already in leadership positions, and the use of case histories or biographical studies (see Stogdill, 1974, pp. 35–100).

Later, improved statistical procedures were employed such as the use of critical incidents (situations that illustrate leadership or the lack of leadership), and factor analysis. Factor analysis was developed by Charles Spearman in his 1904 paper "General Intelligence, Objectively Determined and Measured," that appeared in the *American Journal of Psychology*. The method flowered in the thirties (Harman, 1968, p. 6). Factor analysis, as developed by Spearman, was centered around the idea that intelligence was a single and generalized function that could be analyzed into sub-elements. In a study of leadership these became traits. The idea was that traits were a manifestation of a more generic, testable, and single concept such as "leadership," to be seen in the same manner as intelligence.

Just as Spearman's view of intelligence has been severely challenged in modern times by Howard Gardner of Harvard (who insists that Spearman's assumption was erroneous), so has leadership been debunked as merely a collection of traits.

But in the height of early "scientific" views of leadership, Fred Englehardt (1931), one of the academic leaders in educational administration, published in his textbook a study by Lide (1929), who listed the 25 traits most "desirable and essential to the success of the public-school executive" (see following page).

Not the least of the problems with trait theory was that it failed to have much discriminatory power, and easily lead to tautological statements being sanctified by statistics—i.e., "a leader is someone who leads." Such traits did not always describe what observers identified as leadership. The simple possession of the desirable traits did not ensure that a person would actually be a leader in every situation. There was not much predictive power in using them since it can easily be shown that every person who answered to the description of certain traits would not be a Boy Scout. Tautologies have no predictive power, though they may serve a function as a descriptor or synonym of that which is being considered. This is one of the problems of the so-called school effectiveness research today, and why the elements in them are called *correlates* and not *predictors*. Such nondifferentiated studies demonstrate the fact that science is crippled by language problems—specifically infinite regress—no matter how sophisticated its statistical machinery makes it appear powerful, differentiated, or objective.

Trait theory is far from dead. There are strong vestiges of this approach that still exist in the marketplace today; for example, John Wareham's (1991), *The Anatomy of a Great Executive,* which states that successful people are those who have overall goals, develop work habits and people skills, and possess overall intelligence and emotional adjustment (pp. 197–229), or Stephen Covey's (1991), *The Seven Habits of Highly Successful People.* These two works have strong roots in the psychological studies of leaders who came to fruition in the thirties. While these studies remain as forces in psychology and counseling, their capability to lend content to a

Figure 7.1   LIDE'S 1929 LIST OF THE MOST DESIRABLE AND ESSENTIAL TRAITS
OF PUBLIC SCHOOL EXECUTIVES

Rank	Trait
1	Leadership
2	Good judgment
3	Breadth of interest
4	Resourcefulness
5	Poise
6	Broad mindedness
7	Intelligence
8	Forcefulness
9	Adaptability
10	Purposefulness
11	Sincerity
12	Dependability
13	Health
14	Considerateness
15	Cooperation
16	Definiteness
17	Enthusiasm
18	Refinement
19	Morality
20	Optimism
21	Thoroughness
22	Sociability
23	Promptness
24	Industry
25	Magnetism

more scholarly pursuit of leadership borders on the perpetuation of folk wisdom, or what Blumberg (1989) has called "craft knowledge."

BUILDING A PROFESSION ON THE ROCK OF "RESEARCH"

In the first years of the new century, professors in educational administration, like most everyone else, were transfixed by the blossoming industrial muscles that were evident in the factories. These mechanical meccas lured thousands of Americans from the farms into the cities. They were unlike anything seen before.

The panorama of wheels, pulleys, levers, drills, and lathes were set into rows of work stations. Whistles were installed to signal times to work. The concept of the assembly line in primitive form was already working in Detroit when a young mechanic named Henry Ford began his apprenticeship in the Flower Brothers Machine Shop in December, 1879 (Lacey, 1986, p. 23).

Ford later refined his early ideas into the first mass-produced automobile using a moving assembly line in 1913. Productivity soared. The installation of a magneto flywheel device that had taken 15 minutes to construct eventually fell to five minutes by the introduction of continuous movement along the line of workers who were shifted to side-to-side stations facing a moving belt.

The concept of continuous movement, coupled with breaking down the work into the simultaneous assembly of smaller parts in every division of the Ford Motor Company, enabled Ford to double his output of automobiles with exactly the same work force. Some time later he increased output and lowered the number of employees. "Every piece of work in the shops moves," said Ford. "It may move on hooks, on overhead chains . . . it may travel on a moving platform, or it may go by gravity, but the point is that there is no lifting or trucking." Ford bragged, "Save ten steps a day for each of 12,000 employees, and you will have saved fifty miles of wasted motion and mis-spent energy" (Lacey, 1986, p. 109).

The most important tool for Ford and his engineers was the stopwatch. They worked against the clock. Every motion was analyzed and broken into parts. The idea behind this concept was the creation of Frederick "Speedy" Taylor, who had begun engaging in "time and motion" studies in the 1880s and in 1911 published *The Principles of Scientific Management* (see Lacey, 1986, p. 107). Taylor's idea was to break work into parts—subcomponents—and search for the quickest way to perform the operation.

Ford's new plant became the envy of the nation. It was Ford who installed the five-dollar-day per worker—unheard of in his times. He employed over 9000 men and women who had handicaps—21 percent of his work force. "All these cripples and invalids were paid the full rate of pay, with profit sharing bonus" (Lacey, 1986, p. 126–127). Ford's engineers knew which jobs could be tailored to each type of handicap. Ford also employed ex-convicts, some 400–600 men who he said gave him a "better day's effort . . . than his law-abiding workers" (Lacey, 1986, p. 127).

But what outsiders did not observe, including those smitten with Taylor's scientific management "cure" for waste and inefficiency, was the lobotomization of the humans who toiled in Ford's "utopia." Workers privately complained of nausea, fatigue, and exhaustion. They often became victims of assembly line "speed-ups," where the belts and conveyers were increased little by little each day to squeeze more and more work from each man and woman.

One ambitious auto worker left the Dodge brothers at $3.00 a day to work for Ford at $5.00 a day. He stayed at Ford only a week and returned to Dodge. He wrote that Ford's plant was "a form of hell on earth that turned human beings into driven robots" (Lacey, 1986, p. 128).

This same period of time was one of expanding journalism in the growth of city newspapers. Improvements in printing allowed the development of cheap magazines. Inevitably, they came to emerging social and economic topics of the times.

S. S. McClure founded *McClure's* magazine and began to print stories about developing problems. He employed a young writer, Ida Tarbell, to develop a series of articles about the Standard Oil Company (Brady, 1989). Tarbell took five years, and eventually wrote enough articles to form two books. She exposed the early methods of John D. Rockefeller and his unscrupulous dealings in driving Standard Oil to a near monopoly and mass fortune (Tarbell, 1966). Concluding her epic series, she noted:

> There is something alarming to those who believe that commerce should be a peaceful pursuit, and who believe that the moral law holds good throughout the entire range of human relations, in knowing that so large a body of young men in this country are consciously or unconsciously growing up with the idea that business is war and that morals have nothing to do with its practice (p. 226).

Tarbell's work was joined by other journalists such as Lincoln Steffens, Ray Stanndard Baker, Burton J. Hendrick, and George Kibbe Turner who exposed political corruption in the cities, and the corruption of railroad ripoffs, labor unrest , and racism. These public exposes led to works of fiction such as Frank Norris,' *The Octopus,* Theodore Dreiser's, *The Financier,* and Upton Sinclair's, *The Jungle* (see Link and Catton, 1963, pp. 75–78).

These journalists were called "the muckrakers," and they created in the mass public mind, the awareness of corruption, waste, and inefficiency that was ravaging the nation. They also promised its solution: scientific management in the form of sound business practices. Given this public media blitz, it was not long before scrutiny was turned toward the schools.

The emerging attack was to compare business methods with school methods, noting that school methods consisted of procedures that were described by George H. Martin, Secretary of the State Board of Education in Massachusetts, as "unscientific, crude, and wasteful." These remarks were given before the National Education Association at its 1905 meeting (Callahan, 1962, p. 6).

Although Taylor did not write his first work on scientific management until 1911, he was lecturing widely across the nation. He was vaulted to fame in the national railroad hearings conducted in 1910 in which a future U.S. Supreme Court Judge, Louis Brandeis, lobbied against rail fare increases before the Interstate Commerce Commission using scientific management as his weapon. Brandeis produced an engineer—Harrington Emerson—who stated that if the railroads were run by the principles of scientific management, they could save one million dollars a day (Strum, 1984, pp. 160–161). Emerson became the new national idol: the efficiency expert. The new idolatry was scientific management, and its apostle was Frederick Taylor—a man so driven by the ethic of work and the stopwatch that he invented a device to wake himself up if he ever dozed off in a chair (Lacey, 1986, p. 107).

The same Harrington Emerson who testified for Louis Brandeis in the railroad case, presented the address, "Scientific Management and High School Efficiency," before the High School Teachers Association of New York City in 1912. Emerson's essays were published by Joseph Mayer Rice in 1914, in a collection entitled *Scientific Management in Education* (Callahan, 1962, p. 23).

The combination of muckraking, which established a prima facie case of corruption and inefficiency almost everywhere—the antidote in scientific management—along with the burgeoning expenditures of public education in the cities, and the desire by the youthful professors of educational administration at work in a handful of universities for prestige, respect, authority and monopoly, combined to form the basis for the "scientific" establishment of educational administration as a serious field of study. It produced the rationale for the creation of a distinctive collegiate curriculum as well as the need for a new kind of educational expert in the persona of a scientifically prepared educational leader. Such leadership was based on science and not folk wisdom; it required serious study at the university level; it provided protection against the politics of elected school board members; and it resulted in the creation of a new educational elite with its special language and wisdom. The watchwords were *science, research, the scientific method,* and *efficiency*. These ultimately gave expression to this statement from Fred Englehardt's 1931 text, *Public School Organization and Administration,* in a chapter entitled, "Administration and Costs":

> In the last analysis, and irrespective of the educational philosopohy, cost is the factor that determines whether a service shall or shall not be rendered and whether schools shall be operated. Modern school management is guided largely by the information available on cost (p. 509).

What the new profession promised was cheap education, established by science, using research that was embodied in a step-by-step method. The result was **efficiency,** i.e., the cheapest education possible.

Early educational studies in school administration amounted to organized witch-hunts in the name of the new science of efficiency. The zeal with which it was pursued was suggestive of the establishment of a new religion without miracles or revelations, but a religion nonetheless. The high priests were professors of educational administration. The sacred words were a trinity of belief. Science was far better than superstitution. Only the "facts" mattered. The facts were garnered by investigation using the scientific method. The act of gathering the data was research. The outcome was improved efficiency. The whole process was passed off as science because it had an appearance that resembled science. But upon close inspection, it was never scientific. It was, rather, a series of answers situated in beliefs rather than established facts open to serious question. It was *doctrine*. Such interpretations are now called *ideologies* rather than science (see Boudin, 1986, pp. 28–29). A system of belief that looks like science, but at its core is not, may be called scientism.

One of the earliest examples of scientism was Leonard Ayers (1909) book, *Laggards in Our Schools*. A laggard was an overaged student who was not promoted in a graded school system. A laggard was evidence that the school system had failed. By using uncomplicated data derived from school systems, governmental sources, and other reports, Ayers established a national yardstick for judging school inefficiency. He claimed that his data and methods exposed a failure rate of approximately 33 percent for all school systems nationally. Ayers' work is laced with business and factory metaphors. "If we can find out how many children begin school each year we can compute how many remain to the final elementary grade.

Such a factor would show the relation of the finished product to the raw material" (Callahan, 1962, p. 17).

The 1925 *National Society for the Study of Education Yearbook* contained a section regarding laggards and their effect on school systems. Using a plumbing metaphor, such students "clogged the classes," and became groups that "cause considerable extra expense" (Sutherland, 1925, p. 27). The same author also noted that, "The age grade table, for example, is a method of display of facts of age-retardation. It is objective and accurate" (p. 24). Conceding that interpretion of such data was difficult due to many factors which may not "touch the point of difficulty," it was nonetheless true that "statistical studies do make it evident that something over 35 percent of the children are educationally retarded" (p. 24).

The creation of the concept of *laggards* enabled those examining the efficiency of school systems to construct a standard or benchmark by which "waste" in such organizations could be calculated. Since it was already conceded that most organizations were inefficient—an unwritten belief supported by muckracking writings— one only had to employ an expert and go hunting for it in the schools. Soon, the new "experts" in school administration, mostly college professors eager to establish themselves and their area as "different," were swarming over school systems searching for waste. The peculiar creature born of these efforts was called *the school survey*. Marvin Darsie (1933) commented on the importance of the survey in this movement to legitimize a new profession:

> Of outstanding importance was the application of the technique of the city survey to the investigation of state school systems. . . . The net result of the foregoing lines of investigation was to provide a body of scientific data for the advanced study of educational administration fully comparable in scope and value with the parallel achievements in educational psychology. The foundations had been laid for the professional training of educators on a basis comparable to that required for the professions of law and medicine (pp. 338–339).

Surveys were performed by Paul Hanus in 1911 of the Montclair Public Schools in New Jersey. Elwood Cubberley undertook surveys in the Portland Schools in 1913, and the Salt Lake City Schools in 1915. These scientific attacks on the problems of the schools came to be funded by endowed foundations such as Carnegie and Russell Sage (Darsie, 1933, p. 338). The school survey became the base to legitimate educational administration and schools of education *as scientific*, so much so that Sears (1933) observed that the new superintendent of schools would not say, "Gentlemen of the Board, I *feel* that this should be done," but instead "the superintendent states, not what he *feels*, but what he *knows*, and how he knows it" (p. 248).

The influence of the school survey had many ramifications in public education. Sears comments on some of the dimensions of its impact:

> Standard tests were developed. The survey demonstrated their use and popularized them. Now they are taken as a necessity in school work. The survey has done much to show how to revise curricula and the schools are using it. Surveys have pointed out weaknesses in marking systems. Schools are everywhere giving heed to marks. Similarly, time allotment, promotion plans, class size, and pupil personnel work of all sorts have been rationalized and stimulated by surveys (p. 249).

Sears concluded his list of improvements in education by saying, "The assumption seems fair that the survey has helped in the development of a science of education" (p. 251). The survey was the defining moment for the concept of "research" in public education (Sears, 1933, p. 249) and it was intertwined with the zeal for efficiency laid on a foundation of the assumption of waste with the antidote clearly anticipated in scientific management. Universities founded school research bureaus to continue their efforts to study school systems and eliminate inefficiencies. School systems also established their own bureaus of research to perform research on a continuous basis.

THE BENEFITS OF CENTRALIZATION: THE CONSOLIDATION OF POWER

Fueled by the popular muckrakers, financed by foundations, embued with the doctrine of gathering the facts to support their work, educational administrators and the newly emerging professor-experts, began the work of rooting out corruption in the nation's city school systems. The first attack was the inefficiency of boards of education. They were too large to be efficient. Boston had a board of 116 members (Dutton and Snedden, 1909, p. 133), Philadelphia had 500, and Pittsburgh 234 (p. 137). The reformers pointed out how wasteful such large boards were in early textbooks of school administration:

> The evils and disadvantages of large boards have been seen in nearly all our large cities. They have often presented the appearance of a legislature, with parliamentary procedure, floods of oratory, log-rolling, and those methods of interference which effectually destroy the good intentions of executive officers. Simple matters of management and discipline, which could have been settled in five minutes by a superintendent, have been fought out on the low plane of party politics, and have too often been settled by party vote (Dutton and Snedden, 1909, p. 137).

Michel Foucault (1972) has pointed out that in most discourses there is a structure of relations present that establishes an *enunciative modality* that contains an **enunciative field** comprised of overt and covert relations. These relations are embedded in the order of presentation, verification, and logical validation (p. 57). Such "fields" contain hidden meanings, errors, and assumptions no longer questioned. One can begin to pry open the hidden meanings by asking the questions, "Who is speaking? Who among the totality of speaking individuals, is accorded the right to use this sort of language?" (p. 50)

It becomes clear that the enunciative field is being defined by those who are most likely to gain in that field, i.e., the newly minted educational experts, the professors of educational administration and their major beneficiaries, future school superintendents, supervisors, and principals. In the guise of science, research, and reform, a voice is being projected with new legitimacy because it carries the banner of science. Its allies are the business and professional elites using efficiency as their weapon, and cost reduction as their battle cry. This is the discourse of educational administration. It remains largely intact into present times using the same enunciative field recast as total quality management, which despite appearances and claims to the contrary, still centralizes the power of management and validates the role of the effiency expert as the "quality consultant–statistician" (see Gabor, 1990, p. 37).

Centralizing power in educational systems enabled the expert to have maximum leverage on the system—a theme sung again and again by the Deming people in affirming absolute managerial power in setting quality and productivity (Gabor, 1990, p. 102). The legitimacy of the shift itself to central mangerial power was pointed out by Dutton and Snedden (1909) when they said, "that the crux of the whole thing is in the centralization of power in the hands of competent men. . . . The tonic which is imparted to every part of the work and to every worker by these and other efficient heads of departments is like the life-blood in a living organism" (p. 130).

The discourse of educational administration is that of centralization itself. Using concepts from the emerging field of management and texts such as Henry Fayol's fourteen principles that dealt with issues such as the span of control, unity of command and mangement, administrative hierarchy, and order and stability (Hodgetts and Kuratko, 1988, pp. 36–37), professors of educational administration constructed the architecture of school organization, so that by the 1930s, professors like Oscar Weber (1930) at the University of Illinois could declare, "Organization is but a technical device to assure the attainment of the function of the thing or institution organized" (p. 109). Weber attached to organization wasteful and inefficient practices. Among them was the idea of district organization in which, in Illinois, it had resulted in the creation of 13,000 rural school districts presided over by 39,000 directors (p. 112). One of the antidotes was the rural consolidation of school systems in order to reduce costs. He cited a 1923 study of rural schools in Indiana in which the advantages of moving toward a centralized county school would be to install "statemanlike administration and businesslike management," as well as the complete standardization of facilities, work, and salary schedules, and courses of study (p. 136).

Fayol's ideas were enhanced and expanded in the work of Lyndall Urwick (1943) and Luther Gulick (1948). They were also contained in the ideas regarding administrative practices in texts by Mary Parker Follett (1924), Elton Mayo (1933), and Chester Barnard (1938).

The period was capped by a hard look by Herbert Simon (1945) that derided some of the accepted dogma of these early thinkers. Simon picked apart the so-called administrative principles, likening them to Biblical proverbs, and noting that they usually occurred in pairs. "For almost every principle one can find an equally plausible and acceptable contradictory principle" (p. 20). Depending upon which principle one followed, an administrator could come to different conclusions in the same data field.

EFFICIENCY EXPANDED: ECONOMICS AND BEHAVIORISM

Herbert Simon's works mark a watershed in administrative thinking. Yet the discourse he utilized continued many of the same enunciative homogeneities as previous books in educational administration and management, as for example in the emphasis on efficiency. Simon blended together the perspectives on human relations and decision making of Follett (1924), Roethlisberger and Dickson (1939), Roethlisberger (1941), and Mayo (1945), and coupled these perspectives with a new emphasis on logical positivistic behavioral theory contained in the social psychology of Talcott Parsons (1951), to attack the old "principles" as "unscientific," and to offer the new as again, *truly scientific* instead of simply as paradoxical proverbs. Yet even Simon's new theoretical science contained as much doctrine as the old one that he was attacking and debunking.

Simon utilized the criterion of efficiency as the most important of all principles in developing an adequate theory of administration. Despite taking pains to dissociate himself from the work of Frederick Taylor (Simon, 1945, p. 180), he defined efficiency as, "the ratio between input and output" (p. 180) and one in which, "to be efficient means to take the shortest path, the cheapest means, toward the attainment of the desired goals" (p. 14). Efficiency for Simon involved the metaphor of the balance sheet and conceded that "the criterion of efficiency is most easily understood in its application to commercial organizations that are largely guided by the profit objective" (pp. 172–173).

In this scenario, what is most efficient is simply the cheapest route because the attainment of goals is simply maximizing profit. In this economic model, the means and the ends match. The less money spent up front on costs, the more money one has at the end, or as Simon put it, "In practice, of course, the maximization of income and the minimization of cost must be considered simultaneously—that is, what is really to be maximized is the difference between these two" (p. 173).

Simon's theoretical base is derived from this model of efficiency. From it, he defines **rational organizational behavior** on the part of management:

> The efficiency of a behavior is the ratio of the results obtainable from that behavior to the maximum of results obtainable from the behaviors which are alternative behavior to the given behavior (p. 179).

The implicit value that underscores this identification of efficient behavior is that of *scarcity of resources.* Administrative behavior is rational if it maximixes results at the lowest cost.

To do this, Simon casts out the human dimension of his proffered theory of administration. He eliminates personality as a domain outside of science, and ethics along with it. He engages in a false bit of posturing when he declares that a science of buisness has no ethical content. The statement, "Alternative *A* will lead to maximum profit" is a scientific statement, he asserts. However, he insists that the statement, "'To maximize profit is good' . . . has no place in any science" (p. 250). By defining the maximization of profit as the "best" alternative because it maximizes results (profit) with the lowest cost, the outcome is the same, i.e., what is good is the greatest profit. In this self-deceptive tautological strategem, what is ethical [nonscience] is subsumed under a rational alternative that is stipulated as factual without the so-called ethical component being present. Simon's approach has simply supresssed the ethical component instead of eliminating it. The logic becomes, "what is cheap will maximize profit." The greatest profit is the highest goal of a commercial organization. It is therefore the "best" of all possible alternatives. By default, it is the greatest good to be desired by the organization and its management.

The fallout of this kind of logic is best exemplified by a perfectly rational example of administrative decision making in which profit and cost define and inform "rational and scientific decision making" in an organization. It is an example of Simon's *economic man*—"one who selects the best alternative from among all those available to him" (p. xxv).

When the Ford Motor Company discovered that its Pinto automobile exploded sometimes when rear-ended by another car, it calculated the expense of correcting the design problem. Using a chart to calculate the cost of burn deaths, it used the figure of $200,725 per person established by the National Highway Traffic Safety Administration as the price of human life. Figuring the likelihood of such accidents and resulting damages in pain and suffering, hospital costs, and absence from work of the victims to be roughly $49.5 million, and the cost of sheathing the gas tank with a rubber lining to prevent explosions at $137 million, Ford management refused to change the auto design (Gabor, 1990, p. 133). According to Simon's model, this would be a rational decision by *economic man* based on the maximization of profit. It would be devoid of the problem of ethics and therefore totally "scientific." The idea that such situations are devoid of ethical implications is absurd. The whole concept of a scientific rationality without ethical considerations is in itself a fantasy—a doctrine of belief that is irrational.

Simon's doctrine turns on the tenets of **logical positivism** and its insistence on **objectivity** as a condition in which the observer is separated from the observed. This condition is created when a human perceiver of phenomenona is not believed to be essential to the process of observation itself. The premise itself is unprovable, and is therefore a statement of belief. A perceiver is necessary to create a condition of observation as an act. The objective world is therefore intimately bound to the eyes of the beholder and his or her politics, culture, language, and conceptual–affective awareness state, i.e., consciousness. The presence of consciousness is a necessary prerequisite to engage in perception. The observer cannot be separated from the observed. There is no objective "fact" that stands alone in a field of phenomena without the presence of a sentient human being to bring it into consciousness. All observations are of implicit value and are ethical acts.

By submerging ethics and the so-called "subjectivities" of human perception, pretending perception can be separated from what is perceived, thereby creating a kind of neutral territory in which "facts" can stand alone, and logical positivism/ behaviorism is peculiarly vulnerable to constructing tautologies. The reason is that what one observes, without deferring to contextual variables, is simply named and categorized. One ends up with a thesaurus of correlates, none of which are very precise or final because of the problem of infinite regress.

For example, in describing a leader, early trait theories described that person (the leader) as one who possessed a need for achievement, a desire to excel, a drive for responsibility and taking initiative, a responsibility for pursuing of objectives, an orientation toward tasks, an ability to enlist cooperation, administrative ability, popularity, sociability, tact, diplomacy, and the like (see Stogdill, 1974, pp. 80–81). In short, leaders are people who lead.

The behaviorists would engage in the development of operational definitions. These are supposed to be terms that led to the recognition of that which they (or anybody) can observe and therefore verify independently. They are factual and not ethical.

Simon (1945) engages in a logical circumlocution to explain how this is done. First, he rejects ethical statements because they can't be reduced to factual terms, i.e., reduced to experience following a line of argument by the logical positivists (pp. 45–46). Then he provides an example from the 1940 *U.S. Army's Infantry Field Manual*, which states that, "Surprise is an essential element of a successful attack" (p. 48). It then goes on to mention that surprise is attained by concealing the time and place of an attack shielding such things as deployment from the enemy, as well as not using stereotypical methods.

Simon reduces this passage to three statements. The first, he insists, is an ethical and not a factual statement—i.e., "attack successfully." In the second, he states, "an attack is successful only when carried out under conditions of surprise," which he considers factual. The third statement, "The conditions of surprise are concealment of the time and place of attack" is also factual and not ethical.

Simon never indicates exactly how "an attack is successful only when carried out under conditions of surprise" and equates to "success = surprise"—another form of "attack successfully." He concedes that the decisions a commander might make are both factual and ethical, and that a science of administrative behavior is only concerned with purely factual matters. Simon insists that the factual part of this situation, whether or not the commander takes measures in order to accomplish his aim, are the appropriate content of science. "It is not a factual question whether the aim itself is correct or not, except in so far as this aim is connected, by an 'order' to further aims" (pp. 48–49). But the aim was surprise. Surprise is a value judgment—a desired state of affairs—not a factual condition in and of itself. The behavior adopted by the commander was aimed at this desired condition which was not factual, but ethical. In what way then can these behaviors be considered objective or factual?

Simon counters by insisting that, "Strictly speaking, it is not the decision itself which is evaluated, but the purely factual relationship that is asserted between the decision and its aims" (p. 49). Exactly what the "purely factual relationship" that stands between any decision and the aims of that decision might be are not identified. Then, in a turn on words, Simon circles this linguistic and logical dilemma by saying, "The commander's decision to take particular measures in order to attain surprise is not evaluated; what is evaluated is his factual judgment that the measures he takes will, in fact, attain surprise" (p. 49).

One might say that Simon will not evaluate:

1. the commander's decision to take any course of action
2. specific measures the commander selected to attain his aim (suprise)

What Simon will evaluate are:

1. the factual relationship that is asserted between the decision and its aims (surprise)

2. the factual judgment that the measures taken attain surprise (are congruent with them) (p. 49).

Yet what lies between the decision and its aims is a judgment, hardly factual (neutral or objective), that the measures selected will result in surprise. There can be no factual grounds that exist apart from either the aims or the means, or the decision to adopt those that attain the ends, if by factual we mean able to stand alone untainted by ethical or value judgments. Where then is a science of administrative theory that pretends it is possible?

What is at work here is logical positivism's classic inability to question its own essential premises. While it insists that all things must be observable and factual in order to be considered scientific, the assertion itself cannot be verified by anything that is observable and factual. It is therefore a statement of belief—a powerful, nonobservable metaphysical assertion and not science at all.

Devitt and Sterelny (1987) explain:

> One cannot theorize about anything, least of all language, without implicit commitment to a view of the world. As a result, attempts to eliminate metaphysics lead not to its elimination but to its mystification; the philosopher has to hide or deny his own metaphysical assumptions (p. 190).

The turning on words to separate fact from nonfact results in elaborate explanations that result in logical tautologies touted as science. This kind of "science" is awash in correlations that are simply linguistic permutations—synonyms for the same things—that collectively or individually have no predictive or explanatory power. The impact of behaviorism as trait theory, as the basis for a theory of decision making, or as a basis to prepare or predict leadership, has been a gigantic failure. The quest for contextless situations by which traits or behaviors can be summarized as predictive is a bankrupt strategy founded on premises that only further mystify rather than explain what leadership is. So-called operational definitions have led to tautologies. The method itself—its assumptions and premises—go nowhere. Rost's (1991) admonition should be heeded:

> Leadership studies as an academic discipline needs to come out of the woodwork of management science in all of its guises . . . and out of such discipines as social psychology, political science and sociology (p. 182).

The whole approach to studying leadership rooted in scientific management, behavioral science, and social psychology have been unproductive roads to understand educational leadership. Yet, even as many academics have come to realize this situation, educational administration has been confronted with one more offshoot of its early proclivities to hastily embrace efficiency methods cast in the guise of pseudoscience.

THE NEW DOCTRINE OF EFFICIENCY: TOTAL QUALITY MANAGEMENT

The new managerial gospel of the late 1980s and early 1990s is that of TQM (total quality management) or simply *quality*. It is the modern-day transformation of Frederick Taylor's scientific mangement. Its prophet is W. Edwards Deming. Deming's philosohical roots lie in probability theory, a new kind of statistical structuralism that insists that a "fact" has no meaning until and unless it can be located within acceptable control limits (see Shewart, 1986). Numbers represent reality which is ultimately stable in a Platonic universe. Deming's philosopher– ontologist is Clarence Lewis (1929) who holds that there is a reality outside of human experience and that "experience does not itself determine what is good or bad . . . nor does it determine what is valid or invalid, or the nature of logical validity" (p. 14). This is the rock of all objectivist science, and pseudoscience as well. It is blind to its own subjective ontology (Gadamer's double hermeneutic).

But perhaps the most illustrative of Lewis' (1929) positions is that, "experience does not categorize itself" (p. 14). Deming's work is filled with moral and linguistic binary categories to pigeonhole experience such as true/false, control/chaos, win/lose, system/nonsystem, competition/cooperation, right/wrong, prediction/non-prediction, optimization/suboptimization, common/special causes, trust/nontrust, and perfection/nonperfection.

Because Deming's ontology is stable, his categories are assumed to be stable as well. Attacking the assumption of the stability of reality that is outside human experience has also been called *deconstruction*. The questioning of the Platonic universe and its ideality as reality has occurred in the writings of many contemporary philosophers—from Edmund Husserl to Jacques Derrida (see Evans, 1991, p. 85).

All binary distinctions (or categories) rest on the assumption that they can exclusively accept or reject experience in order to remain stable. One difficulty is that the acceptance of one means the other must be constantly present so that it is not absent. For example, the word *true* makes little sense without holding in one's mind the category of *false*. Otherwise, what does it mean to be *true*? The presence of the oppositional sign creates tension and instability between the two superficially oppositional terms, *true* and *false*.

Let us take an example that Deming uses in his seminars to illustrate the difference between the oppositional pairs—common/special causes. The distinctions between these two types of causes are considered stable. Deming says, "a person falls down reading a gauge because of rickety steps." Is this a common or a special cause? If these were the one set of steps unlike any other in the factory, the cause would be special. If, however, they are like other steps, they would be common.

Now suppose the failure to repair the steps was due to general neglect—a common cause. Suppose, however, the neglect was the result of one worker. This would be a special cause. Suppose that this worker was hired by faulty rules of the personnel department. This would be a common cause. However, the personnel department hired only one worker, the neglectful repairperson. This would be a special cause that occurred because of a common cause. It is possible that the failure to repair the rickety steps is both a special and a common cause. This, of course, confounds the categorical distinction utilized. Theoretically, it would be impossible to be both. Practically, it would be possible.

In the arena of true/false, sometimes false theories generate some truth, and true theories generate false responses. In reality, the categories used in objective science are subject to such scrutiny and may collapse linguistically—i.e., they can't cleanly separate events, data, facts, observations, and the like.

Deming's statistical ontology also suffers from at least one major flaw. Deming (1993) insists that, "management in any form is prediction" (p. 93) and that "the central problem of management in all its aspects . . . is to understand better the meaning of variation" (1986, p. 20). The major means to accomplish prediction is to use a method that identifies patterns because with repetition within statistical control, "a process . . . has a definable identity and definable capability (1986, p. 339).

Truth in Deming's world is established by upper and lower control limits to a given range of phenomena. Truth is repetition within these ranges. Popper (1965) disputes the idea that repetition establishes truth when he observes, "coherence, or consistency, is no criterion of truth, simply because even demonstrably consistent systems may be false in fact" (p. 226). Popper (1985) then draws a distinction in using probabilities or frequencies to establish truth. What is decisive about the use of frequencies in probability is not its results, but the conditions under which the frequencies were obtained. So a probability statement is not about the sequence going on, nor about the results obtained, rather, "it is a statement about certain properties of the experimental conditions" (p. 203). The difference is both onto-logical and methodological. Popper's world is indeterminate. Deming's world is determinate.

Foucault's (1972) *Archaeology of Knowledge* provides the analytical tools to con-nect Taylor's scientific management and W. Edwards Deming's total quality man-agement. Both are part of the discourse of efficiency. The parallelisms between the two movements can be captured by examining the linguistic analogies, logical iden-tities, and enunciative homogeneities employed in both.

The dominant linguistic analogy for both scientific management and total quality management is the assembly line. Frederick Taylor worked with a stop-watch and task analysis to reduce movement and enhance efficiency. W. Edwards Deming employs the statistical control chart for the same purpose. Both were motiviated to reduce variability, enhance control, and attain greater precision. While both proffered enhanced worker latitude, neither approach has emancipat-ed workers.

The logical identity of both movements is centered squarely on order, stability, and hierarchy. Deming's use of statistics, which are measures of central tendencies, reinforces dominant bureaucratic control patterns. He continually insists that, "Quality is determined by the top management. It cannot be delegated" (Deming, 1993, p. 17). He refuses to work with corporations in which top management is not absolutely committed to his doctrine. Hierarchy is reinforced.

Because industrial hierarchy is preserved and protected, the subordinated groups of workers remain captured in their organizations. Androcentrism reigns supreme. When Deming began his work at Western Electric in the twenties, he noted that:

Mr. Coulter exacted out of me straightaway a promise not to get caught on a stairway when the whistle blows: those women with their high heels would trample me to death, and there would be no record. I did not get caught, but I saw what he meant. Of the

46,000 people that worked at the Hawthorne plant, I think that 43,000 of them were women (1993, pp. 177–178).

Deming's work was never emanicipatory of the subordination of women in the organizations in which he worked.

The enunciative homogeneity of both movements is that they are offered as a religion—a doctrine passed off as science. Both systems emphasized the application of numbers to operations. Both Taylor and Deming approached their tasks as preachers. Their works are replete with the tone of scientism, and with disdain for anything that would stand in their way. Deming's apparent democratization of the workforce is simply a tactic to gain tighter central control, in order to construct a system that reduces all forms of in-system variance. The concept of *kaizen* (Imai, 1986), means "continuous improvement," of all things at all levels in an organization (p. 4). The equivalent is simply maximization of the reduction of variation. Unnecessary variance is seen as waste, and kaizen is very much centered on efficiency. Workers are involved because there is no other way to gain entry to reduce variations that are causative in nature, and that are attributed to their decisions. By involving workers, they become as standardized as the parts they produce. Once this occurs, as Deming insists, one does not have to worry about them as a source of variation. The reason is that they have become part of the system and subsumed in its operations.

Figure 7.2 compares Frederick Taylor's scientific mangement with W. Edwards Deming's total quality management (see following page).

Total quality management is the new architecture of efficiency. Both advocates, Taylor at the turning of the twentieth century and Deming in the later period, approached their work with religious zeal, broaching little tolerance for dissent (Gabor, 1990, p. 66). Both developed a doctrine using numerical methods and gave the appearance of being scientific. Both doctrines were metanarratives of power that enhanced the role of the expert and reinforced management's role in dominating discussions of productivity.

Where Taylorism and Demingism differ is on the choice of control methods to reduce variance. Taylor's system emphasizes piece-rate pay systems that rewarded individual productivity. Deming's work takes advantage of the Hawthorne studies performed by Elton Mayo. Deming worked at Hawthorne at the same time Mayo was doing his studies on worker productivity which illustrated the powerful effect group norms have on overall worker output (Gabor, 1990, p. 41).

Deming saw that piece-rate systems were usually subordinated to the social requirements of groups. Control systems that did not include this variable were bound to fail. Deming's statistical concepts were simply amalgamated with the new social psychology of organizations. Empowering workers was merely a way of recognizing the control they already possessed. It is important, however, that Deming did not advocate challenging organizational hierarchy. This would be a threat to his perceived need for order and stability.

So the new "twist" between total quality management and scientific management turned on the abolition of piece-rate systems, and with them such mutations

Figure 7.2   A COMPARISON BETWEEN SCIENTIFIC MANAGEMENT
              AND TOTAL QUALITY MANAGEMENT

Area	Scientific Management	Total Quality Management
Authority	Reinforces top management	Same
Voices legitimated	The expert external to the system	Same
Major metaphor	The assembly line	Same
Primary data source	Stopwatch—task analysis	Statistical control charts
Primary approach to problem solving	Reduction of variance	Same
Employee motivators	External—piece-rate systems	Internal—"empowerment"
Implicit objective	Elimination of waste	Same
Major tactic	Didactic—one right way	Same

as bonus plans, merit pay, management by objectives (MBO), quotas, and the like because they didn't work. They were often counterproductive to raising overall productivity. Such schemes did not recognize the social cohesion of workers—norms that were the key to breakthrough levels of productivity.

What total quality management proposed was to put the statistical control chart in the hands of management, and to "allow" the workers to make choices within acceptable bands of variation. The leverage for such empowerment was always anchored in the statistical control chart. This chart defined and controlled what was permissible. What was valued was the relentless reduction of variation. What was eschewed were any contributions to variation outside the acceptable bands of variance defined by the control chart. This was the new "democracy" of the workplace.

Deming's total quality management is a form of co-optation, where worker antagonism based on concepts of individualism is clearly subordinated to the priorities of the organization. The source of the variation within the decisions of the workers are instead recognized, and allowed some room for play within a new manifestation of organizational control. Deming's use of psychology is strictly manipulative, as was most of the generation of writers that emphasized human relations in organizations without true emancipation (see Gross, 1964, pp. 55–64, and Campbell, Fleming, Newall, and Bennion, 1987, pp. 43–62). The human relations movement made industrial organizations less overtly oppressive, but no less domineering and hierarchical. The visible forms of control were removed, but they remain intact through more subtle means.

The gospel of efficiency is a peculiar combination of fundamental Protestanism with roots traceable to Luther himself, coupled with the rise of the factory and the search for profits mixed with various forms of technology, numeration systems, and calculation models, and mixed with social psychology that continues into modern times. W. Edwards Deming is another advocate in a long line of efficiency prophets who have used techniques affiliated with science to claim that their doctrines were properly *scientific,* when in actuality they were merely ideologies, i.e., closed systems of belief that looked like science. Deming's approach has never courted refutation. It, as well as its leader—the quality expert—claim it to be the one and only correct answer. His doctrine is to be accepted, not challenged.

Perhaps Deming's greatest disservice to educational administration is his shallow portrayal of leadership. The chapter on this topic in his last book, *The New Economics* (1993), is a bare five pages long (pp. 119–123). In it, Deming calls for a leader to transform the organization and indicates, "He possesses knowledge, personality, and persuasive power" (p. 119). He then provides an example of a leader in the person of Morris H. Hansen, and indicates that, "He was thus in possession of some knowledge of the theory of probability, and of errors in surveys" (p. 121). Hansen helped design a survey for postal routes. He later became Assistant Director for Statistical Standards in the Bureau of the Census (p. 123). Deming's leaders are those in the mold of calculators, samplers, statisticians, and problem solvers with probability theory. In fact, his "profound knowledge" is largely a mixture of probability theory along with a smattering of motivational psychology, human relations, and system theory.

Deming's (1986) fourteen points are replete with calls for leadership. For example, in Point Number 2 he says, "take on leadership for change" (p. 23). Point Number 7 exhorts, "Institute leadership" (p. 23). Point Number 11 says, "Eliminate work standards (quotas) on the factory floor. Substitute leadership" (p. 24). He uses the same phrase, "substitute leadership" for dropping MBO (management by objectives) in Point Number 11 as well.

The context of leadership in Deming's work is control, stability, prediction, and hierarchy (see Mann 1989, p. 106, 126). Leadership is primarily technique. It is statistical leadership (see Mann, 1989, p. 178).

Deming talks about transforming organizations. But it is clear from his descriptions of leaders and transformed organizations that he really means a more productive and humane status quo. This fact ought to explain why TQM is so popular in the world of business. While Deming (1993) is fond of insisting that everybody can be a winner—"Everybody wins with optimization" (p. 53)—this is a play on words since in a hierarchical society, those at the bottom can never win as much as those at the top. Deming might call them "little winners." Others might call them "losers." In any scenario, this labeling doesn't fundamentally change the hierarchy.

With TQM, educational administration will have been seduced into believing that the status quo is the best of all possible worlds.

SUMMARY

This chapter highlighted the enduring search for efficiency in American education that is the peculiar progeny of religion, industrialization, socioeconomic relationships, and the continuing coporate hegemony in public life.

Educational leadership was born in the tenets of basic Puritanism, baptized in secular scientism, and continually washed in the river of research dominated by the currents of cost reduction. New prophets Frederick Taylor and W. Edwards Deming arose, which extended the doctrine of cost reduction and efficiency. Both were hailed by the industrial–political leadership of their times as saviors of productivity and democracy. Both espoused doctrines that were profoundly antidemocratic and antiscientific. Neither was recognized as such in those same times.

Educational leadership in twentieth-century America was advanced as a new, scientifically based profession. It therefore required separate preparation in the newly developing colleges of education. The claim to be "scientific" enabled this perspective to prosper and prevail for many generations.

Its intellectual heritage was severely challenged in the Callahan (1962) exposé, *Education and the Cult of Efficiency*. The "theory movement" of the sixties was an attempt to establish a new intellectual base for the profession that implicitly recognized the heritage of efficiency as dead. This attempt was rocked in the late seventies and eighties by writings of T. B. Greenfield (1988) who exposed it as largely barren and just as political. It is to this shift in metanarratives that the last chapter in the book is devoted.

Perception Check and Applications

1. Horace Mann, the Educational Reformer

Compare the life of Horace Mann to any number of school reformers on the scene today. Compare the release of *The Nation at Risk* to any of Horace Mann's twelve public reports as Secretary of Education in Massachusetts. What similarities do you find? In what ways has the discourse regarding the need for change in education remained the same or been transformed? One good source of Mann documents and other American school reform writings is Michael Katz's (1971) *School Reform: Past and Present* (Boston: Little, Brown and Company).

2. The Discourse of American School Superintendents

Pursue writings by and descriptions of the lives and ideas of early American school superintendents (1800–1900). These were men and women who shaped the top school job in the nation. Analyze what the major concerns were in their times. What were the sources of their ideas? What suppressed or hidden metaphors informed their images of needed changes in education? A good source of data exists in nearly every state in the official annual reports of the state superintendents of public instruction. These documents most often included yearly reports from the county and city school superintendents.

3. The Animation of Muckraking and the Public Mind

Obtain the works of popular muckrakers such as Ida Tarbell. Compare their works to modern examples of investigative reporting such as Bob Woodward and

Carl Bernstein's (1976) *The Final Days* (New York: Simon and Schuster) or Woodward's (1979) controversial *The Brethren* (New York: Simon and Schuster). What are the common themes that surround muckracking? How does such writing establish norms, expectations, or suspicions in the public about public officeholders? Can you cite any examples that also apply to school administrators?

4. School Surveys as Educational Research

Early forms of educational research took the form of school surveys. Through the library retrieval system, obtain a copy(ies) of some original school surveys. Examine these documents for their assumptions and biases. What is described as "good," and as "poor"? What overt and covert standards run through them? Compare the rise of the school survey to the concomitant rise of standardized testing in the United States. Are there similarities and parallel, reinforcing currents that inform both?

5. Tracing the Influence of Logical Positivism and Educational Practices

Obtain any source that traces the thoughts and assumptions of logical positivism as scientific thought and method (some authors would be Schlick, Bergmann, Carnap, Feigl, Frank, Godel, Hahn, Neurath, and Waismann). Identify the major lines of argument and link them to at least three major concepts in any one of the following areas: educational psychology, sociology, teaching, instruction, counseling, or school administration. Are these concepts still considered important and relevant? If not, explain how they have been transformed or replaced.

6. The Enduring Legacy of Trait Theory

Obtain any of the popular self-help books in educational administration or business, such as Stephen Covey's (1990) *Seven Habits of Highly Effective People* (New York: Simon and Schuster) or Wareham's (1991) *The Anatomy of a Great Executive* (New York: HarperCollins) that focus on developing habits, approaches, viewpoints, or traits to become successful. Examine the research base for these books. What original research or study informs them? How much research or study was completed prior to their being marketed as personal development tools? Is the base adequate to engage in generalizations? Are such books examples of science or scientism?

7. The Hubris of W. Edwards Deming and the Total Quality Management Movement

Obtain a list of Deming's fourteen principles and his other views of productivity and management. Which aspects of schooling are conducive to the application of the principles and which ones appear to be resistant? What factors in school operations are subject to variance? How have such sources been viewed—both positively and negatively? In what ways do educational systems control sources of variance to focus and connect their work and resource application techniques? How will Deming's ideas be put to use to reduce sources of variance in educational systems? What do you perceive as the most long-lasting impact of Deming's ideas in education?

Key Chapter Concepts and Terms

discursive transformation

The change of a discourse, both spoken and unspoken, that maintains its original assumptions and thrust, but alters its appearence and surface logic, or appeal.

efficiency

A state of affairs in which a goal, process, or outcome has been pursued or attained at the lowest possible cost.

enunciative field

A terrain or discourse in which certain modalities or forms are presented and exist in overt and covert relations to internal and external objects and expressions of power. Such fields are advanced by those most likely to benefit from their adoption, adherence, or extension.

logical positivism

A perspective on research and academic study that posited that what was considered "scientific" had to be observable and verifiable through one of the five senses. Such verification resulted in the production of "facts." Facts, in turn, were not subjectivities, but rather objectivities that could be independently shown to exist apart from human perception or bias. This view has largely been discredited, but remains a strong influence in psychology and in some branches of specialized science.

objectivity

A neutral state that is supposed to exist when the observer is separated from that which is being observed. Posited on the belief that such a separation is possible, and that human perception, which creates the conditions necessary to embody objectivity, is free from bias.

rational organizational behavior

The concept that observable actions on the part of people in organizations are motivated by their desire to accomplish certain goals which are deemed important to the organization in order for it to exist and profit in an economic world.

school survey

An approach to the "study" of educational systems in which outside experts calculated various types of efficiencies, and engaged in reforming them based on their research. Such forms of analysis have been shown to be largely based on simplistic doctrines of assembly line notions of efficiency.

scientism

A doctrine, body of knowledge, theory, or viewpoint that is passed off as science or as scientific, when in reality it is an ideology—a system of beliefs that is not open to refutation because the thing itself would dissolve under such questioning.

trait theory

A view that successful leaders are endowed with certain capacities that would earmark them as different from nonleaders. The concept hinged on the notion of a contextless set of universal characteristics superceding any situation in which it might arise and be observed. The intellectual base has largely been abandoned. Some transformations of trait theory are still in the marketplace, however, as behavioral clusters, habits, or characteristics of successful people or leaders.

References

Ayers, L. P. (1909). *Laggards in Our Schools*. New York.

Barnard, C. I. (1938). *The Functions of the Executive*. Cambridge, Massachusetts: Harvard University Press.

Berman, B. (1983, Fall). "Business Efficiency, American Schooling, and Public School Superintendency: A Reconsideration of the Callahan Thesis," *History of Education Quarterly*, pp. 297–319.

Blumberg, A. (1989). *School Administration as a Craft*. Boston: Allyn and Bacon, Inc.

Bogardus, E. S. (1918). *Essentials of Social Psychology*. Los Angeles: University of Southern California Press.

Boudin, R. (1986). *The Analysis of Ideology*. Chicago: University of Chicago Press.

Bowles, S., and Gintis, H. (1976). *Schooling in Capitalistic America*. New York: Basic Books, Inc.

Brady, K. (1989). *Ida Tarbell*. Pittsburgh, PA: University of Pittsburgh Press.

Button, H. W., and Provenzo, E. F. Jr. (1989). *History of Education and Culture in America*. Englewood Cliffs, New Jersey: Prentice Hall.

Callahan, R. E. (1962). *Education and the Cult of Efficiency*. Chicago: University of Chicago Press.

Callahan, R. E., and Button, H. W. (1964). "Historical Change of the Role of the Man in the Organization: 1865–1950" in D. E. Griffiths (Ed.), *Behavioral Science and Educational Administration*. Chicago: University of Chicago Press.

Campbell, R. F., Fleming, T., Newell, L. J., and Bennion, J. W. (1987). *A History of Thought and Practice in Educational Administration*. New York: Teachers College Press.

Conway, M. (1915). *The Crowd in Peace and War*. New York: Longmans, Green.

Covey, S. R. (1991). *The Seven Habits of Highly Effective People*. New York: Simon and Schuster.

Cremin, L. A. (1980). *American Education*. New York: Harper and Row.

Cuban, L. (1988). *The Managerial Imperative and the Practice of Leadership in Schools*. Albany, New York: SUNY Press.

Darsie, M. S. (1933). "Education Becomes a Profession" in J. C. Almack (Ed.), *Modern School Administration*. Boston: Houghton Mifflin Company, pp. 327–348.

Deming, W. E. (1986). *Out of the Crisis*. Cambridge, MA: Massachusetts Institute of Technology.

Deming, W. E. (1993). *The New Economics*. Cambridge, MA: Massachusetts Institute of Technology.

Devitt, M., and Sterelny, K. (1987). *Language and Reality*. Cambridge, Massachusetts: The MIT Press.

Dutton, S. T., and Snedden, D. (1909). *The Administration of Public Education in the United States*. New York: The Macmillan Company.

Eldridge, B. (1992, November–December). "AirLand Operations: The U.S. Army's Search for a New Doctrine," *Command*, 19, pp. 32–52.

Englehardt, F. (1931). *Public School Organization and Administration*. Boston: Ginn and Company.

Evans, J. C. (1991). *Strategies of Deconstruction*. Minneapolis: University of Minnesota Press.

Follett, M. P. (1924). *Creative Experience*. London: Longmans, Green & Co.

Foucault, M. (1972). *The Archaeology of Knowledge*. New York: Pantheon Books.

Foucault, M. (1973). *Madness and Civilization*. New York: Vintage Books.

Gabor, A. (1990). *The Man Who Discovered Quality*. New York: Penguin Books.

Greenfield, T. B. (1988). "The Decline and Fall of Science in Educational Administration," in D. E. Griffiths, R. T. Stout, and P. B. Forsyth (Eds.), *Leaders for America's Schools*. Berkeley, CA: McCutchan Publishing Corp., pp. 131–159.

Gross, B. M. (1964). "The Scientific Approach to Administration" in D. E. Griffiths (Ed.), *Behavioral Science and Educational Administration*. Chicago: University of Chicago Press, pp. 33–72.

Gulick, L. (1948). *Administrative Reflection on World War II*. Tuscaloosa, Alabama: University of Alabama Press.

Harman, H. H. (1968). *Modern Factor Analysis*. Chicago: University of Chicago Press.

Hodgetts, R. M., and Kuratko, D. F. (1988). *Management*. San Diego, California: Harcourt, Brace, Jovanovich.

Imai, M. (1986). *Kaizen: The Key to Japan's Competitive Success*. New York: McGraw Hill.

Katz, M. B. (1968). *The Irony of Early School Reform*. Boston: Beacon Press.

Katz, M. B. (1971). *School Reform: Past and Present*. Boston: Little, Brown and Company.

Katz, M. B. (1971). *Class, Bureaucracy, and Schools*. New York: Praeger Publishers.

Lacey, R. (1986). *Ford: The Men and the Machine*. Boston: Little, Brown and Company.

LeBon, G. (1897). *The Crowd*. New York: Macmillan.

Leidecker, K. F. (1946). *Yankee Teacher*. New York: The Philosophical Library.

Lewis, C. I. (1929). *Mind and the World Order*. New York: Dover Publications, Inc.

Lide, E. S. (1929, April 3). "Personality Traits of School Administrators," *Educational Research Bulletin of Ohio State University*, 7.

Link, A. S., and Catton, W. B. (1963). *American Epoch*. New York: Alfred A. Knopf.

Mann, M. P. (1937). *Life of Horace Mann*. Washington, D.C.: National Education Association of the United States.

Mann, N. R. (1989). *The Keys to Excellence*. Los Angeles: Prestwick Books.

Mayo, E. (1933). *The Human Problems of an Industrial Civilization*. Boston: Harvard Business School.

Mayo, E. (1945). *The Social Problems of an Industrial Civilization*. Boston: Harvard Business School.

Messerli, J. (1972). *Horace Mann*. New York: Alfred A. Knopf.

Parsons, T. (1951). *The Social System*. Glencoe, Illinois: The Free Press.

Popper, K. R. (1965). *Conjectures and Refutations: The Growth of Scientific Knowledge*. New York: Harper and Row.

Popper, K. R. (1985). *Popper Selections*. Princeton, New Jersey: Princeton University Press.

Ravitch, D. (1974). *The Great School Wars*. New York: Basic Books, Inc.

Roethlisberger, F. J., and Dickson, W. J. (1939). *Management and the Workers*. Cambridge, Massachusetts: Harvard University Press.

Roethlisberger, F. J. (1941). *Management and Morale*. Cambridge: Harvard University Press.

Rost, J. C. (1991). *Leadership for the Twenty-First Century*. New York: Praeger.

Sears, J. B. (1933). "The School Survey Movement" in J. C. Almack (Ed.), *Modern School Administration*. Boston: Houghton Mifflin, pp. 217–262.

Shewart, W. A. (1986). *Statistical Method from the Viewpoint of Quality Control*. New York: Dover Publications, Inc.

Simon, H. A. (1945). *Administrative Theory*. New York: Macmillan.

Spearman, C. (1904). "General Intelligence, Objectively Determined and Measured," *American Journal of Pscyhology*, 15, pp. 201–293.

Spring, J. (1986). *The American School 1642–1985*. New York: Longman.

Stogdill, R. M. (1974). *Handbook of Leadership*. New York: The Free Press.

Strayer, G. D. (1933). "The Superintendent and the Board of Education," in J. C. Almack (Ed.), *Modern School Administration*. Boston: Houghton Mifflin.

Strum, P. (1984). *Louis D. Brandeis: Justice for the People*. New York: Schocken Books.

Sutherland, A. A. (1925). "Factors Causing Maladjustment of Schools to Individuals" in G. M. Whipple (Ed.), *Adapting the Schools to Individual Differences*. Bloomington, Illinois: Bloomington School Publishing Company, pp. 1–52.

Tarbell, I. M. (1966). *The History of the Standard Oil Company*. D. M. Chalmers (Ed.). New York: Harper and Row.

Tharp, L. H. (1953). *Until Victory*. Boston: Little, Brown and Company.

Tyack, D. B. (1974). *The One Best System*. Cambridge, Massachusetts: Harvard University Press.

Urwick, L. (1943). *The Elements of Administration*. New York: Harper & Row.

Wareham, J. (1991). *The Anatomy of a Great Executive*. New York: HarperCollins.

Weber, O. F. (1930). *Problems in Public School Administration*. New York: The Century Co.

Woodward, B., and Bernstein, C. (1976). *The Final Days*. New York: Simon and Schuster.

Woodward, B. (1979). *The Brethren*. New York: Simon and Schuster.

STRUCTURALISM, POST-STRUCTURALISM, AND BEYOND

The Future of Educational Administration

For almost 30 years educational administration has been centered in the **theory movement.** This movement was part of the founding of UCEA (University Council for Educational Administration) in 1956 (see Campbell, Fleming, Newell, and Bennion, 1987, pp. 182–184). The theory movement is a hybrid, combining the metanarratives of behaviorism and structuralism. This metanarrative's intellectual heritage can be traced to the logical positivists of the famed Vienna Circle (1924–1936) (see Runes, 1984, p. 302).

The impact of the Vienna Circle is still felt by the dominance of organizational theory as the force field in which inquiry is to be conducted and judged in educational administration. As a combination of behaviorism and structuralism, organizational theory has emphasized observation as the preferred channel of verification, precise operational definitions, and "logico-mathematical procedures" (Griffiths, 1964, p. 98) which meant largely parametric forms of calculating probabilities anchored in the assumption that numbers representing past occurrences will similarly recur in the future. The metacritical assumption behind the theory movement is that of determinism, i.e., there is an order to things; one merely has to persevere to find it.

The gradual shift from behaviorism to structuralism can be detected in early trait studies of leadership where it became apparent that traits were *situationally defined* (Stogdill, 1974, p. 59). Later studies by Halpin (1966), in which bomber-pilot crew relationships were plotted, produced the concept of school climate. Climates, as *situations qua situations,* were the results of behavioral manifestations of the captain or principal interacting with the crew or teachers, whatever the case may be. Climates, as situations, were grounded in behaviorism because they were caused by observable actions that the school principal exhibited in schools. Pavel (1992) has traced the line of evolution of structuralism through behavioral psychology in the work of Leonard Bloomfield in the 1930s. Bloomfield (1933) rejected human intuition and introspection, as did most behaviorists.

Organizational situations developed by behaviors gave way first to generic managerial beliefs such as McGregor's (1967) *theory x and theory y,* and later to functions that were perceived to be influenced by goals. The varying purposes of organizations were the subject of attempts to classify them as the case with Merton (1951), Blau and Scott (1962), and Talcott Parsons (1966). Functions were finally redefined as structures in the work of Mintzberg (1983), and to the current time, structures as *frames* (see Bolman and Deal, 1991).

Organizational theory may be conceptualized as a form of structuralism. The practical base for a discussion of structuralism is linguistics and semiotics. The theoretical base, however, is what is more important than the actual context in which structuralism as a metanarrative rests.

The roots of contemporary structuralism can be traced to either an obscure Swiss linguist named Ferdinand de Saussure (1857–1913), or to an equally obscure American philosopher, Charles Sanders Peirce (1839–1914). Both brilliant scholars, they pursued the idea that there was to be discovered in language a certain kind of unity and stability, or underlying order of things.

CONSTRUCTING THE TEXT: ABANDONING THE REFERENT

The search for order was one thing. Another thing was Saussure's insistence that once language moved from speech or concept to writing, it could be studied without any particular problem of knowing the context or referents from which the original writing had emerged.

Saussure insisted that language, words, and ultimately *meaning* were to be totally encapsulated in the text itself as independent of reality (Gadet, 1989, p. 33). Once language became writing, it did not matter what the author originally intended. It mattered only what meaning the words had in relation to other words *in the system*. Meaning was independent of the speaker or of history. In this perspective, all contextual references to reality are eradicated. What becomes the central concern for both *structuralists* and *post-structuralists* is what the text is about and how to interpret it. The *context* for discussing meaning is the *text*, and not the referent which may have prompted the author to take pen in hand originally. A structuralist is concerned with relationships and not things (Hawkes, 1977, pp. 17–18). In this sense, structuralism is *ahistorical* (Devitt and Sterelny, 1987, p. 215). Ontologically, by divorcing words from their referents and limiting the discourse to only meaning *within text*, the result is a kind of *radical relativism*. This is the kind of world in which it is very difficult to frame a discussion for moral leadership unless it is some kind of dedication to the process of discerning relations, and not as any kind of absolutes grounded in reality.

THE SEARCH FOR INTERNAL SYNCHRONY: ORGANIZATIONAL THEORY

Structuralism provided, in the words of Foucault (1972), a kind of synchrony, a totality, a world view of coherency, "a sovereignty of the subject" (p. 12). History became a narrative of totalities, continuities, and regularities. Science became a relentless search for the narratives that were expected to run through fields, periods of time, and ideas divided by neat chronologies. Mary Parker Follett (1942) imagined that social behavior within unities provided the knowledge base for "organization engineering," and "the key to history, law, economics, and to business administration" (p. 185). Hers was a search for unity within integration. The latter idea provided "a mechanism for control, a method of decision-making, and a behavior characteristic" (Krupp, 1961, p. 88). Organizational theory provided educational administration with a kind of leitmotif, a whole fabric, upon and within which to examine individual and group behavior, as well as generic functions that are even more far removed from a focus on behaviors.

One of the first definitive works in organizational theory was that of Katz and Kahn (1966). They rejected various forms of behaviorism as being too narrow, and instead found in "open-system theory" the model for their work (p. 8). The intellectual precursors for open-system theory were the works of F. H. Allport (1954) and the general-systems theorists (Miller, 1955). They were also highly influenced by Parsons' (1951) general work in social system theory. What was seductive about these works was the idea that patterns within organizations subsumed and defined individual behavioral patterns. What was at stake in this re-centering of the study of behavior was that the emphasis shifted from the individual and references to what motivated individual behavior (the equivalent of the external referent to text) to what shaped behavior which was within organizations, i.e., to the text itself.

Organizational theory provided a rationale to abandon the search for personal variables that were internal to people, to those forces and patterns in organizations that shaped people (Katz and Kahn, 1966, p. 12). The basic tenets of behaviorism grounded in logical positivism remained. What was different was the emphasis on organizations as texts. It was to be organizations that determined meaning for people, not the meaning people provided for organizations. One consequence was noted by Chris Argyris (1972) who lamented that in some organizational theories, "The 'variable human' seems to be minimally variable and minimally human" (p. 33). Whereas some behaviorists like Freud were concerned with the human interior as the true locus of understanding, organizational theorists were only concerned with how behavior was reactive to organizational functions. In this way, individual behavior could be neglected "(supposedly the real stuff of organizational life) in all its multiplicity and variability" (Perrow, 1986, p. 122).

Structuralism in educational administration has come to be a definitive way of constructing the field for those entering it. The dominant texts in the field are positivistic, behavioristic, and structuralistic in how the field is configured for neophytes (see Owens, 1981; Hoy and Miskel, 1982). It was to this intellectual hegemony that T. B. Greenfield began his series of critiques in 1974 that worked on de-centering the field from its previous structural metanarratives (Greenfield, 1978, pp. 1–23). Greenfield (1991) called organizational theory good at analyzing background variables "that bear upon administrative choice, decision and responsibility" but little else. Greenfield disputed the idea that there was a "science of administration" at all, or if there was, it didn't amount to much. The reason he asserted was "stupefyingly simple: the central problems of administrative theory are not scientific at all, but philosophical" (p. 7).

Greenfield has been joined by a number of other important writers and thinkers in educational administration—notably William Foster (1986) who concluded that "traditional studies have focused on the organization as if it existed in a time warp" (p. 146); Spencer Maxcy (1991) who asserted that "the error made by behaviorism is to attempt to explain away the mental and archival dimensions of leadership" (p. 4); and Joseph Rost (1991) who concluded that leadership was defined *as good management* in the twentieth century because it fit an industrial model. This concept of management was "rational, male, technocratic, quantitative, goal domianted, cost-benefit driven, personalistic, hierarchical, short term, pragmatic, and materialistic" (p. 94). It is clear that the reappraisal of the models for educational administration derived from organizational theory, behaviorism, and organizational sociology are still undergoing reflective criticism in the late twentieth century.

THE FEMINIST CRITIQUE AS CRITICAL THEORY

As a modern movement, feminism is said to have begun with Betty Friedan's (1963) book, *The Feminist Mystique.* Yet history records much earlier protests against the subservience of women, as for example Mary Wollstonecraft's (1792) tract, *A*

Vindication of the Rights of Women, in which she asserted "that the sexual distinction which men have so warmly insisted upon, is arbitrary" (p. 205).

The voice and intensity of feminist thought has waxed and waned since the early sixties, and has undergone various transformations. For example, Bem (1993) notes that for a brief period, feminists (see Heilbrun, 1973) advocated androgyny as a solution to the inequality between the sexes. This inequality produced the rigid sexual polarization that existed in Western society. The idea was that androgyny incorporated aspects that were masculine and feminine, thereby becoming a genderless ideal for equality between the sexes.

The ideal of androgyny was quickly discarded, however, because historically, the male was enhanced by providing him with certain desirable female characteristics such as enriched emotionality, and therefore did not really provide equality between the sexes. Another reason for discarding androgyny was that it failed the political test by not dealing with institutionalized androcentrism. It placed the problem on the personal level where it could be solved, but it left socioeconomic male hegemony untouched. Finally, it accepted gender polarization, i.e., male/female exclusivity, as a given, thus privileging heterosexuality (see Bem, 1993, pp. 123–124). Homosexuality was given a name in 1870 and as Foucault (1990) notes it was moved from "a temporary aberration . . . [to] a species" (p. 43). Positivistic science, with its proclivity to categorize reality, created scales of degradation/abnormality with zoophiles, auto-monosexualists, mixoverts, gynecomasts, presbyophiles, sexoesthetics, and dyspareunist women (Foucault, 1990, p. 43). Once categorized, these differences in sexual preferences became *real,* a stunning example of how reality is preshaped prior to observation or the collecting of data. Feminist thought today not only includes the concept of attacking the socioeconomic–political strongholds of androcentrism, but an assault on the very idea of gender polarization and exclusivity that results in the oppression of homosexuality as "unnatural."

What is important to note is how feminist critical inquiry struggled to find a name for itself. Then, it reacted against the hegemony of androcentrism, worked to find alternatives, abandoned those that did not eliminate socioeconomic–political oppression, and finally turned again on the linguistic and ontological categories that had shaped its own thought patterns about equalization that did not liberate. Friedrich Nietzsche (1887) commented on this tortuous path when he observed, "For all its detachment and freedom from emotion, our science is still the dupe of linguistic habits; it has never yet got rid of those changelings called 'subjects'" (p. 179).

Feminism and critical theorists have served to reengage mainstream thought about so-called "objectivist science" and its tyranny of categories imposed upon reality. Beginning with T. B. Greenfield (Greenfield and Ribbons, 1993), the critical theorists have attacked mainstream thought and patterns of inquiry in educational administration. For a while, they were ignored. Now, there are simply too many of them to ignore. The criticisms must be dealt with. Of more importance are the changes in conducting research in the field and the models it uses to conduct this inquiry. The feminists and critical theorists have served to open the way to consider post-structural ideas. Such ideas were not preshaped by either a priori categorization or values, or blind linguistic traditions (see also Goren, 1993).

THE RISE OF POST-STRUCTURALISM

Post-structuralism is a radical introversion of the structuralist movement that is aimed at discerning synchrony in all fields. In linguistics, post-structuralism was inaugurated by Jacques Derrida's 1966 speech at an academic conference at Johns Hopkins University (Lehman, 1991, p. 47). Derrida's remarks initiated a kind of analysis ultimately to be called deconstruction.

Derrida's position was that any text can be destroyed by a form of close scrutiny that was previously called "close criticism" in the United States (Holub, 1992, p. 84). Derrida's criticisms were new in that they attacked the epistemology of structuralism without altering its centering on textual hegemony.

The epistemology of structuralism is grounded in synchrony—the assumption that there is an order to things. This order is revealed as patterns, unities, strands, and interconnectivities founded on scientific inquiry. In linguistics, Derrida destroyed the concept of stability in language. Language contained infinite shifts, aporias, steppings and slippages, traces, and endless delays. There were no final meanings ever possible within such a system. And translation from one language system to another amounted to scaling the intellectual walls of incommensurability. The order observed in linguistic systems was imposed by some epistemological assumptions, but it was an arbitrary imposition resulting only in constructing smoke and mirror systems that always faded away upon close scrutiny.

Derrida's deconstruction was rooted in Heidegger's notion of *destruktion* (Rapaport, 1989). Heidegger attacked contemporary notions of time in Western ontology. As he abolished time, Derrida and others destroyed the concept of the immutability of linguistic systems founded on demarcations between Aristotle's framework of past–present–future. When these categories were erased, so too were ideas about God, and any final meaning to life. Language and its supporting ontology reveal a process of infinite deferral. There can be no irrevocable interpretation in systems that are incapable of allowing firm conclusions. Deconstruction abolished binary systems rooted in language in such ideas as true/false, good/bad, and theory/practice. Categorically based linguistic systems ultimately were constructed on shifting grounds because they were shorn of linkages to external referents. Language systems themselves are vulnerable to such attacks. Only dead languages maintain stability over time. Lived and natural languages are in the process of constant shifting.

Shearing away structuralism's claim to stability has resulted in a great deal of anxiety in academe. The reactions range from outright refusals to even consider changing epistemological assumptions to deep pessimism. The prevailing mood has led at least one critic to proclaim that a "crisis of belief" exists in the university (Carter, 1992, p. 36). Carter, a history professor at Atlanta's Emory University, had a radio interview on David Duke's (the former Grand Wizard of the Ku Klux Klan) candidacy for public office in Louisiana. Carter said that Duke "made of the truth as he goes along."

A disgruntled Duke supporter challenged him later on the telephone and insisted that such things as the Nazi Holocaust never happened. Each argument put forth by Carter was dismissed by the Duke supporter. Carter finally concluded that mass illiteracy was tacitly supported in the universities by a stance taken by both structuralism and post-structuralism—i.e., their insistence on using only the text as a referent without examining the linkage to what the text referred to. This kind of epistemological stance enabled any one person's interpretation to be as good as anyone else's.

Notes Carter:

> The distinction between fact and fiction is essential both to our sanity and to our ability to make moral judgments. We may never know the truth, the whole truth, and nothing but the truth, but we have to believe that some descriptions of our past and our present conditions are more truthful than others (p. 36).

Carter is concerned about what he calls the "moral and intellectual anarchy" that has swept some academic disciplines. Carter's reaction may be an overreaction since few post-structuralists would posit that any interpretation of a text is acceptable. They would say that interpretation must be ultimately confined to the text because any meaning is locked into the sequence of words as expressed in the text.

What post-structuralism has done is to attack the determinism inherent in structuralism by illustrating that meaning is contingent upon language, which is not stable. Actually, Karl Popper (1957) had attacked determinism much earlier and showed that "real repetition, must therefore be impossible in social history; and this means that one must expect that events of an intrinsically new character will emerge" (p. 10). Popper's attack not only denied any basis for historical determinism (thereby nullifying any claim of the Nazis or communists that their rule was inevitable), but also indicated why statistical prediction rooted in past events could not be considered reliable or true for future ones. Yet Popper's views did not have the contingency of hand-wringers following him around that Foucault or Derrida have in some quarters in American universities today.

One reason may be that the French philosophers have done their work in more mainstream academic areas where powerful vested interests in proffering positions of stability exist. Those who have built their careers on metanarratives of determinism stoutly resist the idea that their systems of positivities may be houses of cards. Writers and researchers in educational administration are certainly among them.

POST-STRUCTURALISM'S SHADOW DANCING WITH TEXT

Post-structuralism had to perform two tasks in order to critique structuralism. They were to: (1) deny stability and order within texts while at the same time stay within them as force fields, without (2) constructing another system in its place that became structural itself. This development would open it to the same criticism as that which it was criticizing.

In coming to an attack on most any idea, one is compelled to develop a coherent set of principles. These principles contain an order, a sequence, and a centering of assumptions. Such principles are then a kind of structural set of ideas in themselves. Both Derrida and Foucault denied that their thoughts were synchronic, or were even systemic in nature (see Pavel, 1992, pp. 68–69). They had to assume this posture, or they too were constructing the very same kind of system they believed to be false. To argue for indeterminism required a text that was not determined by some sort of preexisting order in the system one was using in the language of criticism. It is upon this assumption that post-structuralism is vulnerable.

Derrida and Foucault have insisted that classical science rests upon false pillars of method. The methods, particularly of research, assume an order that will be revealed by continuous study. They rest their case on a concept of linguistics that asserts that language is the image of reality and not of reality itself. This appearance of reality, divorced from any anchoring to it, can be used to dissolve whatever differences there may be between language as an object and reality itself.

Pavel (1992) insists that linguistics, as a field, is entirely unsuited to be able to deliver upon this post-structural assertion. Linguistics, says Pavel, does indeed have a method. And the method is rooted in classical science. In turn, a kind of determinism is assumed to exist in order for the method to be acceptable (p. 71).

Language does indeed have a structure. It may not be objective, as that word is defined. It may be moving, fluid, and incapable of ultimate stability or any finality, but it is indeed a system. To use language as an object and as a field of study upon which to erect an epistemology that asserts pure indeterminism and ultimate randomness is to use an inappropriate and contradictory content field to support this position. To insist that language reveals no determinism in the face of its systemic nature is to take a position that is purely metaphysical.

This dilemma is the one that post-structuralism has failed to resolve. By rejecting any synchrony and a corresponding method as a justified epistemological position, post-structuralists have created a negativity in research that denies their own position any creativity. All they can do is to criticize the positivities that they deny exist without becoming one themselves. Pavel (1992) calls this posture a "shameful parasitism" (p. 84). Ultimately one most not only deny and reject, but also assert an alternative. New knowledge is ultimately built on an assertion—a positivity—and not simply a denial of what it is not or was not. Post-structuralism is a kind of shadow dancing to that which it has chosen to criticize, without advancing any form of its own because it believes one cannot exist. This is the kind of double-bind that post-structuralists have failed to resolve. However brilliant and powerful their denunciations have been, they cannot construct a viable alternative without falling victim to the same set of conditions upon which their criticism has been fed. Jean Hills' (1980) critique of T. B. Greenfield's writings contains a parallel observation He said, "His [Greenfield's] assertions that the essence of organizations is human meanings and that the variability of human meanings precludes the possibility of a theory dealing with them are not defensible" (p. 42).

CHECKING ANARCHISM IN THEORY: RE-ESTABLISHING THE PRIMACY OF PROBLEM SOLVING

Theory, as it has been used in traditional science, entertains the development of postulates that are assertive and engage in forms of positivism. Although forms of scientific positivism have been shown to take extreme positions that become metaphysical in the form of behaviorism, at the other end lie forms of denial that can also become forms of positivism. Post-structuralists have refused to accept this state of affairs. They want to skate "in-between" in the world, denying positivism without becoming positivistic, and hence forcing them to divulge a belief in determinism. The use of language and the field of linguistics was thought to offer support for their position, but it does not. To continue to deny the possibility of language being a kind of positivistic system as an object in itself (through which one denies its existence as a system) is to overlook the fact that the words used to frame the argument presuppose agreement about the meaning of the words before they are ever employed to formulate the argument (an observation Pavel, 1992, attributes to Willard Quine, p. 88).

So any formulation of a theory requires some attributes of positivities at least as assertions to be tested in some way or another. The interconnectivity between the assertions take on the shape of a theory. In order for a theory to be testable in some form, it must be anchored to reality. The linkage to reality is where both structuralists and post-structuralists who depend upon the idea of the independence of text from meaning should be reexamined.

The importance of language is its referents. Words refer to what is believed to be real. Restoring balance to theoretical development in a discipline rests in its capacity to solve real problems in the real world. This means reconnecting theory to that world in a way that both the practitioner and the researcher can act upon and in that world. Language is not the object of meaning. Meaning lies in the linkage between reality, perception, belief, concept, and the world revealed to the language user as *interactive* and ultimately *subjective*. To remove language embedded in the world from this foundation is to embrace a world of shadows. It is to speculate about the meaning of a lost language carved on stone without ever coming to understand to what the words and signs are referenced. Logical positivism denies an essential subjectivity and engages in false posturing. Structuralism divorces the world from the object of study, insisting upon an objectivity found only in that realm of study. Post-structuralists deny the methods used to frame the object of study as objective, asserting that no positivity is anything but a human construct that is ultimately false. In so framing the denial, they reveal prior agreements that outline the possibility of an alternative positivity. The fact that a counterargument becomes a positivity not only refutes their argument by its presence, but also reveals the potentiality of a predetermined response existing prior to their using it. The concept of indeterminism is also voided simultaneously.

RE-CENTERING THE FIELD AND REDEFINING SCIENCE

The "glitch" in the structural/post-structural world is the departure from reality—the idea that language itself becomes the object of study, and that it is not necessary to worry about an author's original intent. Only the text matters. The very same rationale exists for educational administrators studying organizational theory. What people do, understand, feel, believe, doesn't matter, or in the words of

Perrow (1970), "the structural viewpoint considers the roles people play, rather than the nature of the personalities in these roles" (p. 2). If people's feelings or their personalities don't count, what does matter? What matters is *the system*. Viewed as a collectivization of universals, organizational theory becomes a way of moving large parts around in search of greater organic economies (Scott, 1973, p. 114). Behavior is specified, routinized, and standardized, because as Mintzberg (1983) notes, "Organizations formalize behavior to reduce its variability, ultimately to predict and control it" (p. 34).

Organizational theory becomes the *text* for the organizational–administrative "scientist," in the same way that structuralists and post-structuralists conceptualize the text as the only thing that matters. The motivation or intent of the author is irrelevant.

Balance has to be restored to a discussion of systems or structures by: (1) re-establishing the primacy of speech in language, and by so doing, (2) linking texts to actions that have meaning in the political world. The French structuralists upended the classical notion regarding the primacy of speech. For the text to be primary, it had to be divorced from speech (Pavel, 1992, p. 69). Derrida claims that "writing is indicative in its own sphere" and therefore "reading is speaking" (see Evans, 1991, p. 120). Derrida takes the position that "The structure . . . supposes both that there are only contexts, that nothing exists outside context" (Critchley, 1992, p. 32). Context is designated in writing.

Speech is central to ideas and to the expression of ideas. Writing follows. Speech is anchored in a world of the living. Speech is the expression of life as it is lived. Reconnecting science to life means to re-center the primacy of speech and politics in studying educational administration. As Holub (1992) proffers, "Politics brings an end to and pins down what otherwise might be judged elusive and infinitely regressive" (pp. 136–137).

Politics is the world as it is encountered. It is interactive, dynamic, and fluid. Meaning can be encountered, contextualized, and understood in context. Because of the vagaries of language instability, it can never be viewed as completely finalized. And meaning will change and shift over time. But for the participants at the time, meaning can be fixed in their frame of reference as they understand it, as they understand others to understand it, and as a person standing aside can reconstruct the interrelationships and understandings in a specific time frame. Objectivity is relational and limited. Objectivity is interruptive by an outsider because that person is using a knowledge of consummative events that were not present in the field of perception of the participants at the time they were interactive. It may be analogized as opening a closet door to let the light in to see what is there. The entrance of light represents a circumstance that was not present before the door was opened. It was thus a condition that did not exist if anyone had been in that closet prior to the door being opened. Objectivity is therefore a reconstruction of things, and not an act implying no bias or interference in events or phenomena. Objectivity is hermeneutical.

Scientific knowledge is inevitably a reconstruction of events. It represents a careful reconstruction, and always ultimately false in the sense that it is a human artifact—either a simplistic reconstruction or a delimitation of the field of variables and, hence, traceable interactions. The extent to which it is truthful is the extent of the overlap to that which is meaningful and useful. Those values are ultimately contextualized as well. Meaningful science in medieval times may be considered irrelevant in contemporary times. Science, like most other human activities, is situationally dependent, i.e., as supremely political as any other human endeavor. Unmasking science as a political activity—situationally dependent and human—is central to demythologizing it and re-centering it as a worthwhile activity for pursuit in colleges and universities. It is also the key to restoring its morality in human affairs. Science cannot stand apart from its use. It can never be objective in the old logically positivistic frame.

Abandoning the stance that science proceeds apart and independent from humanity and its politics will not only restore the essential morality of the enterprise in educational administration. It should also go a long way in breaching the gap between science and the arts in educational administration. It ought to reunite the study of human situations and problems with the role of the schools in perpetuating or solving them. It ought to restore humanity to a study of organizations and schools by re-establishing the primacy of individuals and their unique humanness to the center stage, as people both shaped by their contexts, but also capable of simultaneously altering them.

Finally, it ought to frame the basis for a realistic definition of social and political emancipation of the schools acting within and upon the larger political arena in which they are dependent, but ought to interact with and change the structures that relegate them to simply cloning existing social structures and all their inequities. Re-centering educational administration is intimately linked to re-centering the activity called "science." Nietzsche (1887) observed, "The more emotions we allow to speak in a given matter, the more different eyes we can put on in order to view a given spectacle, the more complete will be our concept of it, the greater our 'objectivity'" (p. 255).

WHERE EDUCATIONAL ADMINISTRATION NEEDS TO GO

Educational administration as a field is the product of a contextual "double hermeneutic" (Outhwaite, 1991, p. 34) with which it is finally coming to terms. Educational administration began as an offspring of scientific management (see Gresso, 1991). Its early adherents in universities were thoroughly imbued with the doctrine of efficiency and established their hegemony by using the language of science in pursuing a definition of the field that advanced their own needs for organizational independence and legitimacy, enhanced their prestige and power, and wrested the field from the clutches of corrupt boards of education. The new educational administrators—trained in universities—were the epitome of scientifically prepared educational engineers. They were the agents of change, using science as a doctrine to reform the schools.

This conception of science has been shown to be scientism—i.e., "sciencelike," but not science by any means. Later, educational administration became thoroughly captured by the behaviorists, and in turn the organizational sociologists. Neither behaviorism nor organizational sociology has provided the explanatory or predictive power of either understanding or advancing the field, or its graduates, to solve the myriad of political, moral, and technological dilemmas the schools face in late twentieth-century America.

Too many educational administrators see themselves as continuing the legacy of efficiency in systems theory and now total quality management. Educational administrators are not agents of moral leadership. Both schools and society continue to be plagued with racism, sexism, poverty, and expanding wealth differentials between classes. These misfortunes are reinforced by standardized tests and many instructional practices such as ability grouping and whole class instruction dominated by the lecture method. Administrators of our schools look for solutions inside the confines of behaviorism–structuralism that preclude moral leadership because these positivities have never considered values and morality fitting topics of science and hence of doctoral study.

The myopia of the field precludes it from expanding its borders to the arts, where moral dilemmas have been the topic of discussion for thousands of years. Institutional autonomy and even accreditation standards preclude universities and colleges from interdisciplinary work. "Research" has been thoroughly appropriated by the behaviorists to the point where too few studies that deal with the human dimension are permitted or labeled "too soft" to be endorsed by many professors directing graduate research. Many graduate students have been discouraged from using anything but behavioral–structural premises in their work. Statistical packages dominate the methodologies selected in these circumstances. Blind-reviewed journal and conference presentations indicate that dominance and pervasiveness of behaviorism–structuralism to perpetuate its own hegemony in thinking about how the field shapes problems and reinforces its own power–knowledge position simultaneously.

This book has been aimed at clarifying how educational administration began and where it has been as a discipline. The field is unlikely to progress any further until the tenets that have served as both tether and blinders are removed. The old administrative science is dead. It must not be replaced by a new administrative science, but by a critical reflective approach that is centered in the humanities (see Hodgkinson, 1991).

The first move is to expand the idea of appropriate content in the study of leadership. Leadership without morality is little more than bureaucratic technique. Leadership centered in morality is distinctively aware of its own values, and those of the people who are also working in organizations such as schools (see Kimbrough, 1985). Moral leadership is centered on people as centers of action, not merely as recipients of action. Moral leadership re-centers people as agents of change who can shape their environment and the organizations they live and work in to become more fully humane, not simply technocracies devoted to ever more refined efficiencies. Moral leadership asks questions about *ends*. It asks questions such as, "Who benefits from schools as they now exist?" and "Who does not benefit from schools as they now exist?" Moral leadership is rooted in a context of values that rejects factory–manufacturing metaphors as inappropriate to the main goals of education. Efficiency as an objective is also rejected. The nature of objectivity must also be reappraised. Methods do not assure objectivity. A search for a kind of meta-objectivity has been as futile in science as it has nearly everywhere else. No such state exists in human affairs, nor is likely to in human studies centered on human affairs.

BIOGRAPHY AS A LOGICAL CENTER FOR THE STUDY OF LEADERSHIP

Ever since Plutarch was describing the likes of Alexander, Caesar, and Cicero, the lives of leaders have been instructive and inspirational sources of guidance for aspiring neophytes. Portraits of leaders serve as models. The ancients believed that character resided in people and resulted in moral attainments (Whittemore, 1988, p. 6). The ancients always joined morality and character. Plutarch did not assess thought so much as he was interested in conduct. Conduct was considered the bellwether of greatness. Plutarch was an "ethical biographer"—a source of inspiration to the likes of Shakespeare, whose characters walked the Globe Theatre and into the theatre of the world (Whittemore, 1988, p. 33).

There is more to Plutarch and Shakespeare than in the hundreds of studies about leadership cited in Stogdill's (1974) *Handbook*. Yet there is scant evidence that most professors of educational administration consider these more time-honored sources of leadership anything but curious oddities at best. They certainly do not consider the sources "science" or worthy of any study. Professors of educational administration have been called "complacent" by those who have studied them (McCarthy, Kuh, Newell, and Iaconca, 1988, p. 170). The continuing habit of embracing leadership from the viewpoint of behaviorism and structuralism in the name of science produces studies that have been insignificant in preparing leaders for tomorrow's schools (see Rost, 1991, pp. 69–128). Administrative science may have produced skilled bureaucrats, but it has failed to produce leaders (see National Commission on Excellence in Educational Administration, 1987).

Biography provides a rich source for understanding context and thereby establishing the meaning of leadership (English, 1992, p. 430). It is able to describe how and why leaders made decisions and how others reacted to them. As a source of data it is certainly not any more flawed than so-called "scientific" studies of leadership have been shown to be seriously compromised, including the contention that they are or were "objective" or more rigorous. Every study has a point of view. Science is no exception. Biography's point of view is perhaps a little more obvious and honest.

There should come a time when a well-constructed biography as a doctoral dissertation about a school leader will provide a data source regarding educational leadership that is far richer and more instructive than some of the studies now passing for science can ever approach.

Biography as an activity includes history, language, politics, and many of the social science fields such as sociology, anthropology, and psychology. Biography is multidisciplinary. Doctoral studies grounded in biography could provide a rich contextual fabric to inform the field about the nature of leadership in a variety of times and circumstances. To be sure, it is not "administrative science." This rubric has excluded anything worth knowing about leadership since it was initiated into educational administration. Re-centering educational administration on leadership means abandoning the academic boxes and specialities that have come to dominate its configuration in most colleges and universities that prepare and certify school administrators. It will also mean a deliberate abandonment of the business literature that continues to wash it in the seductive perfume of efficiency, whether in the form of frame theory or statistical probability theory wrapped with incense from Japan.

SUMMARY

Structuralism in the form of organizational sociology/theory has long managed to lock educational administration into its intellectual grasp. Structuralism is both a point of view about systems, as well as a kind of epistemology about the composition of administration. Structuralism was concerned about discovering the unity behind systems, believing in the ultimate determinism of all that was finally discerned in the process.

Critical theory, and much of feminist writing, has exposed the androcentrism that is inherent in structuralist approaches, and sought to re-center educational administration around more egalitarian themes.

As a kind of *nouvelle critique,* post-structuralism emerged in France as first reinforcing a structural perspective, but then veering away into a radical attack. Post-structuralism came to doubt the categories and methods of science and of the research that informed it. While science focused on central themes and patterns, post-structuralism found such themes and patterns imposed rather than "discovered." They were artifacts that served to enhance the power of those using them, revealing intricate and sometimes hidden "power–knowledge" linkages (see Gordon, 1980).

Structuralism was concerned with unity. Post-structuralism become obsessed with dispersion and discontinuity. The contribution of the post-structuralists was that they showed the instability of language to convey truth. Linguistic categories lacked permanency and therefore could not stand close analysis. Binary opposites dissolved before the practice of deconstruction. Distinctions became blurred. Meaning was first textualized and then obscured. The idea of one "right" interpretation or "grand narrative" was ridiculed. Certainty and finality were the victims.

Yet even as the post-structuralists insisted that determinism was dead, and indeterminism the only alternative, their new language revealed certain regularities, including the embrace of a series of opposites as in "systems of dispersion" (Pavel, 1992, p. 90). Discursive formations that revealed modalities and coherency were discussed.

Post-structuralism and deconstruction are powerful analytical approaches. Their insistence on referencing only the text without linking the text to reality, and their refusal to establish a new text (or the denial that they are doing so), severely hampers their view to create an alternative. It shears the approach from major, creative advances except as doctrines of denial and negativity.

Post-structural analysis of patterns and the sources of their information and formation have, however, been instructive. Ruptures, dispersion, discontinuities, and transformations are part of pattern as well. Language contains power relations, domination and subordination, and paradoxes—even as it is being used to conceal them. Language is no objective mirror of reality. Even as the post-structuralists searched for a kind of arche-writing that would be objective as a metanarrative, their contribution has been to destroy the grounds for considering anything *objective* as a metanarrative. As long as those pursuing truth in the social sciences insist on objectivity, they will be vulnerable to post-structural critique to reveal their essential subjectivity, including the post-structuralists themselves. Objectivity as the binary opposite of subjectivity is perhaps the ultimate deconstruction in science. It is also the basis for a re-centering of the discipline of educational administration with the arts. If there can be no scientific objectivity, then the reconnection with the arts as the penultimate human narrative is both possible and desirable. In this "turn" we may have made the study of leadership a reality in academic settings.

Perception Check and Applications

1. Assessing the Impact of Structuralism: A Search for Synchrony

Structuralism is a search for unity within systems. Examine any academic social science system—sociology, anthropology, or psychology—and identify the major systems of thought within it. Can you trace them to Saussure?

2. Organizational Theory as Text

Compare the idea that text is to a structuralist or post-structuralist as organizational theory is to a researcher or an administrator. What are the similarities and dissimilarities in the comparison? Can the post-structuralist idea that no author is necessary to consider a text be the same as a researcher using organizational theory to examine a school?

3. Determinism vs. Indeterminism

If a researcher believes that no order is necessary to examine a set of phenomena (i.e., no a priori pattern exists), but then finds such a pattern or patterns, how is the researcher to know if it was: (1) really in the phenomena observed, or (2) created by the observer to make sense of the observations? Which one would be determinism? Indeterminism?

4. Politics and Ultimate Meaning

Explain why politics is a way to end "infinite regression." Is politics a way to establish finality of meaning at the same time? Explain why or why not finality and politics can be established.

5. Science and the Reconstruction of Events

If science is a reconstruction of events, how is anything then discovered? What is a scientific discovery? If everything is ultimately false, can anything be true?

6. Conduct, Character, and Morality

Linking conduct to morality and using it as a basis of establishing character was a perspective advanced by Aristotle. In what ways is this idea still dominant in assessing leaders in comtemporary society? What other approaches are there to assess the morality of leadership?

Key Chapter Concepts and Terms

close criticism

A kind of literary analysis based on a very "tight" or rigorous reading of selected passages of an author's works.

incommensurability

The position that translation from one language to another is ultimately impossible because of syntactical differences. If languages cannot ultimately be translated from one to another with some accuracy, perception is not universal, but relative. A position regarding incommensurability is used to support a position of extreme relativism in philosophy and epistemology, supporting a claim that there can be no universal truths (see Devitt and Sterelny, 1987, pp. 172–183).

a positivity

A claim or proposition that is assertive, not simply a negation of another proposition or explanation, so that it can be analyzed, extended, tested, applied, and utilized to advance the production of knowledge. The major problem with positivities is that one must confront the dilemma of determinism, i.e., whether a cluster of propositions represents a pattern that preexisted or one constructed by the claimant. Preexisting patterns indicate a view of determinism. Imposed patterns as constructions can be indicative of indeterminism. The latter position can also make no claims to truth that can be considered universal. Indeterminism is based on radical relativism.

the text

An idea adopted by both structuralists and post-structuralists that writing, as a text, can be considered independently from its author or source. This stance was supported by their belief that the meaning of words is not derived from the intent of the author, but rather, from the relationship of the words, one to the other, in any given passage. Later, the idea of text was lifted from linguistics and applied to any dogma or belief that had been written—i.e., so a metanarrative can be called a "text."

theory movement

A point of view adopted by academics in educational administration that insisted that research should be theory driven. Furthermore, the theories that were most acceptable were those from the metanarratives of behaviorism and structuralism. To a large extent, despite the work of T. B. Greenfield and others, this perspective is still dominant in the discipline.

synchrony

The idea that things arise in patterns such as personages in histories in some sort of chronology. Synchrony rests on the assumption of determinism—an idea that there is preordained arrangement to things. Post-structuralists rigorously denied the existence of synchrony, and claimed not to have erected it in the analysis of structuralist thought. Such claims have been disputed.

References

Allport, F. H. (1954). "The structuring of events: outline of a general theory with applications to psychology," *Psychological Review,* 61, pp. 281–303.

Argyris, C. (1972). *The Applicability of Organizational Sociology.* Cambridge, MA: Harvard University Press.

Bem, S. L. (1993). *The Lenses of Gender.* New Haven: Yale University Press.

Blau, P. M., and Scott, W. R. (1962). *Formal Organizations.* San Francisco: Chandler Publishing Company.

Bloomfield, L. (1933). *Language.* New York: Holt.

Bolman, L. G., and Deal, T. E. (1991). *Reframing Organizations.* San Francisco: Jossey-Bass, Inc.

Campbell, R. F., Fleming, T., Newell, L. J., and Bennion, J. W. (1987). *A History of Thought and Practice in Educational Administration.* New York: Teachers College Press.

Carter, D. T. (1992, November 18). "The Academy's Crisis of Belief," *The Chronicle of Higher Education,* 39:13, p. 36.

Critchley, S. (1992). *The Ethics of Deconstruction.* Cambridge, MA: Blackwell Publishers.

Devitt, M., and Sterelny, K. (1987). *Language and Reality.* Cambridge, MA: MIT Press.

English, F. W. (1992). *Educational Administration: The Human Science.* New York: HarperCollins.

Evans, J. C. (1991). *Strategies of Deconstruction.* Minneapolis: University of Minnesota Press.

Follett, M. P. (1942). *Dynamic Administration,* H. C. Metcalf and L. Urwick (Eds.). New York: Harper.

Foucault, M. (1991). *The History of Sexuality: An Introduction.* New York: Random House.

Friedan, B. (1963). *The Feminine Mystique.* New York: Simon.

Gadet, F. (1989). *Saussure and Contemporary Culture.* London, England: Hutchinson Radius.

Gordon, C. (Ed.) (1980). *Power/Knowledge*. New York: Pantheon Books.

Goren, J. M. (1993). *The Struggle for Pedagogies*. New York: Routledge.

Greenfield, T. B. (1978, Spring). "Reflections on Organization Theory and the Truths of Irreconcilable Realities" in *Educational Administration Quarterly*, 14:2, pp. 1–23.

Greenfield, T. B. (1991). "Foreward," in C. Hodgkinson, *Educational Leadership*. New York: SUNY Press, pp. 3–9.

Greenfield, T. B., and Ribbins, P. (1993). *Greenfield on Educational Administration*. London, England: Routledge.

Gresso, D. W. (1991). "Implications for Future Preparation of Leaders," in B. G. Barnett, F. O. McQuarrie, and C. J. Norris (Eds.), *A Focus on Human Decency*. Memphis, TN: National Policy Board for Educational Administration, pp. 76–86.

Griffiths, D. E. (1964). "The Nature and Meaning of Theory," in D. E. Griffiths (Ed.), *Behavioral Science and Educational Administration*. Chicago: University of Chicago Press, pp. 95–118.

Halpin, A. W. (1966). *Theory and Research in Administration*. New York: The Macmillan Company.

Hawkes, T. (1977). *Structuralism and Semiotics*. London: Methuen.

Heilbrun, C. G. (1973). *Toward a Recognition of Androgyny*. New York: Norton.

Hills, J. (1980). "A Critique of Greenfield's 'New Perspective'" in *Educational Administration Quarterly*, 16:1, pp. 20–44.

Hodgkinson, C. (1991). *Educational Leadership*. Buffalo, New York: SUNY Press.

Holub, R. C. (1992). *Crossing Borders*. Madison: University of Wisconsin Press.

Hoy, W. K., and Miskel, C. G. (1982). *Educational Administration*. New York: Random House.

Katz, D., and Kahn, R. L. (1966). *The Social Psychology of Organizations*. New York: John Wiley & Sons, Inc.

Kimbrough, R. B. (1985). *Ethics: A Course of Study for Educational Leaders*. Arlington, VA: AASA.

Krupp, S. (1961). *Pattern in Organization Analysis*. New York: Holt, Rinehart and Winston, Inc.

Lehman, D. (1991). *Signs of the Times*. New York: Simon and Schuster.

Maxcy, S. J. (1991). *Educational Leadership*. New York: Bergin & Garvey.

McCarthy, M. M., Kuh, G. D., Newell, L. J., and Iaconca, C. M. (1988). *Under Scrutiny: The Educational Administration Professoriate*. Tempe, Arizona: University Council for Educational Administration.

McGregor, D. (1960). *The Human Side of Enterprise*. New York: McGraw–Hill Book Company.

Merton, R. K. (1968). *Social Theory and Social Structure*. New York: The Free Press.

Miller, J. G. (1955). "Toward a General Theory for the Behavioral Sciences," *American Psychologist*, 10, pp. 513–531.

Mintzberg, H. (1983). *Structure in Fives: Designing Effective Organizations*. Englewood Cliffs, New Jersey: Prentice Hall, Inc.

National Commission on Excellence in Educational Administration (1987). *Leaders for America's Schools*. College Park, PA: University Council for Educational Administration.

Nietzsche, F. (1887, 1956). *The Genealogy of Morals*. F. Golffing (Trans.). New York: Anchor Doubleday.

Outhwaite, W. (1991). "Hans-George Gadamer," in Q. Skinner (Ed.), *The Return of Grand Theory in the Human Sciences*. New York: Cambridge University Press.

Owens, R. G. (1981). *Organizational Behavior in Education*. Englewood Cliffs, New Jersey: Prentice Hall, Inc.

Parsons, T. (1951). *The Social System*. New York: The Free Press.

Pavel, T. (1992). *The Feud of Language*. Oxford, England: Basil Blackwell.

Perrow, C. (1970). *Organizational Analysis: A Sociological View*. Monterey, California: Brooks/College Publishing Company.

Perrow, C. (1986). *Complex Organizations*. New York: Random House.

Popper, K. R. (1957). *The Poverty of Historicism*. New York: Harper and Row.

Popper, S. H. (1990). *Pathways to the Humanities*. Tempe, Arizona: University Council for Educational Administration.

Rapaport, H. (1989). *Heidegger & Derrida*. Lincoln: University of Nebraska Press.

Rost, J. C. (1991). *Leadership for the Twenty-First Century*. New York: Praeger.

Runes, D. D. (1984). *Dictionary of Philosophy*. Totowa, New Jersey: Rowman & Allanheld.

Scott, W. G. (1973). "Organization Theory: An Overview and an Appraisal," in F. Baker (Ed.), *Organizational Systems*. Homewood, Illinois: Richard D. Irwin, Inc., pp. 99–119.

Stogdill, R. M. (1974). *Handbook of Leadership*. New York: The Free Press.

Whittemore, R. (1988). *Pure Lives*. Baltimore, Maryland: The Johns Hopkins University Press.

Wollstonecraft, M. (1792, 1989). *A Vindication of the Rights of Women*. New York: Prometheus Books.

ABOUT THE AUTHOR

Fenwick W. English is a Professor in the Department of Educational Administration and Supervision at the University of Kentucky, Lexington. He has also been a faculty member at Lehigh University in Bethlehem, Pennsylvania, and the University of Cincinnati, Ohio, where he was department head.

Dr. English has authored or co-authored twelve books in educational administration, among them *Educational Administration: The Human Science* released in 1992, also by HarperCollins.

In his more than 20 years of service as practitioner, Dr. English has functioned as a classroom teacher, assistant principal, principal, coordinator, director, assistant superintendent, and superintendent of two school districts in New York State. He is a former partner in the international accounting and consulting firm of Peat, Marwick, Main, as well as an associate director of the American Association of School Administrators in Arlington, Virginia.

In his current capacity, he serves as chairperson of the Curriculum Advisory Council of the National Association of Secondary School Principals, and as an advisor to the Chicago School Finance Authority. He has worked and/or consulted in 48 states, Puerto Rico, and the U.S. Virgin Islands, as well as nine foreign countries, including Japan.

Dr. English is a frequent platform speaker for many national educational associations, including the American Association of School Administrators, National School Boards Association, Association of Supervision and Curriculum Development, and the National Association of Secondary School Principals. He has presented papers at the University Council of Educational Administration and Division A of the American Educational Research Association. He received his B.S. and M.S. at the University of Southern California, and his Ph.D. at Arizona State University.

NAME INDEX

Achilles, 139–140
Albert, H., 17
Allport, F., 222
Altman, L., 53, 165
Apple, M., 70
Aquinas, T., 178
Argyris, C., 120, 223
Aristotle, 3, 45–46, 72, 87
Asante, M., 67, 138
Athens, 115
Ayers, L., 109, 201

Bainton, R., 176–177
Ball, S., 21
Banfield, S., 151–152
Barber, D., 122
Barnes, R., 117
Bell, A., 5
Bell, C., 119
Bell, T., 16
Bem, S., 124, 145, 224
Berman, B., 194
Bernal, M., 138, 143
Bernasconi, R., 3, 11, 13
Bernstein, B., 53
Bernstein, C., 215
Bertalanffy, L., 121
Beveridge, W., 34, 39–40, 50
Billington, R., 80–81
Blakeslee, S., 45
Blau, P., 123
Bloomfield, L., 221
Blumberg, A., 198
Bobbitt, F., 19
Bogardus, E., 197
Bolman, L. 123, 221
Borgia, C. 161
Boudon, R. 45–50
Bowles, S., 196

Brady, K., 200
Brandeis, L., 18, 200
Brougham, H., 191, 194
Buddha, 113
Buenger, C., 20
Burns, J., 122, 151
Button, H., 195

Callahan, R., 18–19, 29, 51, 112, 194–195, 200, 202
Campbell, J., 113, 141
Campbell, R., 110, 212, 221
Canguilheim, G., 49
Cantor, N., 148
Capper, C., 118, 120
Carter, D., 225–226
Champollion, J., 66
Charlemagne, 148
Chaucer, 116
Cherryholmes, C., 4, 34, 68
Chomsky, N., 61
Churchill, W., 166
Cicero, 147
Cimon, 147
Clausewitz, C., 83–85
Coe, M., 35, 60
Collison, M., 74–75
Columbus, 81
Comte, A., 88
Conway, M., 196
Cookson, P., 54
Covey, S., 197
Cremin, L., 189
Critchley, S., 229
Cuban, L., 53, 103, 193–194
Cubberley, E., 19, 100–101, 137, 202
Culbertson, J., 16, 87–88, 102
Cunningham, L., 19
Cyert, R., 120

d'Arc, Jeanne, 150–153
Darder, A., 15
Darsie, M., 218
Darwin, C., 36, 41, 49, 61, 67, 69, 71–72, 80
Davidow, L., 147
Davidson, J., 81–82
Deal, T., 123, 221
de Bono, E., 8–9, 24, 26, 90
DeCamp, L., 67
de Grazia, S., 137, 161–164, 166–167
DeLoughry, T., 71
Deming, W. E., 20, 29, 51, 118, 204, 209–213
Demosthenes, 114
Denzin, N., 77
de Pisan, C., 153
Derrida, J., 6, 9, 26, 125, 225
Devitt, M., 208, 222
Dewey, J., 83, 167
Dilthey, W., 61, 91, 137
Douglas, W., 183
Duesberg, P., 71
Duffy, J., 37, 68
Dunn, W., 17
Durant, W., 14
Durkheim, E., 121
Dutton, S., 110, 203

Eaton, W., 19, 51
Eco, U., 61, 64–65
Edmonds, R., 26, 51
Einstein, A., 39–41
Eiselen, F., 23, 67
Eldridge, B., 194
Elliot, E., 19
Emerson, G., 102
Englehardt, F., 197, 201
English, F., 20, 100, 232

240

Subject Index